Coaching the Pistol Spread Option Offense

Chris Paulson
Jeff Glessner

©2014 Coaches Choice. All rights reserved. Printed in the United States.

No part of this book may be reproduced, stored in a retrieval system or transmitted, in any form or by any means, electronic, mechanical, photocopying, recording, or otherwise, without the prior permission of Coaches Choice.

ISBN: 978-1-60679-296-4
Library of Congress Control Number: 2013957798
Book layout: Cheery Sugabo
Cover design: Cheery Sugabo
Front cover photo: Tom Jones Photography

Coaches Choice
P.O. Box 1828
Monterey, CA 93942
www.coacheschoice.com

Dedication

To my wife, Amanda, and daughter, Ava. Thank you for all your love and support.

—Chris Paulson

To Don Joy: For selling me on the wishbone.

To Stan Clements: For selling me on the triple option.

To Bob Oliver: Whose brilliant school of defensive thought molds how I think of offensive football.

To Ritchie Saltz: For teaching me the technique aspects of football.

To Emory Bellard and Glenn "Tiger" Ellison: Two of the most brilliant coaches in football history, who innovated football to another level.

Ultimately, to my father, Thomas Glessner: My hero and my inspiration for everything I do.

—Jeff Glessner

Acknowledgments

I would like to thank:

My parents, Scott and Kristi Paulson, for allowing me to follow my dreams.

Mike Price and Bill Doba, for demonstrating genuine love and care for every player in their program.

Howie Martin, for leaving a legacy in which I can only hope to aspire.

Gordy Elliott, for being a mentor to not just me, but any coach who asks.

—Chris Paulson

I would like to thank my family and friends in Fredericksburg, Virginia. The love and support I have received from them makes it a very special place to me.

—Jeff Glessner

Contents

Dedication 3
Acknowledgments 4
Preface 6
Introduction 8
Chapter 1: Measuring a Play's Effectiveness 11
Chapter 2: The Triple Option 29
Chapter 3: The Pistol Spread Option Passing Game 79
Chapter 4: Complementary Plays 114
Chapter 5: Game Management 146
Chapter 6: Option-Specific Drills 167
Chapter 7: Option Offense Practice Schedule 180
Conclusion 187
About the Authors 188

Preface

This book wouldn't have been possible to create without specific influences on the content. As will be soon demonstrated, the principles and theories in this book are from old school option football coaches. The "spread guru" movement of the past 10 years has minimal to no influence on the content. Original principles of the option are the staple of this book.

To be more specific, several coaches deserve recognition for their influence on the authors. The first three would be Emory Bellard, Don Faurot, and Bud Wilkinson. These are the three pioneers of option football. Although many people don't know who these people are and what influence they have had on the game, they set the standard for principles and the theoretical realm of not only option football but the entire game itself.

The running game is influenced by many sources. The first is the Paul Johnson school of coaches. These are the coaches who have kept option football alive and running. They've had great success with the weaponry of the spread (flexbone/double slot) offense. The second influence on the running game are the old-time wishbone coaches: Barry Switzer, Paul "Bear" Bryant, Ken Hatfield, and, most especially, Emory Bellard, Homer Smith, and Franklin "Pepper" Rodgers. These are the coaches who ran the option successfully in the day and age where everyone ran the option. Needless to say, they were some of the most successful in their approaches.

The passing game is influenced by several sources. The first in principle would be the original wishbone coaches. The first in practicality is Tony DeMeo. DeMeo helped develop a complementary passing game to the option that hadn't been used before. Tom Moore, Norm Chow, Glenn "Tiger" Ellison, June Jones, and Darrel "Mouse" Davis have had an impact on the philosophical and technical realms of the passing game. Although the passing game shown doesn't have these coaches' direct ideas, they have subtly had an influence on the content.

Although many have influenced this offense, most of the ideas and concepts come from the authors. Although they have been heavily influenced in their thought processes, the authors have undoubtedly become very opinionated on why and what they believe in. Although coaches have been acknowledged here for their influences, the authors still state that some disagreement exists with some thought processes, techniques, and schematic fine tuning that will be argued for and against in this book.

The goal of this book is to be theoretical, philosophical, and, most importantly, open to debate. The problem with football literature in the past 30 years is that most of it leaves out theories and philosophy. A football book with just diagrams, anecdotes, and clichés doesn't mean anything. Any coach can put a bunch of diagrams together and create a book. Showing the different methods and thought processes behind the option is important to understand the overall structure of the option. This book is aimed at readers who want a much more in-depth look at the actual option philosophy itself.

Introduction

The Pistol Spread Option: How Did We Get Here?

The option play has had a dynamic history and relationship to the game of football since the 1940s. The idea of eliminating defenders by reading them rather than blocking them is as revolutionary now as it was in the 1940s at the University of Missouri and the University of Oklahoma. Over the course of time, football evolves and even goes through cycles. One of the reasons why football didn't evolve much until the 1950s was because "movies" weren't widely available. What adds insult to injury about the evolution of football was that for 30 to 40 years, most of the evolution occurred because of rule changes. The main point is that the more accessible technology has become, the faster information and ideas move along in the football world. Now we've reached a point where football has combined the triple option with the pistol formation.

It's true to say nothing is new about the triple (three-way) option. Or about having two slotbacks in the spread option formation. Or about a systematic approach to running the option. And barely anything new with techniques. The idea of reading two defenders on a play has been around since the 1960s. What's new is the idea of marrying the best of the under-center option game with the best of the passing game in the shotgun. The theory of this attack is to activate all the areas of the field and stretch the defense horizontally and vertically to get as close to one-on-one match-ups as possible. Trying to get the best of both worlds is difficult in itself, and if anyone expects perfection in either area, he's going to be disappointed. But the power of combining the two, sacrificing a little bit of the passing game and a little bit of the running game, makes running the triple option out of the pistol a very deadly weapon.

History of the Option

The single wing, the Halas T, and the Shaughnessy T were on top of the world back in the 1930s and early 1940s. The single wing was prominent in college football and in the pros. The Halas T proved to be dominating with the Chicago Bears under Coach George Halas, destroying opponents left and right. Clark Shaughnessy with Stanford University won the 1941 Rose Bowl, owning the western part of the United States. These offensive attacks were very effective for their time, but they were rightfully dethroned once the option hit the scene in college football.

The split-T, designed by Don Faurot, had the idea of faking close to the line of scrimmage and eliminating defenders. This is where the original option play got its start. It was originally called the running pitchout. Running the option and eliminating a defender—usually the end man on the line of scrimmage—were aspects that turned the college football world upside down. Bud Wilkinson at the University Oklahoma took the idea of the split-T and had the most success with it. The attack was predicated on maximum speed, deception on the line of scrimmage, and elimination of a defender by optioning him. With the success of the attack, the single wing offense was soon eliminated in college football. Several reasons caused this: The point of attack was predetermined, speed was slow, and the formation failed to attack all the dimensions of the field. Another reason—which football history has shown to be ironic—is that the single wing was considered a poor passing formation because the ball wasn't already in the passer's hand immediately following the snap. The T formation was something that facilitated the idea of throwing the ball because the ball was in the passer's hands immediately. The past decade of football has shown the opposite trend.

Once the split-T had dominated college football, defensive minds finally caught up with the offense. Wilkinson, who helped master this offense, devised a defensive game plan to stop the split-T. The defense he developed was the Oklahoma (Okie) defense. Using new principles of defensive line play, linebacker play, and secondary rotation put the effectiveness of the split-T on hold. By the mid-1960s, the split-T had faded quickly from the scene of college football. One problem that the coaches of that era had was opening up the passing game. Back then, throwing the football was looked down upon. Thus, when split-T teams refused to throw the football, the offense went dead.

By 1968, a pioneer named Emory Bellard came to his head coach Darrell Royal with a new idea. With Royal being in trouble for several mediocre seasons, Bellard came to him with a new idea: running the T formation with a triple option, moving the backs closer together, moving the fullback up, and splitting a receiver out. Bellard said he had experimented with the formation when he was still a high school coach. As football history has shown, when a coaching staff is desperate, it will try anything to get back up on its feet. Royal approved of the new offense and they went on to install it at the University of Texas.

Bellard took his new offense and revolutionized college football. The defense that had taken the split-T out of college football was now being destroyed. The triple option play out of the wishbone helped defeat an Oklahoma defense that had hurt many offenses in the past. The resume for the wishbone speaks for itself: Eight Associated Press national championships in 17 years shows how effective the offense was and is. During the 1980s, the flexbone became more popularly used. Many claim to have been one of the first to install the triple option out of the spread (flexbone/double slot), but the fact of the matter is that Ellison was the first person to create a triple option play out of the spread. He called it his "cowboy on the run" and a "three-way option."

At Georgia Southern and the military academies, the spread formation (flexbone) was becoming more popular. The only fault with the original wishbone offense was the limitability of the passing game. Believe it or not, using option principles, the passing game out of the wishbone isn't bad. But if two minutes are left in the game and the defense knows the offense is going to throw the football, the offense is in trouble. Also, football coaches are copycats. The average football coach naturally runs what the most popular offense is at the time. In the 1980s, the modern passing game was being developed by Bill Walsh, Dennis Erickson, Mike Price, and Darrel "Mouse" Davis. Selling these new concepts out of the wishbone is impossible because of the structure of the formation. As a result of that and how hard recruiting is for the wishbone, by the end of the 1980s, the wishbone was bleak. The spread (flexbone) was one of the main tools to run the triple option from, including the I bone at the University of Colorado and Tom Osborne at the University of Nebraska. But the idea of running a systematic option offense in college football was gone by the 1990s. Nebraska was still running the option, but it wasn't part of the wishbone system. Once the year 2000 hit, the option as a system was a lost cause in major college football.

Although the option seemed to have vanished from major college football, it was still being run by lower-division programs. While that was going on, spreading the field and throwing the ball became more and more popular in college football. At the same time, Paul Johnson at Georgia Southern and the Naval Academy dominated the ground game with limited talent. The option was then given a chance: Paul Johnson took his 2009 Georgia Tech Yellow Jackets to the Orange Bowl. Georgia Tech, Army, Navy, and Air Force have dominated the ground game by using the same offensive principles that the wishbone had established.

The past decade has shown the trend to wide-open football. That's where the pistol and the spread connect with each other. The University of Nevada first broke the scene running the pistol and the University of West Virginia and the University of Texas helped popularize the "zone read" out of the shotgun. The idea of running the spread option out of the pistol (to the authors' knowledge) was tried first by the Virginia Military Institute around 2005 and 2006. This shows this idea has been around for some time now. This book is meant to be a way to show how the original themes of the option, established by the split-T and the wishbone, put together with some modern ideas can give an offense a theoretical, numerical, angular, and space advantage against any defense.

At the core of the option is the wishbone. The wishbone is the gold standard of option football. Hopefully, this book shows that using old principles established not by "spread gurus" of the past 10 years but old school option coaches is the theoretical gold standard for moving the football.

1

Measuring a Play's Effectiveness

Coaches can measure a play's effectiveness in several ways. While the term *effective* can be subjective, certain factors need to be considered when evaluating a football play. Many great football plays can be executed very well in a variety of offensive systems. However, an effective football play isn't merely about drawing up a play on a chalkboard. An effective play must be based on sound theory, philosophy, and reasoning for it to be consistently successful. Thousands of football plays have been run throughout history. Some have stood the test of time and are still in use today, while others have disappeared from modern football. The plays that have stood the test of time measure up when considering the following factors of measuring a play's effectiveness.

Determining a Play's Effectiveness

Attacking the Defense Horizontally

The football field is 53.3 yards wide. To achieve maximum effectiveness, a play should threaten the field from sideline to sideline. Two significant reasons exist for this. The first reason is simple spacing. By stretching the defense horizontally, the offense can create as close to a one-on-one matchup as possible. The most difficult thing to do in football is to tackle in space. By utilizing the field's entire width, an offense can force defenders to tackle in space. The role that open space has can be illustrated in the fact that if the football field were 100 yards wide, the offense would have the advantage over the defense because more room would exist for the defense to cover. But if the field were 25 yards wide, the defense would have the advantage.

Another dimension to the principle needs to be mentioned. The fewer number of players involved in a play, the greater the advantage the offense has. If football were played with five players on each team, the defense would be at a great disadvantage. If football were played with 17 players on each team, the offense would have a difficult time moving the ball up and down the field. The best example of this is six, seven, or eight-man football. The scores of these games are very high because of the limited number of players on the field. Arena league football also bolsters this.

Creating one-on-one matchups through the use of spacing and limiting the number of players involved in the play are two strong principles that should be applied when examining a play's effectiveness. Based on those principles, an effective play is one that stretches the defense with multiple points of attack. Figures 1-1 and 1-2 provide a comparison of the triple option to a conventional power play.

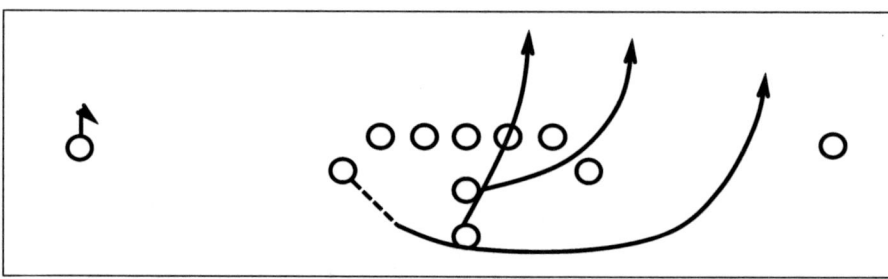

Figure 1-1. Triple option

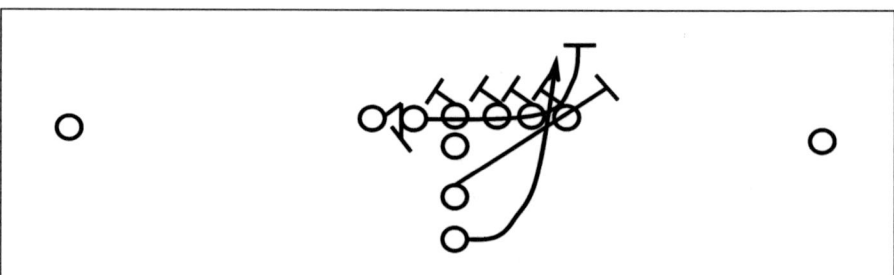

Figure 1-2. I formation power

The two examples clearly show which play attacks the entire width of the field. The power play out of the I formation can be a great play, but in terms of attacking a defense horizontally, it's not as effective as the triple option. The triple option stretches the attack from sideline to sideline, which means the defense has multiple points of attack it must account for.

Holding Off Defensive Pursuit

The next factor to consider when measuring a play's effectiveness is how well the play holds off defensive pursuit. Pursuit is the enemy of offense in the sense that defensive pursuit allows a defense to gain numbers at the point of attack. For defense, it's simple: Pursuit equals numbers—and numbers equal a defensive advantage. The pursuit principle goes hand in hand with the first principle of having multiple points of attack. If a defense is stressed at multiple points, an offense can hold defenders and slow down defensive pursuit. The triple option is a play that holds off defensive pursuit by attacking the entire width of the field.

When the option first came to being in the early 1940s, the single wing was the dominant offense in college football. One of the issues that single wing offenses ran into was holding defensive pursuit. Defenses could immediately run to the point of attack—whether it be the spinner series, the buck lateral series, or the trap series. In contrast, early option offenses were able to hold off pursuit. Defensive pursuit caused the single wing to fall out of favor and put the split-T option in charge of college football for a decade.

Because the early double option play had two points of attack, it was impractical for the defense to simply run to just one point of attack. When the option play was first introduced into college football by Don Faurot, collegiate coaches were stunned by how much they could hold pursuit on a defense. When Bill Yeoman added the triple option, more parts of the defense were frozen for two reasons. The first is the natural "freeze" of certain members of the defense when they're being read. The second is that the offense added another point of attack to the offense to combat the defense. Combating the principle of pursuit is key in measuring a play's effectiveness. Eliminating pursuit means fewer defenders at the point of attack. The fewer number of defenders at the point of attack for the offense, the greater advantage the offense has on that particular play.

Can Smaller, Below-Average Offensive Linemen Succeed?

Championships are won and lost on the offensive and defensive lines. In measuring a play's effectiveness, the level of difficulty of each player's responsibility should be considered. Because it's practical to assume that championships are won and lost at the line of scrimmage, it's also practical to first consider the difficulty of an offensive lineman's responsibility. Figures 1-3 through 1-6 show comparisons of the triple option with common power, iso, and inside zone plays.

Power, iso, and inside zone are predicated on creating movement and winning one-on-one blocks along the line of scrimmage. The power play requires the playside guard and tackle to double-team the 3 technique all the way to the backside linebacker. This is a difficult skill to accomplish with average linemen. The splits are very tight, so the

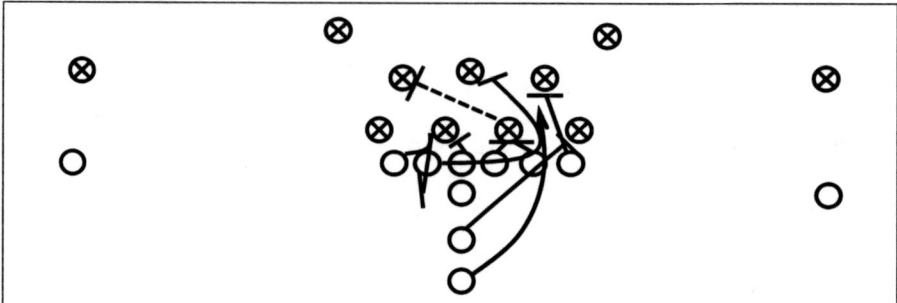

Figure 1-3. Power

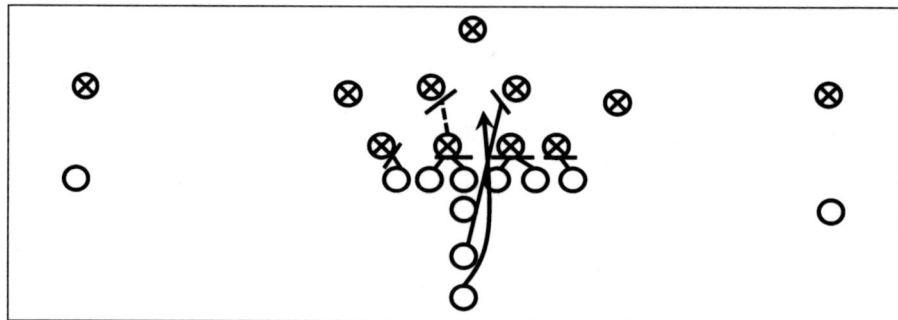

Figure 1-4. Iso

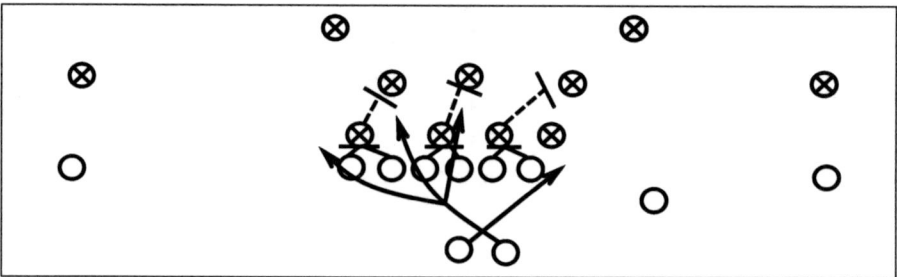

Figure 1-5. Inside zone

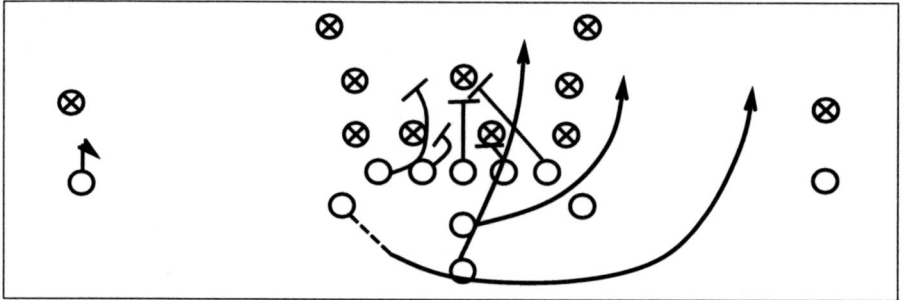

Figure 1-6. Triple option

entire play hinges on the idea that offensive linemen will move the defenders off the ball. While the power play is one of the most utilized plays in football today, it requires a high level of ability on the offensive line.

The isolation play requires a very similar skill set to the one needed to run the power play. The isolation play out of the I formation depends on everybody on the line of scrimmage to win one-on-one blocks. While the isolation play is one that has stood the test of time, it also heavily depends on offensive linemen being superior to their counterparts.

The inside zone play is different. Inside zone has more leeway when it comes to dominating defenders at the point of attack. It's a physical play. However, it can be successful with linemen who simply stay engaged with defenders. Quicker linemen will have a better chance at succeeding with the inside zone scheme than power and iso. While the inside zone doesn't require the same level of physicality as the power or iso play, it does require that linemen be able to maintain contact with defenders for a significant amount of time.

The triple option is designed to allow inferior offensive linemen to succeed. Many of the blocks required for the offensive line are technique blocks. Even so, for the sake of argument, unlike power, iso, and inside zone, the triple option only needs to win one block on the line of scrimmage. If the offense can't block that one defender, an answer within the option system requires that the defender be read instead of blocked. When running any other running game, at some point, the offense has to win blocks at the point of attack. If a 3 technique is used, the offensive line can't move, meaning the offense can't run the ball inside. The service academies have shown that inferior offensive linemen can be successful within the spread offense.

The Difficulty of the Play for the Skill Positions

If the triple option gives the offensive line an advantage, it also shifts the burden to the skill positions. While more is required from the skill positions than from offensive linemen in this system, the triple option requires very few techniques from these players relative to other offensive systems.

Many critics of the option offense claim that to run the triple option, the offense must have superior athletes. This statement is far from the truth. Is it true it can enhance the threat to the defense? Absolutely, but it doesn't hinder the offense to a status of useless. Many offenses require tailbacks that are 4.5 runners and under with receivers that range from 6'1" to 6'4" and tight ends who can block, stretch a defense vertically, and make tough catches over the middle. It also requires a quarterback who can make all the throws and has above-average height and a cannon arm. The triple option requires none of these traits. As already stated, would these characteristics help the option? Of course, but does the offensive system being run depend on having a stud quarterback year in and year out and big, strong, lengthy receivers who can beat any secondary? Does the offensive system require a tight end who can do everything?

Does it require a broad range of personnel traits needed by five to seven competent skill positions? It's fantastic if a school can fill these requirements, but the reality of the situation is that a majority of football programs aren't blessed with these characteristic traits. The option is open to many different body types. For example, what value in a pro-style offense does a 5'6" player have? Absolutely none to that offense. Within the scope of the option offense, if he's a hard worker with speed, he could be a valuable asset to the offense.

Illustrating the difficulty of base plays within other systems will show the difficulty that's placed on the quarterback and other skill positions compared with the triple option. For the sake of argument, the triple option will be compared with other offensive base pass plays. The reason is that other offensive base run plays, the quarterback does nothing but hand the ball off and boot away from the play.

Many West Coast offenses feature the "stick" concept as a core play in their playbook (Figure 1-7). The quarterback must come up to the line and determine whether it's man or zone. The primary side he's looking at is the stick route to the tight end side if it's zone. He has the freedom to go to the double slants side if it's man. He can also stick to the tight end side if it's man. The quarterback will take a three-step drop with no hitch and read the flat defender and the ball will be gone by his third step. Many moving parts exist in this play. The tight end will run a stick route. Versus zone, he'll sit in the hole. If it's man or if he's attached, he'll stick his foot in the ground and turn out. In many West Coast teams' philosophy, this is an efficient play designed to get four to seven yards. Countless techniques are taught in every facet of this play to gain only four to seven yards. A coach must teach the quarterback where to go depending on whether it's man, cover 2, 3, 4, 6, or 10, or press. That's a lot on the quarterback's plate to gain only four to seven yards. This is also but one play of an infinite amount in the West Coast offense.

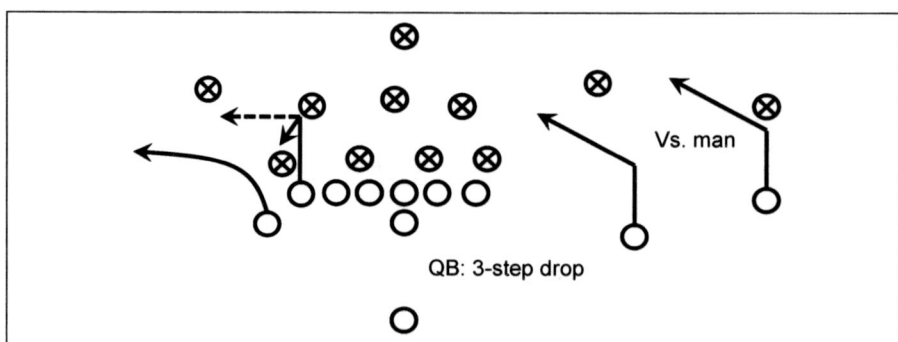

Figure 1-7. West Coast stick route

The bench route (Figure 1-8) has many facets to it. The quarterback drop varies from coach to coach, but it would be a five-step drop and the hitches to the drop would vary from coach to coach. The split end will run a curl route, unless it's cover 2, in which case he converts it to a fade. The flanker will run an 8- to 12-yard speed out depending on the cushion the corner gives him. The tight end will read the middle of the field. If the middle of the field is open, he'll run a short post, splitting the safeties. If the middle of the field is closed, he'll run a seam route about two yards outside of the hash. Both running backs will check-release off the outside linebackers. If the linebackers come on a blitz, the running backs have to pick them up. If the linebackers drop in coverage, the running backs run swing routes. This play presents the same predicament as the stick route: It has a lot of moving parts. This play can become an efficient and explosive play depending on how the defense reacts. However, this is one of many plays in the West Coast offense that skill players and quarterbacks have to master for the offense to work. This route is one of many for which the quarterback, receivers, and running backs have to be on the same page for it to work.

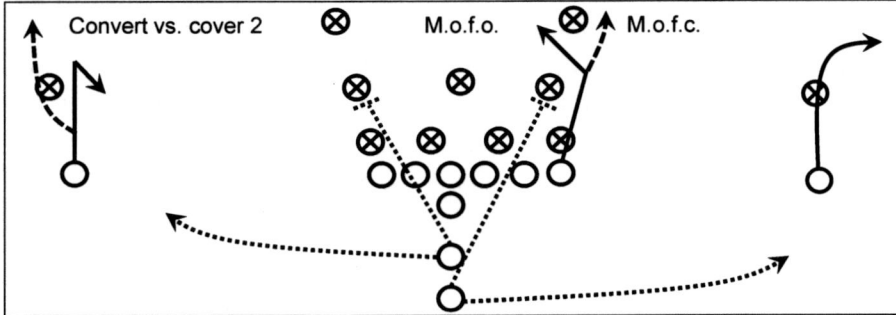

Figure 1-8. Bench route

Compared with West Coast plays, the base 4 vertical play (Figure 1-9) is much more explosive and is used more for teams who run a 2x2 spread. Most teams who run a 2x2 spread have this as a staple play, which is theoretically better than the West Coast philosophy. However, this is being compared with the difficulties of all skill positions compared with the triple option.

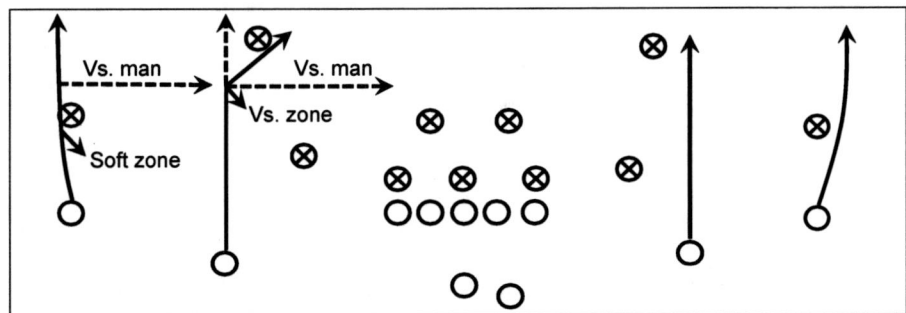

Figure 1-9. Base 4 vertical

The play's details vary greatly from coach to coach. However, the way it was originally invented is shown. The quarterback will look at the right slot receiver first and he'll throw the football on his third step if the receiver is open. If not, the quarterback then shifts his eyes to the left slot receiver. The slot receiver will read the coverage and react accordingly. If the quarterback is uncomfortable or if he has a cloudy read, he'll pay attention to the left slot receiver and see how he reads coverage. Again, compared with West Coast plays, this play in theory is much better to hang the offense's hat on—assuming it's a huge part of a team's game plan every week. The point is that the skill positions in these other offenses have a lot more to work on than triple option skill positions, especially more technical and specific aspects to the entire realm of those offenses than a team that specializes in the option.

Critics will say that the triple option has a lot of moving parts to it for the skill positions. They're correct in their assertion. However, the triple option play will always consist of 40 to 60 percent of a team's game plan every week regardless of what kind of defense the opposition runs. The triple option is covered in more detail in Chapter 2. However, theory, history, and results have proven that the triple option quarterback doesn't need a rocket arm, infinite knowledge about every coverage, stunt, and front the defense will show, and doesn't need to be an all-world athlete. It's also understood that once the quarterback masters the triple option, everything else in the offense is very easy to pick up because everything flows together.

Are All Defenders Accounted For?

Many base run plays are predicated on dominating the line of scrimmage. However, another downfall of many run plays is the inability to account for every defender on the field. The triple option almost never has this predicament, whereas many other run plays do. For example, in a power play vs. 4-3 cover 4 (Figure 1-10), the safeties are unaccounted for. What's the answer for wanting to run the ball if the defense is playing cover 4 where the safeties are primary run support? Theoretically, none.

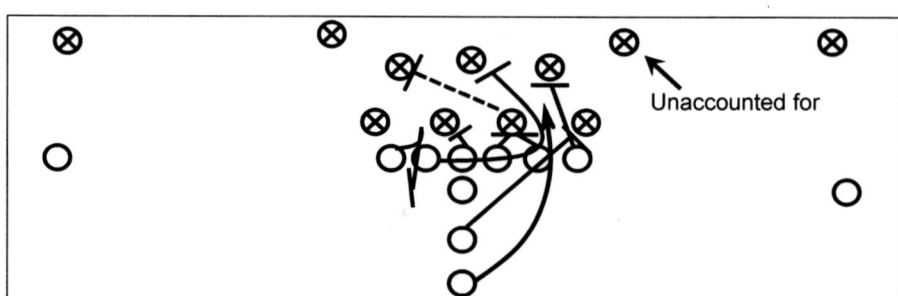

Figure 1-10. Power vs. 4-3 cover 4

Against cover 3 (Figure 1-11), again, in theory, no answer exists in the run game for this unaccounted-for defender. Not only does the power and isolation play require big, strong linemen, but it doesn't even account for everybody on the field. The offensive line could theoretically dominate the line of scrimmage and the play could still go for no gain. The normal depth for an I formation running back is usually seven yards deep. It's not difficult to grasp the concept that safeties at seven or nine yards deep can come up and make a tackle for no gain or a three- to four-yard gain.

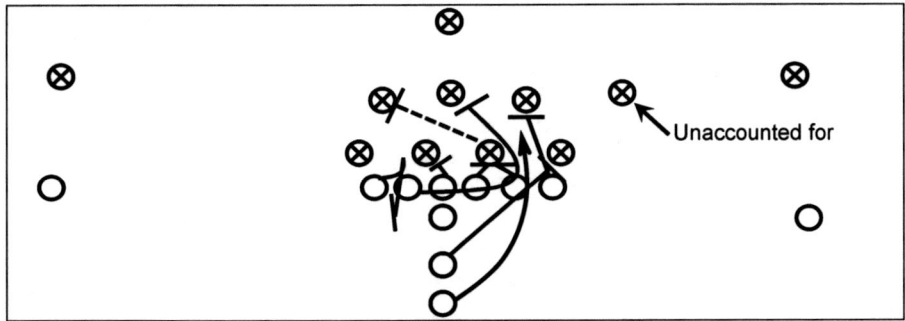

Figure 1-11. Power vs. 4-3 cover 3

The inside zone (Figure 1-12) and outside zone (Figure 1-13) are better answers than power and isolation. Because the running back has the freedom to bang, bend, or bounce or read the alphabet, he has more leeway to get away from unaccounted-for players. Because the running back's path isn't necessarily pre-determined, safeties who have a wrong run fit can be giving the offense an automatic six points. However, the point remains the same: The safeties still aren't accounted for. In a cover 4 situation, the safeties could be free to be run stoppers. Or if the defense is in a cover 2 shell and correctly "spills" the play to the unblocked corners, the play will go nowhere.

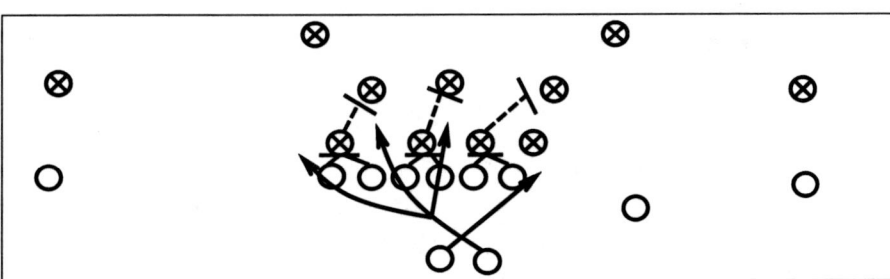

Figure 1-12. Inside zone

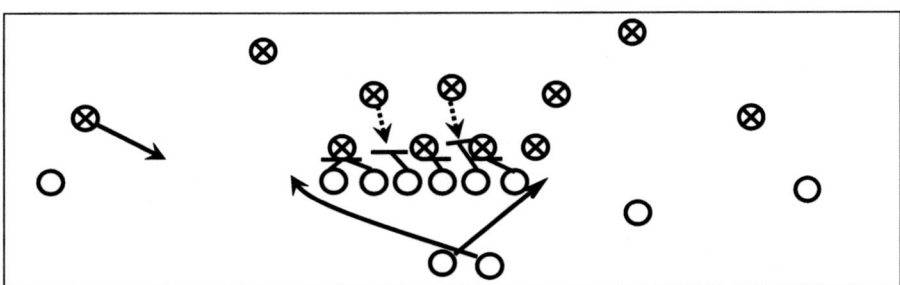

Figure 1-13. Outside zone

Theoretically, in running zone, the tight end and tackle should be able to combo the 5 technique to the corner. But practically, when has that ever happened on inside zone? Even if they correctly combo the 5 technique to the corner, the safety is still unaccounted for in the box. Again, unlike power and iso, this play has more leeway and is stronger in theory because it's blocking gaps. But the reality of the play is different. At some point, the running back is going to have to run somebody over or make somebody miss for the play to be successful.

Against a sound defense, the triple option will almost always account for everybody in the defensive picture. Figure 1-14 illustrates the triple option vs. the 4-3. (More frontswill be discussed later.) Compared with the other run plays that have been reviewed, the triple option accounts for everybody in the picture.

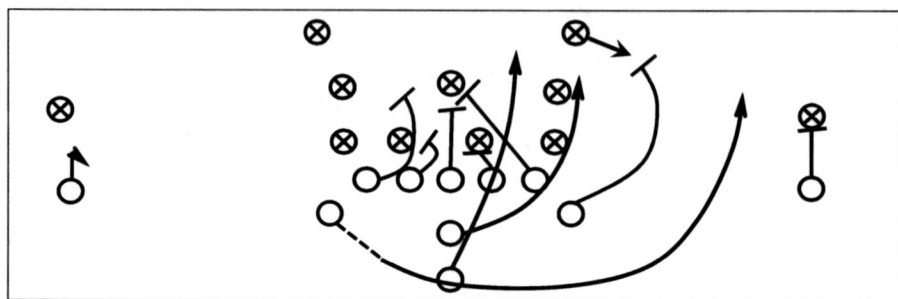

Figure 1-14. Triple option vs. 4-3

In What Situations Can a Play Be Run?

Most offensive plays are usually good only in certain situations. The triple option play is good anywhere on the field and on almost any down. Many plays are situational plays. The triple option is as good on third-and-10 as it is on first-and-10. Once perfected, this play can be run from goal line to goal line. This is a key measurement of a play's effectiveness. The more situations and field position markers the play can be successful in, the more practical it is to run. The triple option can score a touchdown on any part of the field if executed 100 percent.

Is the Play Based in a System?

A great wishbone coach once said "90 percent of offenses don't run an offense—they just run plays." That statement is one of the sad truths of football. Most teams don't run an offense with core plays. They just run random plays that don't fit in the realm of a well-oiled offensive machine. A lot of offenses have no answer for what a defense does with its base play. Running the triple option as the base play of a system gives a clearer picture to the coaches and players. Everything begins and ends with the triple option. Whatever the defense does, the system has an answer. Whether it's another running play, a tweak in the blocking scheme, or a pass, the triple option as a system has concrete answers to all defenses. Other systems may have answers, but at the end of the day, if the offense can't move a 3 technique from point A to point B, it really doesn't matter what the supposed answer is. It's pretty simple: When a play is part of a system, the effectiveness of the play can only improve.

Does the Offense Have the Chalk Last?

Running the triple option will always give coaches and players on offense the chalk last. The concept of the offense having the chalk last comes from the great Darrel "Mouse" Davis, the co-inventor of the run-and-shoot offense. Many core similarities exist between a run-and-shoot offense and an option offense, but the most common theme is that both systems will always have the chalk last. Running the triple option always gives the offense strategic moves during the play (which is the same with the run-and-shoot offense). When West Coast teams run power or iso or when wing-T teams run belly or bucksweep, the second the quarterback receives the snap, the play is already pre-determined. The revolutionary idea of the option offense is that nobody on the field knows who'll get the ball. It all depends on the defenders' reactions. This principle also unintentionally gives offensive players a lot of confidence and power. Knowing and understanding that no matter what the defense does the offense is right and the defense is wrong are revolutionary and empowering concepts to football players.

Measuring the Effectiveness of a Formation

Measuring the possibilities of a formation is important when trying to come up with sound fundamental football. A formation should be measured by many key aspects.

Balance

A balanced formation forces a defense to be balanced. An unbalanced formation naturally forces a defense to be unbalanced. A strong suit that the offense can use is balance because being balanced will give the offense its greatest advantage. Tendencies are highly exposed in unbalanced formations. But if an offense is simply balanced, it can kill whatever tendencies a defense can key on. Balance makes the spread and wishbone hard to defend. Proper formation balance will make the defense play 5.5 defenders on each side (Figure 1-15).

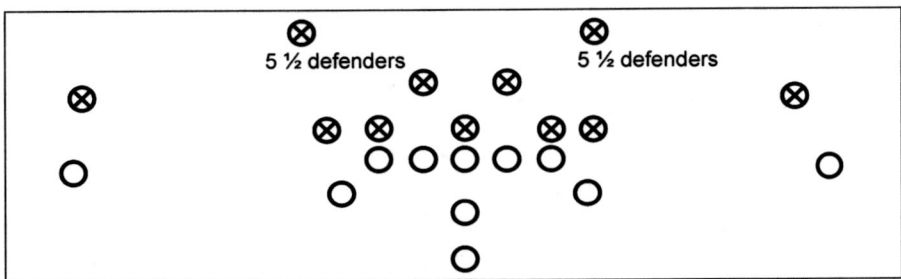

Figure 1-15. 5.5 defenders on each side

This makes the counting system within the option much simpler. An unbalance in numbers will many times lead the offense to miscount the defenders. If the defense is overloaded to one side, the offense should run the triple option to the other side. With quick motion, the offense can automatically outnumber the defense. However, if the defense shifts with motion, that makes it vulnerable to the backside option game

Stretching the Defense Horizontally

As stated before, the football field is 53.3 yards wide. Stretching a defense to defend every inch of the field is important in moving the football. The principle that will be restated in this book multiple times is that the fewer number of players in a football play, the greater the advantage is to the offense. The more players, the more the advantage is to the defense.

What gets lost in attacking the defense horizontally is how many gaps the defense has to defend (Figure 1-16). The more gaps, the greater the advantage the offense has. If a defender misses an assignment with his gap responsibility, a big play will occur. The spread option formation offers a unique challenge for a defense to prepare for within the structure of gaps.

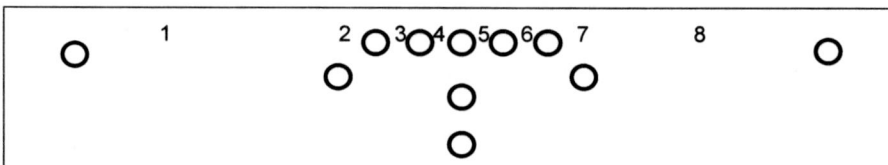

Figure 1-16. Spread gaps

The gap structure begins to weaken the defense by stretching it throughout the width of the field. Technically speaking, eight gaps require eight defenders to play gap responsibility before either slotback goes in motion. Figure 1-17 compares this with the wing-T formation.

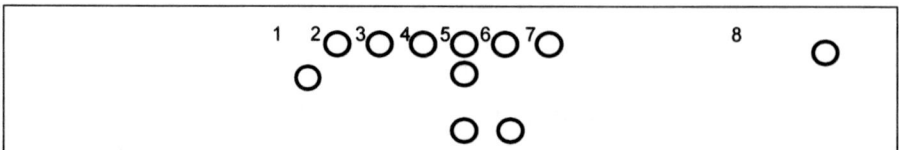

Figure 1-17. Wing-T gaps

Both formations require eight gaps to be covered efficiently by the defense. However, a key difference exists in defending these formations. The base wing-T formation is a compressed formation with relatively small splits. This doesn't necessarily stretch the defense horizontally. Attacking the width of the field is key in having an explosive offense. With crowding an area, the defense has the advantage in numbers. Pursuit is numbers—and numbers is defense. The fewer one-on-one match-ups the offense has, the greater the advantage to the offense.

Why are the spread option gap responsibilities more effective than a base 4 wide receiver spread? Do they have the same number of gaps the defense has to cover? Yes, but the spread option is superior for one reason: The slot receivers in a base 4 wide receiver spread formation are spread out too wide to control their gap to the inside (Figure 1-18).

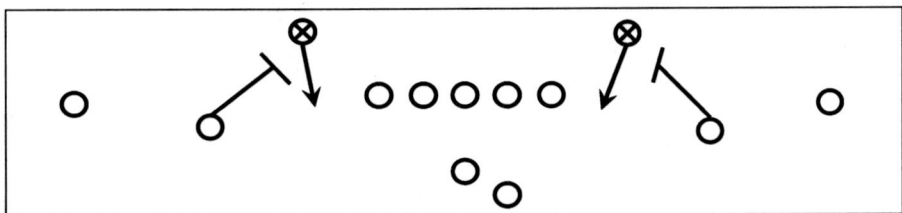

Figure 1-18. Base 4 wide receiver set

Yes, the defense has to defend eight gaps, but two of them are difficult to control. In essence, the defense isn't scared to be threatened within these gaps. Slotbacks are close enough to the line of scrimmage to be able to theoretically control the gap inside of them and the gap outside of them. The advantage of the spread is that eight gaps are created horizontally and the formation is stretched out far enough to threaten the entire width of the field, but it's also compressed enough to control all eight gaps.

Does the Formation Attack the Field Vertically?

The importance of attacking the field horizontally has already been talked about. But a vertical threat will completely threaten all 11 defenders on the football field. It's impractical to say that a formation needs to threaten the field vertically for 100 yards or even 60 yards. However, the vertical stretch of a defense for 30 to 40 yards is very practical for an offense to get the proper stretch on a defense. The question then becomes "How many immediate vertical threats does the offense present to the defense?" The I formation has only three vertical threats (Figure 1-19).

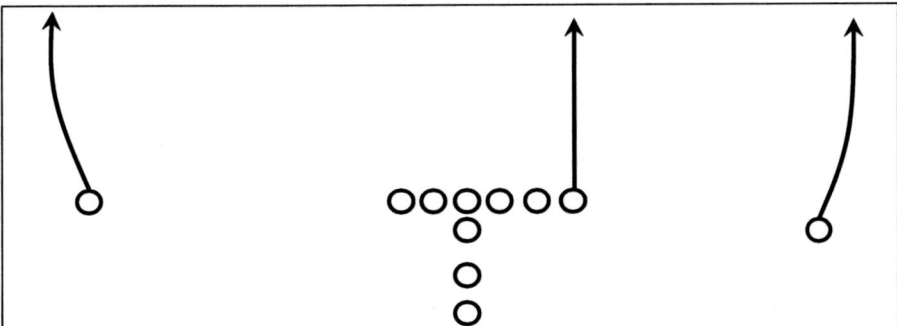

Figure 1-19. I formation vertical threats

In theory, this only stresses the defense vertically in three areas, which means the defense only has to worry about three vertical threats. Pre-motion in the spread threatens the field with four vertical threats (Figure 1-20).

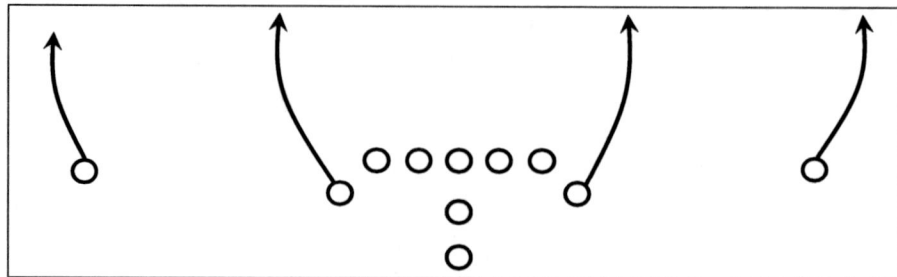

Figure 1-20. Spread option vertical threats

This is what sets the spread apart from the wishbone. Running the triple option with a lead blocker is the reason for the wishbone formation. Running the triple option with eight horizontal gaps and four vertical threats is the reason for the spread formation. Both approaches have costs and benefits, but the following theoretical reasons for the triple option and the spread formation need to be understood: to create gap conflict, to have balance, and to have four vertical threats. For those reasons, the triple option with the spread formation is a deadly weapon.

The Marriage Between a Formation and a Play

The theories stated are only good if a play and a formation can fit together. Given the theoretical arguments shown, it makes sense that the spread and the triple option go together better than any other play with any other formation. The success of this marriage has proven itself on the football field. Making the defense defend eight gaps and four verticals and also having to defend the best play in football put a defense in a bind. On short motion, the defense must defend all these areas that are based on the pistol spread option attack (Figure 1-21).

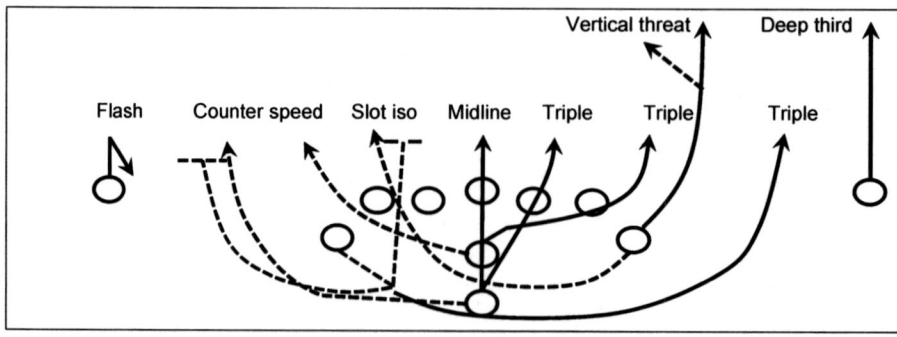

Figure 1-21. Pistol spread option points of attack

With quick motion, these are all the immediate places the defense must defend against. If a defense shies away from one of these points of attack, it will be burned. This is in contrast to the original points of attack with the wishbone formation (Figure 1-22).

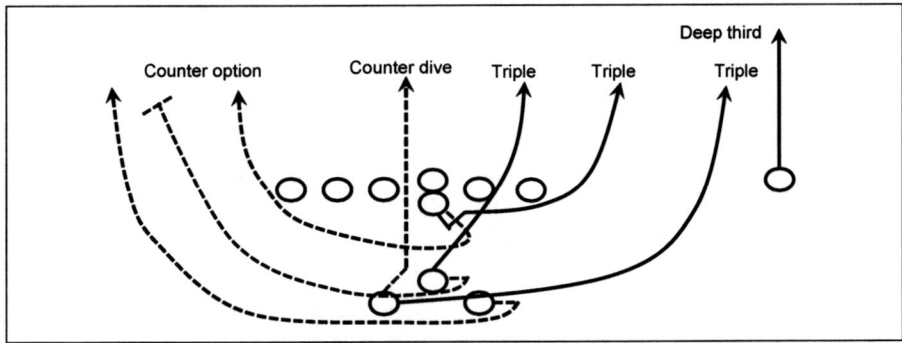

Figure 1-22. Wishbone points of attack

Comparing the two shows what a bind the defense is in. Both are using the triple option to create horizontal and vertical stretches on a defense—a technique that's seldom talked about.

The Truth About the Spread Formation

An unsaid truth about the spread formation is almost never talked about. Maybe it's not talked about because in today's football world, people can't fathom the triple option being run from any other formation. However, if the passing game through the spread isn't consistently attacking the defense vertically and the offense doesn't consistently attack the defense at all areas of the line of scrimmage, the spread is a very keyable offense. The same goes with the wishbone—except in the opposite direction. Without the triple option, it's a poor formation because of principles of a formation and its plays. If a team doesn't spend half its time perfecting its passing game with the spread, the team is running the wrong formation. The advantages of the spread are lost when it's only merely a running formation. If the offense consistently shows the defense a vertical passing game, the defense will defend those areas of the field. If not, the wishbone formation is the best at triple optioning.

Along the same lines, if a strict adherence to maintain attacking all areas of the line of scrimmage doesn't occur, the spread is a keyable formation. The reason is because of its use of quick motion. *Motion is a good that can turn evil.* That's a huge key defenses can and will use against the offense. Keeping the defense honest will make the offense sound. If the defense is unsound in its linebacker or defensive line play or is playing with unsound secondary rotation, a play will be open. However, not restricting the defense to these plays will make running the spread suicide against teams that are only out to stop the triple option. Even though the wishbone requires the same adherence to attacking all areas of the line of scrimmage because of stagnant backfield play, it's a better formation. The spread formation can magnify the wishbone's original principles, but straying away from these principles will make it an easy offense to figure out during the course of a game.

The Truth About the Pistol Formation

Fads come and go, and in today's football world, the fad is the pistol formation. It's the hip new thing everybody's excited about. However, most of that excitement is just the fact it's something new, not something that's theoretically sound. The reason for the pistol and the triple option being married together is to boost the effectiveness of the passing game. Pass protection has always been a problem for teams who are under center, especially double slot spread teams who have wide splits that the defense will take advantage of. *The main reason for the pistol and the spread being married is pass protection.* Too many coaches want to run the pistol because it's what's new, but if that's the reason they line up in the pistol, then they'll fail. They're not doing something with philosophy or theory on their side. They're doing something because they've been talked into being modern in today's football world.

A subject in football that's rarely talked about is the importance of pass protection. It's pretty simple: A coach can draw up all the cool-looking pass plays in the world. At the end of the day, if the quarterback has no protection, the play won't work. A vast majority of football coaches neglect pass protection because it's a dry subject to talk about. Most offensive coaches coach offense because they love the intricacies of offense. Most offensive line coaches love pounding defenses into submission, so it's understandable why most coaches neglect pass protection. But it must be understood that pass protection is the number one priority whenever the offense is throwing the football and that pass protection is everyone's responsibility. The pistol spread option activates the entire field. It's true that if a team wants to fully utilize the advantages of the gun, the pistol spread isn't the best option. It's easier to protect the quarterback when he's at five yards instead of three. But that's the sacrifice of running this particular offense. The triple and midline are much more effective under center and an all-out passing game is better with the quarterback five yards behind the center.

However, three yards is the happy medium where the quarterback can effectively run the triple and midline while having better pass protection than under center. It's true that critics can say this offense is sacrificing too much to marry two ideas. But the success of this offense speaks for itself. Sacrifice a little bit of the running game by starting the quarterback three yards behind the center with the tailback in a two-point stance at five and sacrifice a small portion of the passing game by having the triggerman line up two yards closer than he normally would. The point being is that the marriage starts with the importance of pass protection. Lining up in the pistol isn't a perfect answer nor is it the best theoretical answer for pass protection, but combining the best of the under-center option game with the benefits of good pass protection is the goal of this offense. Sound pass protection must be preached from day one.

The truth is, if the passing game is used as something to completely attack the defense—especially out of the pistol spread—it's the wrong thing for the offense to do. The reason for the spread formation is to attack the defense vertically and keep it honest—theoretically and philosophically—against the option game. However, operating out of the pistol gives a small extension of that attack. Being able to throw quick passes along with a dropback passing game can amplify an offense as long as it's not long or extensive in a West Coast–style manner and is strictly used as a constraint on a defense.

If a small extension of the passing game through better pass protection isn't a priority for an offense, then the pistol spread isn't for that particular team because the advantages in the option game are lost going to the pistol. The speed of the read is affected. The read can be cloudy because of where the mesh is taking place. It can be argued that the counter game out of the pistol is better because of depth from the line of scrimmage. But the advantages of the triple and midline option plays will be lost to the wind if the reasons for fully going to this offense aren't utilized.

The pessimism isn't shown for the sake of being pessimistic and the theories espoused here aren't simply theories for the sake of theory. This theory of the under-center game compared with the shotgun isn't backed up by theory but also by football history. As already discussed, one of the reasons why the single wing folded to the T formation was because of pursuit. Pursuit helped defenses defeat the single wing. Another reason for the extinction of the single wing is the shotgun snap. Because the single wing and the split-T formation were predicated on misdirection, the immediate placement of the ball was important within the mechanics of these offenses (Figures 1-23 and 1-24).

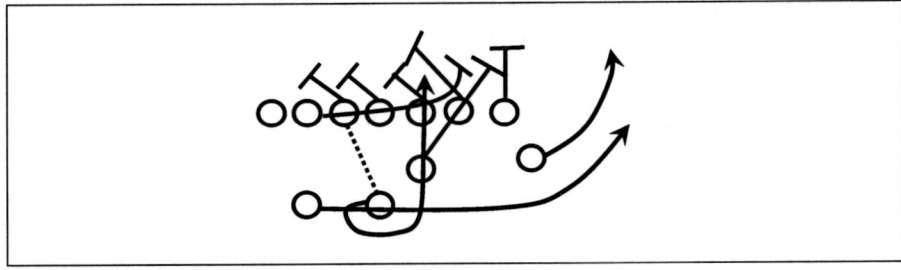

Figure 1-23. Single wing

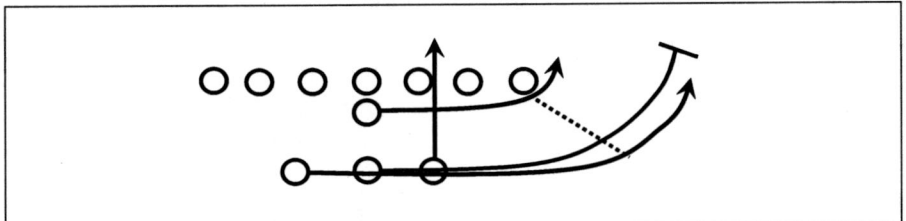

Figure 1-24. Split-T

When deciphering these two diagrams, the split-T fakes are operating closer to the line of scrimmage. The staple of the split-T offense is to have good fakes close to the line of scrimmage because deception would be better hidden from its closeness to the line of scrimmage and the attack would hit the perimeter faster because its faking would be on the line of scrimmage. The single wing faking takes place five yards beyond the line of scrimmage, which gives defenses time to recover from the initial fake.

There are specific reasons for going 60 to 70 years back in football history. The pistol, operating under the assumption of trying to be sexy rather than being theoretically sound, isn't a good offensive choice. However, without a clear explanation of theory, this is only snappy clinic talk. The offense is only out to please the man running the offense for being "sexy" and "cool" and "cutting edge," when the truth of the matter is that very little is ever invented in football. New coaches come up with "new ideas." However, the principles of "new ideas" have been around forever. The pistol spread option is no exception. This offense is a direct descendent of Don Faurot and Bud Wilkinson's split-T, Emory Bellard's wishbone, and Glenn "Tiger" Ellison's double slot formation. The pistol is added to acknowledge that the principles are still the exact same but that pass protection is better.

To summarize, the reasons for running certain option offenses are these: If an offense wants to run the ball the majority of the time, the wishbone triple option is second to none. It controls the perimeter of the defense by using the "run off" technique to attack the deep third of the field. The "lead back" principle makes perimeter blocking and variations of triple option blocking deadly. If the offense wants to run the ball but also wants to catch the defense off-guard from time to time, then the spread under center is the best option. This system has eight gaps and four vertical threats pre-motion. If the offense wants an extension to the spread option, it's out of the pistol while keeping the same spacing of the under-center option game. The extension consists of better pass protection, easier quarterback footwork in the passing game, and a small extension of the dropback, play-action, and screen systems. As already stated, the goal is to marry the best of the under-center option game with the best of the short shotgun. The key phrase is "small extension." The option offense is a repetition offense and the practice time required to perfect these techniques is scarce. If the offensive coordinator wants to run football's best 100 plays out of football's best 20 formations, this offense isn't for him.

Anyone who's interested in this offense is in for a steep change in offensive thinking, play calling, game planning, and attacking defenses. However, once this offense is utilized to its maximum potential, coaches won't want to go back to traditional football. The option principles started by Don Faurot, amplified by Emory Bellard, Franklin "Pepper" Rodgers, Paul "Bear" Bryant, and Barry Switzer, and enhanced by Glenn "Tiger" Ellison's double slot formation added to the short shotgun will give offenses principled and theoretical advantages over every defense they see.

2

The Triple Option

The specific origin of the triple option is unknown. However, in football literature, the first three-way option play shows up in Glenn "Tiger" Ellison's book *Run and Shoot Football: Offense of the Future*. Something can be said about the two parts of the triple option being created separately. Obviously, the split-T created the pitch option. Don Faurot famously called it the "running pitchout." In the early to mid-1950s, the split-T went through a structural change, causing the creation of the inside belly series. On this play, the quarterback rode the fullback all the way through the line and then rode the off back coming between the tackles. How this play is connected with the triple is that the defensive tackle wasn't blocked and the pre-determined handoff kept the defender guessing. Obviously, combining the two would eventually come in the form of the wishbone-T formation. In a more precise measure, Bill Yeoman must be credited with creating the triple option in college football. It was an accident that was caught on film, but that accident of giving the ball on a dive play with the defensive end screaming upfield gives the official collegiate creation to Yeoman.

The triple option has its name because three possibilities can happen on a given play. The first is the give to the fullback in the middle of the defense, the second is the quarterback keep, and the third is the ball being pitched to the perimeter. In his phenomenal book on the Cincinnati split back veer, Homer Rice noted that the origin of the triple option isn't important. Herein lies a good point: It's not important to know if the team has decided that its triple option structure is the split back veer. The split back veer had no evolution. It appeared out of nowhere. However, it's very important for a wishbone or a spread team to know and understand the evolution of the triple option through the "bone" or errors could occur because of the fault of not understanding the original thinking of the triple option.

When Emory Bellard first came up with the wishbone, he based it on solid football principles. The first idea was to send the split end downfield to attack the deep third of the field. Consistently attacking the deep third of the field theoretically forces the first defender to the sideline to take the receiver downfield to protect the deep third of the field. With that in mind, the second defender outside must be responsible for the pitch, the third defender is responsible for the quarterback, and the fourth is responsible for the fullback. This is significant because the overall goal of the option is eliminating defenders. If the corner is being sent downfield, three possibilities with a blocker exist, and only three defenders are left, the defense is theoretically destined to fail because of the numbers game. This is the original thought process of the triple option: Dictate how perimeter defenders can play and the offense is in control. Perimeter defenders are dictated because of the first principle of the triple option: Send the wide receiver downfield to attack the deep third of the field. This is a principle that has been lost in the wind in the realm of option football but is important because this is the principle that keeps defensive coverages in check. (This will be further covered in Chapter 3.)

The triple option requires five outside (on or outside the tackle) defenders to stop the play: one for the dive back, the wide receiver, the pitch, the quarterback, and the lead (arc) block. If all these are met, the defense is extremely vulnerable between the tackles, the backside counter game, or the passing game. Many spread option attacks can become victims to certain defensive schemes if the original wishbone principles aren't used. It's important to emphasize these principles and make the defense defend the field's entire width and 30 to 40 yards vertically. For an option offense to be successful, these standards must be met.

The triple option out of the pistol spread is illustrated in Figure 2-1; player assignments are listed in Table 2-1.

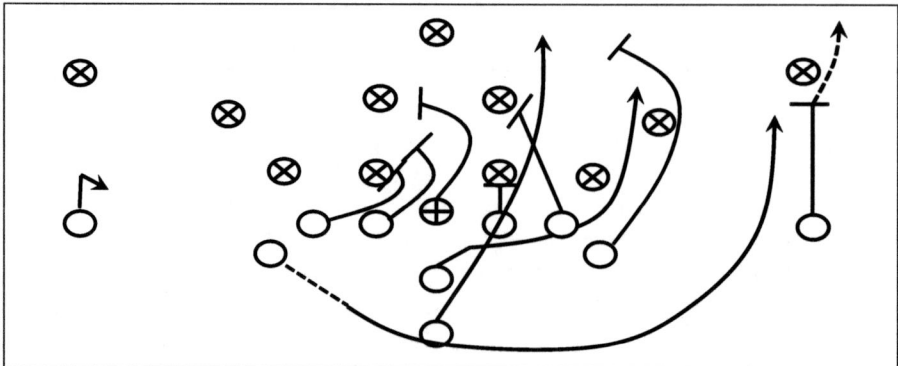

Figure 2-1. Triple option out of the pistol spread

QB	Triple footwork, reads #1, replaces, leverages pitch off #2
TB	Mesh, runs the wall, squares up shoulders as soon as possible
PSSB	Arc blocks #3
BSSB	Option route, three flat steps after passing tailback and works downhill
PSWR	Threatens the deep-third defender, then stalks
BSWR	Backside flash, then works to cut off
PST	Covered: loops to backer; uncovered: veers to backer
PSG	Base
C	Covered: 0-scoop; uncovered: playside backside technique
BSG	Vs. nose: scoops through the nose; vs. no nose: scoops, cuts if possible
BST	Scoops, cuts if possible

Table 2-1. Assignments for the triple option out of the pistol spread

Personnel Considerations

Skill Positions

Quarterback

Ever since the wishbone hit the scene in college football, an option quarterback's most important attribute is being an aggressive runner. An aggressive runner comes in all shapes and sizes. However, without an athlete who'll aggressively pull and replace or who'll take a small crease on an option play, this offense will be dead. Good option quarterbacks have been 6'2" and 215 pounds and can run a 4.6. Others have been less than 5'9" but have been quick and fast. Good option quarterbacks have also been athletes who aren't very athletic. A popular argument against running an option offense is that a team must have an all-world athlete at quarterback. That's far from the truth. Some of the best option quarterbacks have been slow quarterbacks who honestly aren't that quick, but they were aggressive runners and understood the offense.

Another important characteristic that helps an option quarterback is functional intelligence. The ability of a quarterback to functionally process information on the fly is important for an option offense. Sometimes, things on the football field don't happen the way they are drawn up on the chalkboard. In those cases, you need a quarterback who operates functionally and can perform in different situations. Football is not played on the chalkboard; it's played on the field.

The burden of this offense falls upon two skill positions. The quarterback is one of them and is the most important. The quarterback must believe, trust, and understand the offense. Without a quarterback who understands the mission of this offense, this offense will be hard to execute during a game.

Slotbacks

As stated, the quarterback is one of two skill positions on which the burden of this offense falls. The slot position is the other one. Without great slot play, this offense will fail. The slot position can literally be played by almost any size. Some of the best slotbacks in option football history have been shorter than 5'8". The best high school slotback to play in this offense was a player who was 5'6" and 145 pounds. The will to play hard is the most important attribute in playing slotback. Taking pride in blocking is something all slotbacks must have. This starts with the coaching staff and is something that can be infused into players. Having a full understanding of the offense is something that will carry significant weight with the success of this offense.

Tailbacks

The tailback position requires good vision and quickness through the hole. Quickness through the hole is much more important than top speed. As in the case with slotbacks, good tailbacks in this offense come in all shapes and sizes. Good ones have been 5'11" who run 4.5 or have been 6'0" and 230 pounds. Good ones have been short, stocky players who have the will to smash through the line of scrimmage and they've also been skinny players who have top speed. All high schools and colleges will have no problem filling this position. Some years, the offensive line positions will be something to worry about, but this will seldom be a problem with tailbacks and slotbacks.

Wide Receivers

Wide receivers in the option offense are primarily blockers. However, they'll catch many touchdowns in the play-action game. The will to stalk block, crack, and threaten the deep third of the field is important for them to succeed. As with the slot position, the will to play hard is the absolute most important attribute of a wide receiver. A wide receiver doesn't have to be the fastest, quickest, or biggest. Those attributes will help, but they're not a requirement.

Offensive Line

Guards

The best big-on-big blockers in the offense should be put at the guard spots. The most difficult block in this offense is one where the guard has to base block a defender over the top of him. Size, girth, and all the essential offensive line characteristics would be preferred here. Again, if those kinds of players aren't available for every spot, answers in this offense will help deal with this predicament.

Center

The center is a tricky position to fill. He doesn't need to be big and overpowering, but he does have to be quick. Quickness with decent size is the most important attribute to this position. He'll rarely have a situation where he has to block a noseguard one-on-one, but he'll usually have help. But quickness is something that must be assessed before assigning a player the position of center.

Tackles

The tackle spot is the easiest spot in the offense to fill. Tackles will mostly only block linebackers. This fact is significant because the offense can get away with putting small, slim players here. The tackle spot is a position where the offensive line is often trying to hide weak players from the defense. They'll occasionally have to kick out a 5 technique on midline. However, that's an angle block. Angle blocking doesn't require a monster offensive lineman.

Quarterback Play

No position in football is more important than the quarterback. Every offense has its intricacies regarding what the quarterback must do. But in the option offense, the quarterback is responsible for eliminating two defenders on a single play. For the option offense to be successful, the quarterback must make good decisions at least 90 percent of the time for the offense to work.

The Snap and Stance

This offense requires no prescribed quarterback stance. No evidence has verified that a tight, very-coached-up quarterback stance in the shotgun has any significant effect on how he plays. A comfortable athletic position with a slight knee bend that makes him agile is fine. Some mild coaching points can be used, such as locked-out knees. If a quarterback's knees are locked, it's difficult for him to perform his steps and work downhill. Other obvious coaching points exist, but a comfortable athletic stance from the quarterback is just fine.

The second the snap is performed, the quarterback starts moving downhill. Legally, once the ball is moved from the center, any action from any offender is legal. One goal of running the spread out of the pistol is working downhill. Thus, legally, it's best for the quarterback to immediately start his steps once the center snaps the ball. Attacking the football puts the quarterback in attack mode. The quarterback needs to be in the mindset that he's attacking the defense, not the other way around. Once a quarterback believes that the defense is dictating offensive flow, the offense is in trouble. This is a good start for the quarterback's thought process.

As already explained, the quarterback's heels must be three yards away from the tip of the football (Figure 2-2). Any deeper and the quarterback has put the offense in a position to where the goal of meshing the under-center option game and passing out of the pistol becomes foggy. Any closer and the advantages of pass protections are lost.

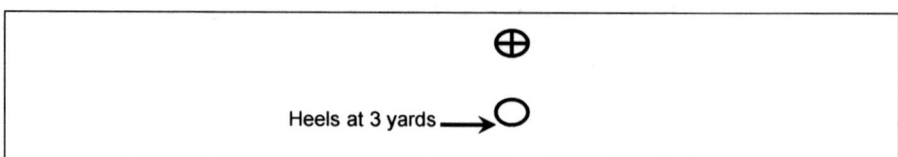

Figure 2-2. Quarterback's heels three yards from tip of the ball

Quarterback Steps

The quarterback's first steps in the attack set the tone for every play. If the steps are wrong, everything else is wrong. The first step occurs with the quarterback's playside foot (Figure 2-3). It needs to be at a slight angle. Something that must be explained is that out of the pistol, angles are exaggerated. Unlike under-center wishbone quarterback footwork where the quarterback takes a large step back at a 45-degree angle, the quarterback must recognize that when operating with depth beyond the line of scrimmage, if his first step is too wide, then the entire play is busted. No prescribed precise angle—just a slight angle, working downhill for the quarterback, is the best way to start operating in the pistol.

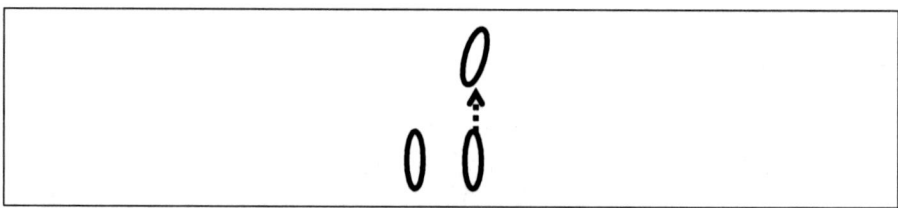

Figure 2-3. Quarterback's first step with playside foot

The quarterback's second step follows the first step and must be maintained on the angle the first step has placed. Once the quarterback's second foot is in the ground, he'll mesh and make sure his feet are underneath him. His feet must be underneath him because he must be able to take a small "slide" step. The slide is performed for several reasons. First, it gives the quarterback more time to read. Second, it helps him work downhill and keeps his transfer of weight downhill and attacking. Third, it allows the quarterback to "mesh" and start to accelerate on his path at the same time. One of the goals of operating out of the pistol is that the quarterback is a magician. A really well-coached quarterback out of the pistol is able to start to accelerate downhill while still meshing with the tailback. He's able to pull the ball or give it at the last second while transferring his weight and accelerating downhill.

Once the quarterback has pulled the football after his small slide/shuffle with both feet, he needs to perform his "depth step." This step puts the quarterback on a direct path downhill. His outside foot needs to be on a downhill 45-degree step from the line of scrimmage and aggressively replace the handoff key (Figure 2-4).

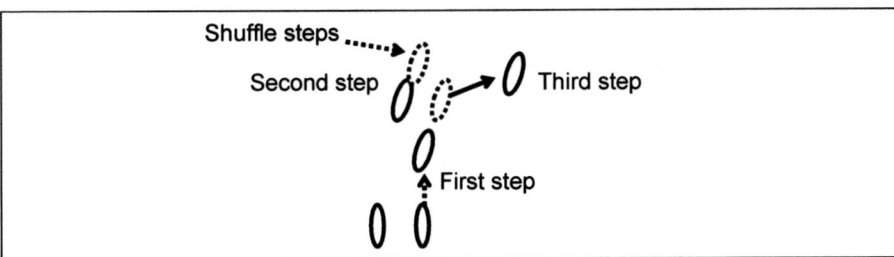

Figure 2-4. Quarterback's footwork

Who Are the Defenders to Be Eliminated?

Where does the count start? The first down lineman outside of the B gap. Another way to put it is the first defender from a 4i out. That defender is labeled #1. Back in the day, option football counted everybody on the side of the defense and the offense would eliminate the #3 and #4 defenders. Evolutionary thought processes led by spread option coaches have changed that confusion and have made a simpler way of identifying defenders.

The quarterback and tailback will eliminate #1 by reading him with the dive phase of the triple option. He'll be a complete nonfactor because the offense is reading him instead of blocking him (Figure 2-5).

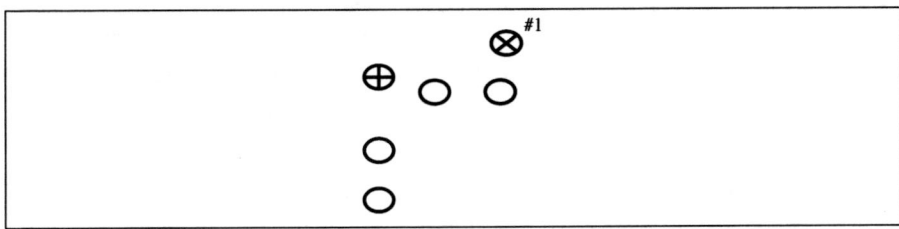

Figure 2-5. Handoff key

The next question is who's #2? Defender #2 is simply the next defender outside #1. The offense will eliminate #2 by reading him in the pitch phase of the triple option. Again, as in the case of #1, the offense is eliminating him by reading him (Figure 2-6).

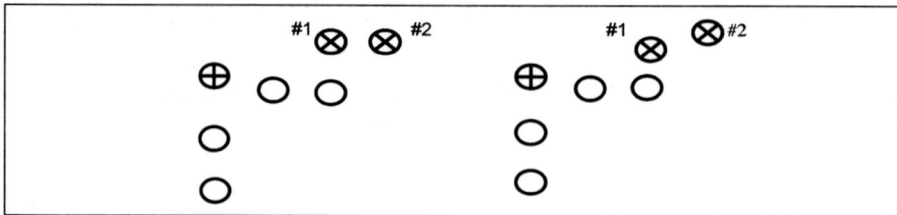

Figure 2-6. Handoff and pitch keys

The last question to be answered is who's #3? Defender #3 is the next most dangerous man. If that's too broad of a rule, another way to put it is simply the third man outside of the B gap (Figure 2-7).

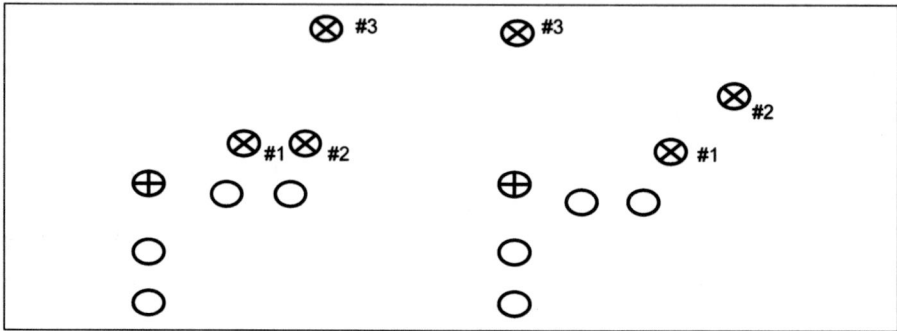

Figure 2-7. Read keys and the #3 defender

The Mesh

The most important part of the triple option is the mesh and the read of the dive key. Throughout the history of the triple option, many different theories or techniques have been used to run the triple option. To be thorough, many popular ways to mesh the quarterback and the fullback must be talked about for a coach to have enough information about the advantages and disadvantages of each use.

The most popular way to mesh in today's college football world is the "point method" technique. This method is used at Georgia Tech, Navy, and Georgia Southern—just to name a few. The technique is simple. After taking his steps, the quarterback will point the ball at the handoff key. Once he points the ball at the read, he'll simply read "Is the handoff key attacking the fullback?" Once he does that, he'll make his decision to give. This next technique is different depending on who's teaching it. Some coaches teach that the quarterback must make his decision by the time the fullback reaches his front foot. Others teach that he must make his decision by his back foot. Once the fullback has reached either one of these points, the quarterback must live or die by his decision. No ride is taught. If contact occurs between the quarterback and the fullback, it's an automatic give.

This isn't a good way to "hook up" between the quarterback and the fullback. The main selling point of the "point method" is that fumbles won't happen. That's far from the truth. Point method teams fumble the mesh roughly the same number of times the "ride and decide" teams do. Obviously, ball security is the number one priority for any offense, so in theory, this is an excellent reason to choose the point method. But this method doesn't give the quarterback the best tools available to make a consistently good decision. If a defender is executing a mesh charge, the point method can make defeating this difficult and can put a quarterback's mind in doubt. Point method could be summed up as the doctrine of best guess. The act doesn't give the quarterback enough information to thoroughly make the right decision. It's true that to some extent, quarterbacks can handle deception used by the defense and it isn't a problem, but the goal is to maximize the tools for the quarterback to make the best decision.

Another reason exists for not using the point method technique. This is specifically from the pistol formation. In the pistol, the quarterback is working downhill. He's not hopping his first two steps. He's actively working downhill with his footwork. He has no efficient way to "point" the ball working downhill. Also, because the mesh is working from the pistol, room for error exists. When the quarterback is under center, it can be argued that he's close enough to the read for there to be no room for error, which in most cases is correct. From the pistol, a layer of deception has to exist because of the depth between the line of scrimmage and the quarterback.

Some option teams teach the "hip method." They teach that if the quarterback is going to give the ball, he'll slide the ball to the fullback's far hip and that if he's going to pull the ball, he's going to ride on the near hip. The fullback will have his far hand as a stopper and his near hand on his inside hip. Once the football is "slid" into the fullback's near hand, he'll slide his bottom hand to meet the football. The obvious problem with this technique is that the fullback will slide his bottom hand and then rearrange his top hand to compensate for a different position of the football. If it's a short-yardage situation or if a gray read occurs, the fullback could very easily fumble.

The "ride and decide" method has withstood the test of time. This has been around almost since the inception of the triple option. The ride and decide technique works like this: While working downhill, the quarterback will push the ball back to the fullback. To illustrate how simple this technique is, the quarterback is simply moving the ball back as competently as possible. The quarterback doesn't swing the ball back. He just needs to get the ball in the "soft squeeze" as quickly and as easily as possible. The quarterback pushes the ball back as far as possible. Shifting his weight downhill, the quarterback rides the ball all the way through the line (except in situations that will be later explained). Most option coaches teach that once the ball reaches the front foot, no decision needs to be made. It's a give read. The honest truth is that the quarterback has the full authority on what he decides. Riding the football all the way into the line gives him a clearer read. Obviously, the quarterback doesn't need to ride the ball fully into the line every time, which isn't necessary. But the freedom is always there for the quarterback to receive greater information about the defenders' reactions.

The tailback's technique isn't difficult at all. For the initial "hook up" between the two, he starts with his hands much bigger than what the size of the ball is and with his inside arm up. He rapidly molds the "soft squeeze" to the point where the quarterback can give the ball efficiently and pull it—even doing so at the last second. Many option coaches teach different methods, such as only ride with the ball on the bottom hand. Or once contact is made, clamp down on the ball and no read occurs. The truth is, every relationship between the quarterback and the tailback is different. The efficiency of the tailback and the quarterback operating the "soft squeeze" is a result of repetition. Repetition after repetition will get the correct feel between the two. In all honestly, the mesh could be called a feel. It's something that's individual and coaches should only give some structure to the act itself. Everything will work out great if freedom is given to the two players who are performing the technique.

Giving the players freedom to fully mesh adds another dimension to the ride and decide: deception. While deception isn't the goal of the triple option, it can add an amazing dimension to the offensive attack. Many times, a quarterback has fully ridden the mesh and the defense doesn't know where the ball is. Initially showing the ball to the defense is powerful. Following defensive "instincts" shows how powerful deception can be in this offense. A great man once said "If you know where the ball is going with a triple option attack, the quarterback isn't doing a good job." The quarterback is a magician. The coach must allow the quarterback to be a magician.

Execution of the Read

The execution of the read with the tailback is the hardest part of a quarterback's job. The easiest part of the triple option is when the quarterback decides when to pitch. The hard part is the first phase of the option. This phase must have hundreds to thousands of repetitions to be mastered. The quarterback is the triggerman in this offense. If he isn't proficiently prepared to read the defense 80 to 90 percent of the time, the coaching staff isn't doing a good job of getting him prepared.

As a general rule of thumb, if a defender is aggressive, he's easy to read. If a defender is passive, he's at times cloudy to read. However, if a defender is hard to read, he's easy to block. Well-coached handoff keys are still easy to read with the proper thought process given to the quarterback. If a handoff key is cloudy, the offense will have a field day burying him into the ground.

In the simplest terms, many option attacks have rules, such as "Give unless …" or "Pull unless …" or "Is the handoff key attacking the tailback?" These are good ways to teach a quarterback how to read a defense.

One-way decisions can be good for the quarterback in most situations. Coaches such as Tony DeMeo advocate these types of methods. However, a downside to such methods exists. At a higher level of football or throughout the course of the game, the quarterback needs more information to consistently make the correct decision against a handoff key. The quarterback is given the freedom to ride the football all the way to the line. The falsehood of the premise "A wrong read is better than a wrong read" isn't a good slogan for an option quarterback. It's wrong because the offense needs to be right 100 percent of the time.

The quarterback will be given two keys to read the handoff key. The first is that he'll be peripherally reading the aggressiveness of the defender. "Is the handoff key attacking the dive back?" is what will be going through the quarterback's mind. Peripherally, this is enough information for the quarterback to quickly disconnect with the dive back and continue to the next phase of the triple option. Seeing a giant collision isn't complicated for the quarterback to figure out.

The next thought process is what the quarterback will be specifically looking for. Specifically, the quarterback will be reading the defender's eyes. As a rule of thumb, the defender's eyes almost never lie. The mesh is taking place while the quarterback is already working downhill and starting to replace. If the handoff key changes his decision at the last second, the quarterback will simply hand off the football. It's true that to some extent this technique is in itself "clinic talk," but given the necessary and proper tools to defeat the handoff key, the quarterback will figure it out on his own. The strict coaching point remains the same: The quarterback will peripherally read the aggressiveness and nature of the handoff key's attack and will specifically be reading the defender's eyes. Combined with a full mesh, sliding downhill, and being aggressive, this makes any read for the quarterback easy.

Quarterbacks have many ways to read the mesh—and many of them are good. But the goal is to give the quarterback as many tools as possible to help him succeed. The goal of coaching is to put players in the best position to succeed. Anything else isn't good coaching.

Difficult Reading Situations

It's not always as simple to read a defense as a reference football book might tell someone. Specific instances might cause a person to come into a situation where he doesn't know what to do because the situation isn't specifically explained. Several problems will be discussed that will hopefully clarify these possible problems.

Blood Stunt

Since the beginning with the wishbone, the blood stunt is one of the most popular ways to attack an option offense. The idea is to have the two defenders come so hard at the quarterback that a bad play is inevitable. The blood stunt is shown in Figure 2-8.

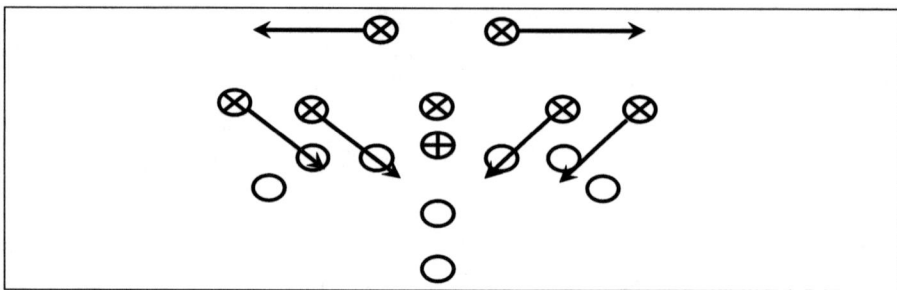

Figure 2-8. Blood stunt

The first thought process that should be in the quarterback's head is that he's expecting a quick pull and pitch when defenders #1 and #2 are on the line. To make this read easy, making it an "area" read gives the quarterback an easier time reading the situation. If the quarterback sees #1 and #2's shoulders aimed toward him, he immediately pulls and pitches the football (Figure 2-9).

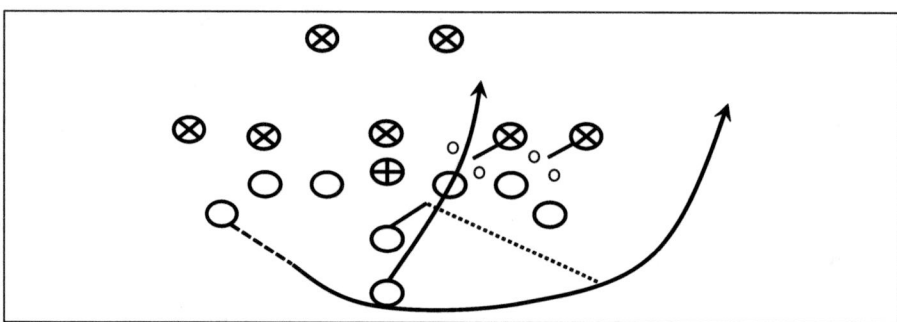

Figure 2-9. Two shoulders inside = pull and pitch

It's true that this won't always happen. The quarterback must still go through his regular progression because it could look like #1 and #2 are coming hot and something else happens. As will be explained later, the fadeaway pitch isn't taught in this offense. However, when #1 and #2 come hard, the quarterback should have his weight on his front foot so he can simply pitch the ball and push off his front foot to absorb the hard hit coming from either #1 or #2. If his weight is on his back foot, he won't be able to push away and absorb the defender being left unblocked, which could result in a disaster for the quarterback.

The quarterback must understand that the defense won't always come hard on a blood stunt when it aligns like this. Defensive coordinators are smart. They'll mix things up. Thus, the quarterback must be ready to pull and replace the handoff key. He must be ready for everything. The problem with the blood stunt is executing the hardest part of it: #1 and #2 coming hard at the quarterback.

Cross Charge

Many different terms are used for this stunt, but a cross charge is simply #1 and #2 in a stack alignment exchanging respons ibilities. This is one of the most difficult reads for a quarterback, which means it must be worked on throughout the season and the off-season. The cross charge is illustrated in Figure 2-10.

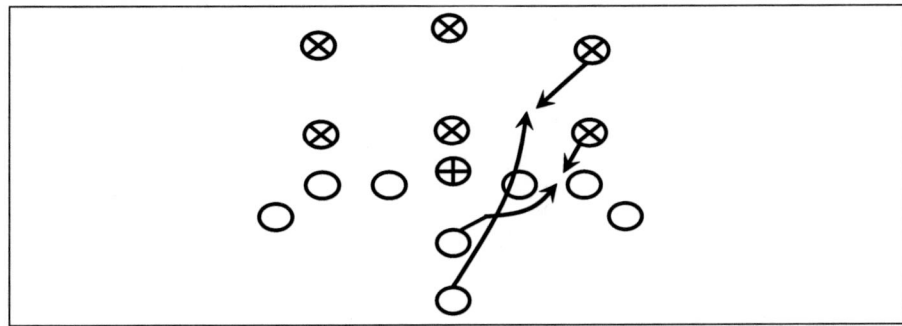

Figure 2-10. Cross charge

Before any discussion on how the quarterback will execute this read, the offense must do three things to attack the stack defense adequately:
- The offensive line must widen its splits. This creates a better picture for the quarterback to perform his read.
- The tailback must tighten his path by a hair (which will be explained later). Also, his shoulders will square up to the goal line sooner than normal.
- The quarterback always fully meshes into the line of scrimmage (point of emphasis).

The stack read can be executed in two ways. The first is the easiest way to do it: to make it an "area" read. The area read against a stack defense can be summed up as "air or no air." If the quarterback is meshing with the tailback and air is in the hole, give the football. Otherwise, pull the football. These methods are shown in Figure 2-11.

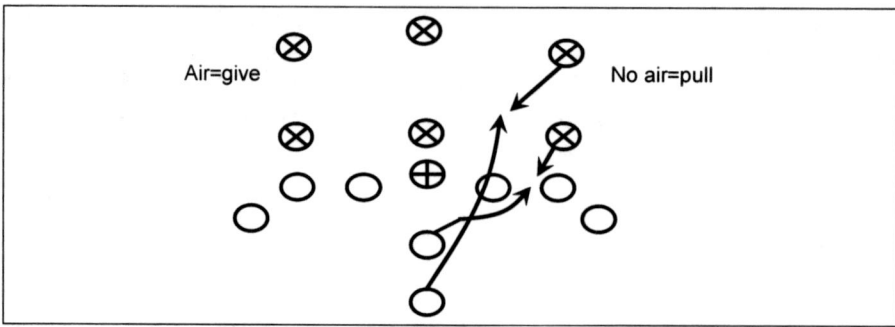

Figure 2-11. Air and no air methods

The main coaching point of reading a blood stunt also goes with reading the stack. Once the quarterback sees two defenders' shoulders turned inside facing him, it's an automatic pull and pitch (Figure 2-12). Another coaching point remains the same: The weight of the quarterback must be on his front foot in order to push off and absorb the blow against a defender.

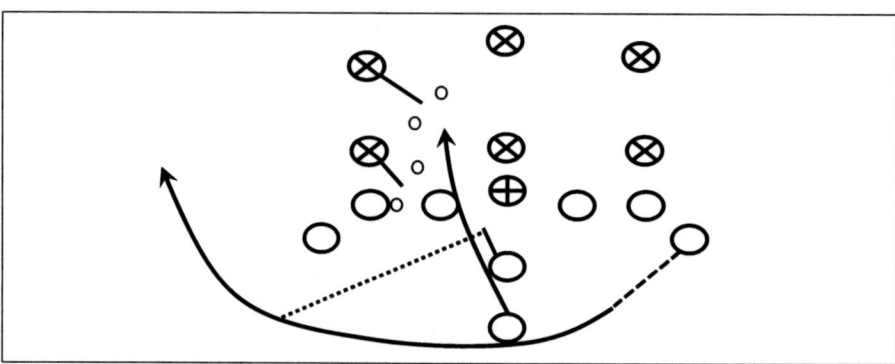

Figure 2-12. Pull and pitch

The air and no air methods are the easiest to perform. However, they have their theoretical shortcomings. The main problem is that sometimes, it's not as easy to simply read air or no air. It has to be more specific. The next way to teach reading the stack is to read it from the stack backer to the down defensive lineman. The quarterback will first look at the stack backer's reaction. If the backer stays there or turns his shoulders inside, the quarterback's eyes will immediately turn to the down lineman. The quarterback will simply react accordingly.

Two variables need to be discussed. It's true that reading a defender off the football can be hard and sometimes cloudy. That's why against the stack, the offensive line will widen out its splits and the tailback will tighten his path a bit. If the stack backer is trying to play games, the exaggerated structure has given him several predicaments. The first is that he must cover much more ground, which means his movements have to be sharper and more aggressive. The next is that the tailback has more room to operate in making the defender wrong. If the quarterback is in doubt or if the stack linebacker's angle is cloudy, the ball will be given. The change in angle puts the linebacker in a bind. Against a stack defense, the tailback's shoulders will become square to the goal line as soon as possible. This is illustrated in Figure 2-13.

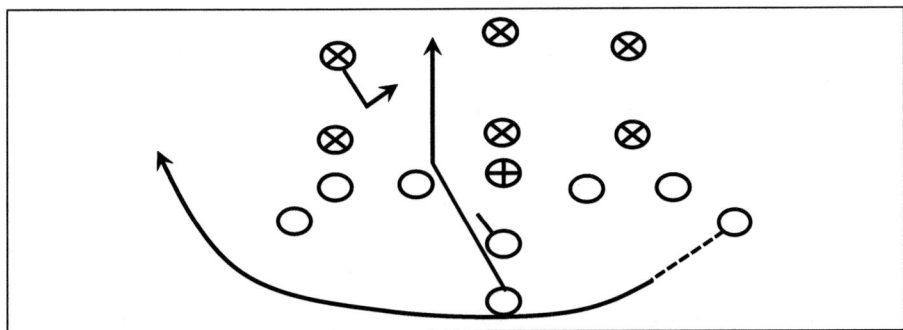

Figure 2-13. Tailback making the stack linebacker's angle wrong

The point of this figure is to show that if it's a cloudy read, the mechanical changes of the line splits and the tailback's path have put the defense in a bind. The stack backer now has a lot more space to account for if he's trying to play games with the quarterback. The tailback against a stack should look to square up his shoulders as soon as possible, which makes the stack backer wrong.

The Most Important Technical Point

Whether the quarterback has given or is keeping the football, the quarterback must accelerate 100 mph off the tailback's rear end. The most important aspect when faking is whether the quarterback is running like he has the ball or if he's running like he's given the ball. The acceleration off the tail eliminates defenders squatting to take the tailback and then popping up at the last second to take the quarterback. The easiest way to defeat a defender who's trying to get the quarterback to pull the ball and then take him is for the quarterback to give the ball and accelerate out like he's on fire. The defensive end will be confused. It's easy to toy with a quarterback who has two distinctly different reactions. However, if the quarterback's reaction always remains the same, the defense will be taken advantage of badly.

The Pitch Phase: Different Quarterback Path

When option football was in its infancy stage in the split-T, the standard way to execute the pitch phase of the option was for the quarterback to go straight down the line (Figure 2-14). The thought process was simply that the defender couldn't take the quarterback running down the line of scrimmage and the pitchman in a 45-degree relationship. Or if the defense wasn't gap sound, a running lane would be created because of the flow toward the outside. The quarterback would simply cut it up.

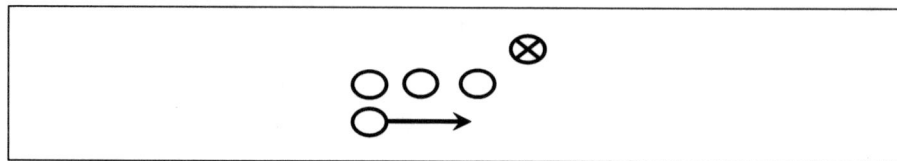

Figure 2-14. Down the line

The obvious problem with this technique was that by the 1970s, teams had seen the option so much that they had adapted and adopted a technique called "feathering the pitch" (Figure 2-15). Because of this, it seemed as if defenses had an advantage over teams who ran the option because repetitions was all that was needed in order to stop this two-way go play. The defender being optioned on would sit and wait for the quarterback to move his shoulders, indicating he'll always pitch the ball. Once that happened, the defender would go straight to the pitchman and tackle the ballcarrier. This defeats the option because it strings the play to the sideline, helping the defense create erratic pursuit to the football.

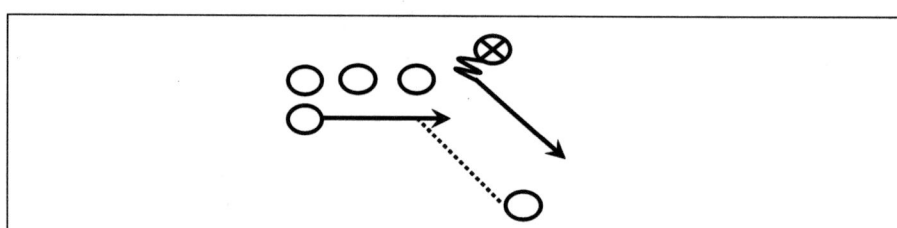

Figure 2-15. Defender feathering the pitch

A way to combat this problem was an option theory that has lasted a long time. The idea was that the quarterback would attack the defender's inside shoulder. This is the main way to teach an option quarterback in today's game. It's a very basic way to teach a quarterback to run the option. However, some shortcomings exist with this way of teaching the quarterback to run the option.

The basic problem of this way of thinking is when attacking a naturally wide defender. When the quarterback is attacking a close defender, it's a perfect design, but the old enemy of feathering the pitch comes up once again when it's a naturally wide defender. The reason for this predicament is angles because angles make it possible for a wide defender to take the quarterback and pitchman. Feathering the pitch is possible and maybe even better than before because the quarterback's path is taking him more toward the sidelines. The difference is shown in Figure 2-16.

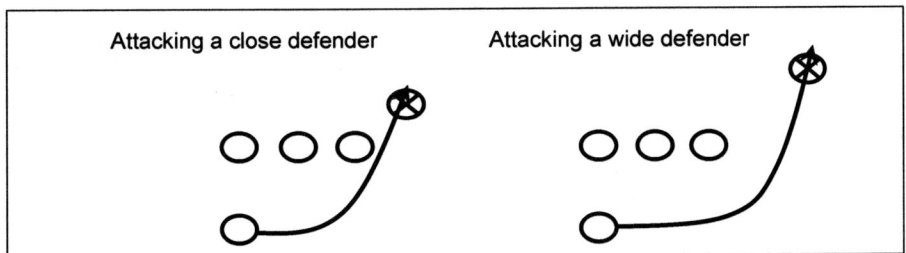

Figure 2-16. Difference with a close defender and a wide defender

Another big problem is the way the slots are taught to run their option course. They always need them to be downhill, making the option aggressive and more productive. When the quarterback attacks a wide defender, it changes the slot's path. The idea of an aggressive option is that the offensive players want to get downhill as fast as possible. When the quarterback attacks a wide defender, it changes the angles on how fast he gets downhill (Figure 2-17). This is also true from a slot's perspective.

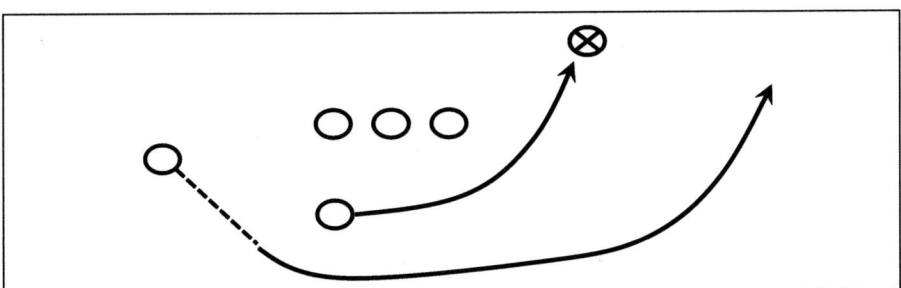

Figure 2-17. Option path too wide

This method strings out the option attack. On option plays, *never go to the sidelines*. The offense is always attacking downhill. The offense always has to put more pressure on the defense. A defensive principle being combated is "pursuit." Just about every good football team in America does a pursuit drill with its defense. The idea is very basic: Numbers is defense—and defense is numbers. If a defense can defeat an offense by having all 11 defenders flow to the football, the offense is destined to fail. This method of attacking a wide defender takes a lot more time to option a defender, which in turn creates more time for defenders to either get off blocks or fulfill their gap responsibilities so they can flow to the football and create numbers the offense can't account for.

Pull and Replace Method

The pull and replace method has combated the problem of feathering defenders and defensive pursuit. This method is espoused by the spread option coaches at Georgia Tech, Georgia Southern, and the U.S. Naval Academy. When it comes to Division I college football, defenders are much faster than anticipated and can execute simple defensive techniques of feathering the pitch and pursuit.

The method is very simple: Once the quarterback pulls the ball from the tailback, he's now replacing the defender and is running downhill. Once he pulls the ball, his objective is to score. The difference is shown in Figure 2-18.

Figure 2-18. Different attack angles

It's obvious that pulling and replacing is the best method because it allows the quarterback to play downhill and it keeps the defense on its toes because he's attacking the defense instead of the defense attacking him. The quarterback (as discussed before) must have an accelerated and aggressive third step in order for this method to work. He must play a thousand miles an hour when performing this technique.

The quarterback will never under any circumstance run to the outside. Many quarterbacks think that once they pull the ball that they're just running without any guidance. A quarterback will pull and replace because the tailback takes the inside running lanes and the slot has the outside running lanes (as will be discussed). *Never run to the outside—pull and replace only.*

Leverage Pitching

Coaches can use many different ways to teach a quarterback when to pitch the ball. The most basic way of teaching an option quarterback when to pitch is to tell him if the defender takes him, pitch the ball, but if the defender takes the pitchman, cut it upfield. That method doesn't necessarily correlate with the way an option quarterback's downhill path should be. That method of thinking generally goes with the down-the-line option crowd because when a quarterback is running down the line, he has to cut it up in order to gain yardage (Figure 2-19).

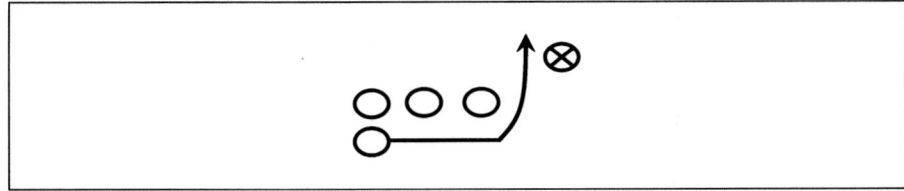

Figure 2-19. Down-the-line quarterback keep

The best method to teach a quarterback in conjunction with his instructed path is the leverage pitch. The idea is very simple and is an easier idea to teach and execute with quarterbacks. While the quarterback is coming downhill, he'll ask himself this question "Does the slot have leverage to the outside of the pitch key?" If he does, the quarterback will pitch the ball and the slot will run to the outside. If the pitch key has outside leverage on the slotback, the quarterback will keep the football and gain as many yards as possible (Figure 2-20).

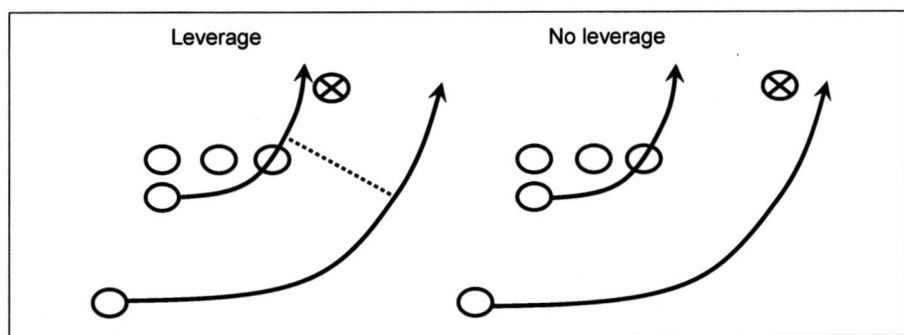

Figure 2-20. Leverage vs. no leverage

Because the offense is truly attacking two different points of the field, it's impossible for the pitch key to feather the pitch. Even after the pitch, the quarterback will continue downfield. When the quarterback adds the pull and replace path and the slot is attacking downhill, the defense has to truly defend three parts of the field. Because other option methods teach coming down the line and attacking defenders, they really aren't attacking an area of the field. These three distinguished parts mixed together give the triple option the best chance to succeed against all defenses.

The Quarterback's Pitch

Once the quarterback pulls the football from the tailback, he'll put the football away in his third hand. His third hand is carrying the football about six to eight inches away from his chest with two hands on the football. When he does decide to pitch the football, he simply pitches the ball with his thumb down. It needs to be a dead pitch. It can't be a fast ball or have rotation on the ball. It also needs to be emphasized to the quarterback that the ball is pitched "heart to heart." When executing the pitch, the quarterback will have a loose wrist. This is important so the wrist of the quarterback is agile enough to perform a "thumb under" pitch. A static wrist will require the quarterback to "push" the ball to the pitchman. A dead pitch needs to occur so the running backs can run through the pitch at full speed instead of chasing the ball before accelerating to score.

Different thought processes exist on how to finish the pitch, including two dominating theories.

Step and fade away is a classic way to pitch the ball on the option. This has been done for decades and has had success. The thought process behind this way of finishing the pitch is that once the quarterback decides to pitch the football, he'll step at the pitchman, pitch the ball, and then fade away. The fadeaway portion is there so the quarterback can "absorb" the hit taken by the defensive man in his face, thus causing less punishment for the quarterback throughout the game and season (Figure 2-21).

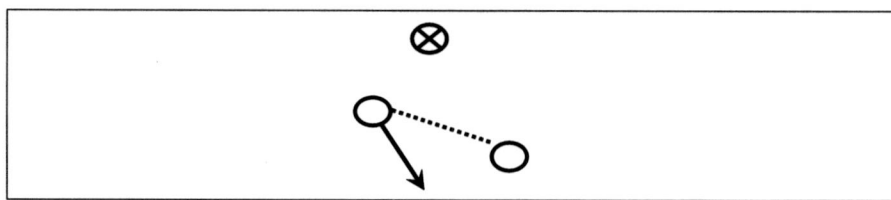

Figure 2-21. Step and fade pitch

The *sit, step, and pitch* is almost as simple as it sounds. Once the quarterback decides to pitch the football, he'll simply sit, step, and pitch. Another part that's important to this method is the idea of "If the defender plays fast, we play slow, but if the defender plays slow, we play fast." That's a good method to go by if a team decides to use this method. However, downsides do exist to using these two methods as a part of option football.

Like a giant elephant standing in the room that nobody wants to acknowledge, the fake pitch is completely obsolete while using these two methods. Defensive pursuit angles change once the ball is pitched. Once the quarterback's shoulders have turned, the defense is now chasing the ball to the sidelines. The step and fade method is the worst for this part of the option. When executing the step and fade, 90 percent of the quarterback's weight is transferred to the back portion of his feet, thus causing him to not having a chance to respond to a feathered pitch player.

The sit, step, and pitch is somewhat better to add the fake pitch, but it's not adequate enough to have in the arsenal of an option offense. Because the quarterback "sits," he's now taking his momentum from going forward to stagnant. It's better than the fadeaway concept, which takes the momentum going backward, but it's still not a good method if the fake pitch is in the weaponry of the offense. As talked about earlier, once the defense sees the quarterback sit and open his shoulders, defensive pursuit angles will immediately change to the sidelines. The downfall for this method is that once the quarterback's shoulders open up, it is obvious to the defense that he will no longer carry the football.

The movement pitch is theoretically the best way to pitch the football (Figure 2-22). The biggest reason for this is that it correlates with the way the quarterback is taught to get downhill, not attack defenders, and use leverage pitching. The fake pitch is always in the arsenal because the quarterback is moving forward. Not only that, but the quarterback will take less punishment by the defense. Because he leverage-pitches the football as soon as the pitchman has leverage on the defender, the ball is gone. If the defender is sitting waiting for the leverage pitch, the quarterback will now not get hit and the ball will be on the outside with no chance of the pitch key feathering to the pitch. This is a win-win situation for the offense.

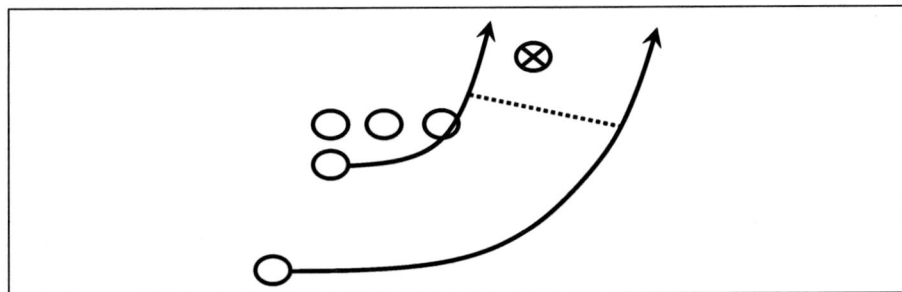

Figure 2-22. Movement pitch

Even though the ball has been pitched, the quarterback remains on his path, accounting for pursuit from the defense and keeping the fake pitch in the equation. This method has again diminished techniques the defense can play against an option offense.

Some confusion exists for quarterbacks who are performing the movement pitch. Many of them think that because they're staying on their tracks that they're not stepping and pitching. On the contrary, they're still stepping at the target, but it's different. If the quarterback has decided that the slot has leverage on the pitch key, once the outside foot of the quarterback has hit the ground, he'll pitch the ball and remain on his track (Figure 2-23).

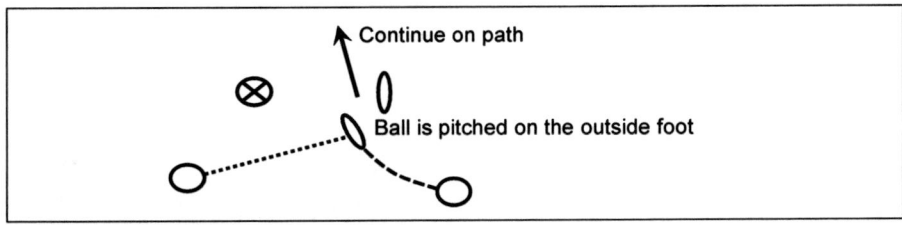

Figure 2-23. Movement pitch footwork

Running Back Play

Many offenses require very little coaching of its running backs for the simple reason all they do is run to an assigned hole and "run to daylight." This isn't the case for any option offense. The burden of this offense falls on three players: the quarterback and the two slotbacks. The tailbacks have few assignments that require many repetitions. A rule of thumb for this offense on picking the personnel is this: The smart backs play slot and the dumb ones play tailback. The slotback position requires blocking, catching, running, and smarts. The tailback position requires running and some blocking. If a player can't handle the load at the slot position but is very athletic, he should be moved to tailback.

Tailback Play

The tailback's number one job in this offense is to "run the wall." With veer blocking or loop blocking, the offensive line is creating a wall for the tailback to run. The question now becomes what's needed to accomplish this task.

Stance

The tailback will be in a two-point stance with his heels approximately five yards from the tip of the football and approximately two yards from the quarterback's heels (Figure 2-24).

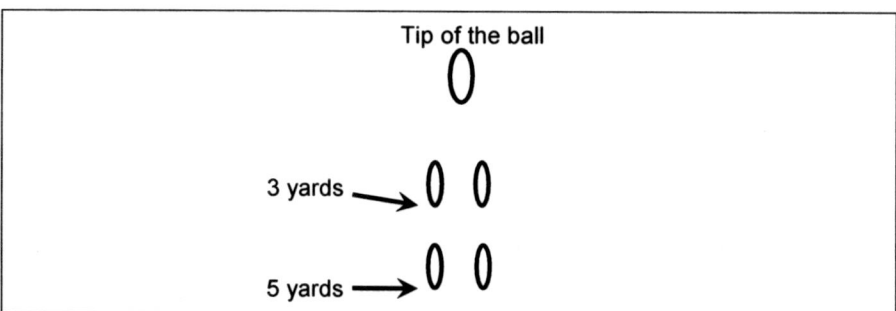

Figure 2-24. Quarterback and tailback spacing

Spacing is something that must be stressed every day to the tailbacks. This isn't a suggestion. It's a demand. As noted, if spacing is too deep, the problems of the single wing come about and this offense is sound in theory but not sound in mechanics.

Footwork

An important point in teaching a tailback is his opening step. This is important because if this is wrong, his angle of departure is wrong. If the play call is triple right, the first step will be with his left foot. He wants to replace the heel of the quarterback, whose first step is with his right foot (Figure 2-25).

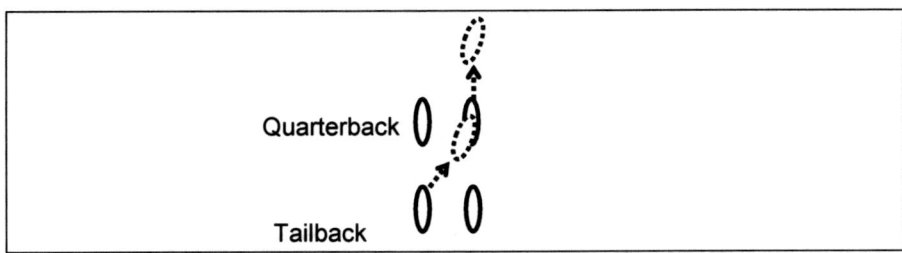

Figure 2-25. Tailback replacing the quarterback's heel

This step should be taken at a slight angle. However, the angle shouldn't be so great that he's running right at the handoff key. If that happens, no read occurs and the handoff key will play the quarterback and tailback. False steps will destroy the timing and angle of the mesh. Many players have problems training their feet this way because it feels unnatural. To prevent false stepping, the tailback should curl his playside toes, which will force his body to move with his opposite foot first. He should curl his toes until his body has gained the muscle memory to perform the step automatically. Many coaches believe he always needs to curl his toes, but because the player has cleats on, it's impossible for coaches to enforce such a rule. Also, once a player has mastered the technique, he no longer needs to curl his toes. However, in the beginning stages of installing the triple option, it is a valuable tool to use in correcting the footwork. Coaches must demand proper footwork from their tailbacks. If a tailback is unable to correctly perform the opening step, he's not capable of effectively playing tailback. The good thing is that anyone can master this technique with repetition.

Running the Wall

This is the path the tailback will take every time the triple option is called. Many other teams call this the veer path or the attack path. Those terms can be used, but they don't mean anything to a 16- or 22-year-old playing football. "Running the wall" is a term that means something to the player because he knows and understands the blocking scheme.

The aiming point of the tailback is the inside leg of the guard. Many option coaches object to this because they believe it's too tight. However, a specific reason why the aiming point is the inside leg of the guard is if the aiming point is the guard's rear end, his path will be too wide for one reason: The linemen in this offense are as far off the ball as legally allowed. Figures 2-26 and 2-27 show the reasoning.

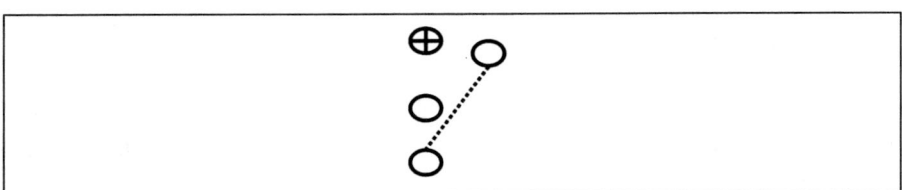

Figure 2-26. Aiming point = guard's rear end—before the play

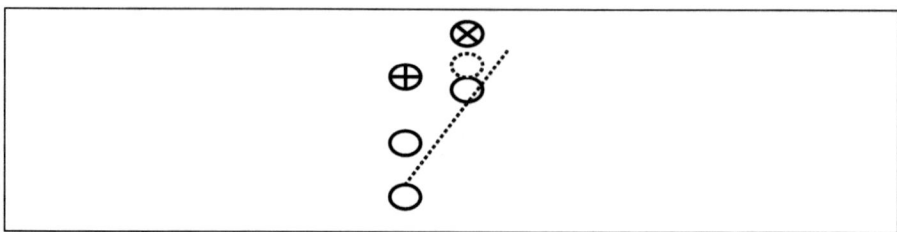

Figure 2-27. Aiming point = guard's rear end—when contact is initiated

The point the figures are out to prove is that with the aiming point being the guard's rear end, this path turns into an outside leg/B gap path. This is too wide. One of the goals of the tailback's path is to be as far away as possible from the handoff key in order for a clean read of the handoff key. If that's not the case, the handoff key can just stand up after the snap and successfully tackle the tailback for a minimal gain of three to four yards. Having the tailback as far away from the handoff key as possible is what makes the triple option a well-oiled machine.

The inside leg of the guard is perfect for several reasons. The first is because it places the tailback as far away from the handoff key as possible. The second is it puts the tailback in a great position to be as tight to the blocking scheme as possible (Figures 2-28 and 2-29). The third is something that will be gone over later in more detail, but the tailback will be able to square up his shoulders to the end zone quicker and more efficiently with this method.

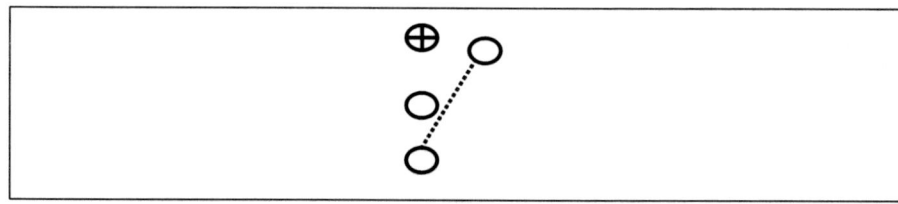

Figure 2-28. Aiming point = guard's inside leg—before the play

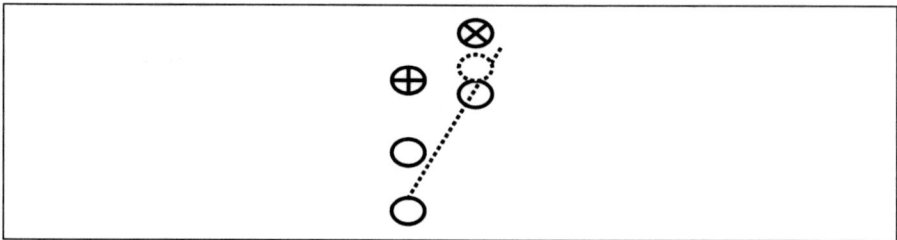

Figure 2-29. Aiming point = guard's inside leg—when contact is initiated

The only danger of this path is that the tailback will be too tight, which is a concern. However, repetition after repetition will naturally teach the tailback how to specifically run the wall with great success.

Many option football coaches simply pick an aiming point for the tailback/fullback just because they were told to do so, which is fine as long as it's the inside leg of the guard. But the point here is to illustrate specific mechanical reasons for this positioning. It also helps when a coach is coaching players who need a "why" to everything. This offense is perfect for the "why" players a specific why exists for everything in this offense.

Shoulders Parallel to the Goal Line

Once the tailback has successfully "run the wall," he wants his shoulders parallel to the goal line. Several scenarios and reasons make this needed action. The first and obvious reason is because the offense wants to score now! No dancing—just go. Many option coaches teach that once the tailback/fullback has the football he wants to run to the "option alley." However, this can lead to defenders successfully playing this offense correctly. Once the tailback has cleared the initial blocks that create the wall, he'll immediately square his shoulders and score a touchdown (Figure 2-30).

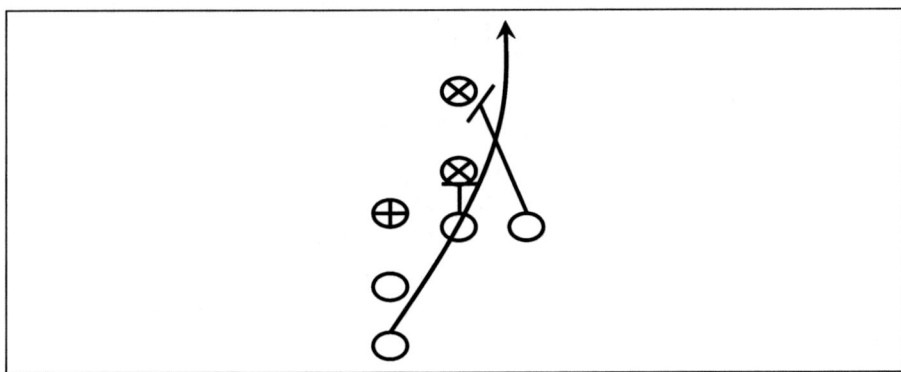

Figure 2-30. Tailback's path

A good reason for this technique goes back to how the split-T operated its principled mechanics. A player gets from point A to point B faster by running a straight line, which is why the split-T handoff play went straight ahead. The mechanics of the wishbone and the spread requires the tailback to take a slight angle in order for the mesh to be successful. Thus, the goal of the tailback is to run the wall. Once he clears the wall, his shoulder's become parallel to the goal line. The fear of this is that the tailback squares up his shoulders too fast and runs into the defender the tackle is veering to block. This technique takes repetition after repetition to perfect and is a "feel" that the tailbacks must instinctively have.

This technique has other benefits that must be understood in order for it to reach its maximum potential. When linebackers are "scrapping" over the top to stop the perimeter option game, this technique allows the tailback to run right by them (Figure 2-31). Once the linebacker has committed himself to running lateral, the linebacker has no chance to change his angle for chasing the tailback.

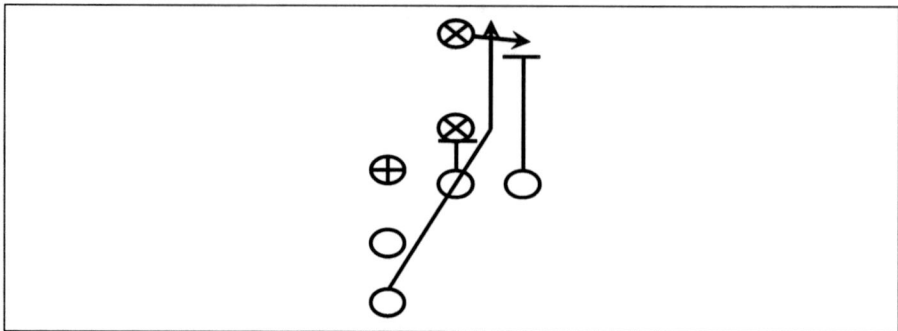

Figure 2-31. Tailback defeating scrapping linebacker

The tailback has the freedom to square up his shoulders immediately if he "feels" the linebacker running laterally. Running the football is 90 percent a natural trait. Some techniques can be acquired from finishing runs, setting up defenders, and sideline running, but the vast majority of running the football can't be taught. Many tailbacks do this without even knowing it. The natural ability to square up the shoulders against a linebacker who's running lateral is something the animal instincts of a runner "feel" and react to accordingly.

A squat defender in the triple option is a defender who's sitting in the hole and is trying to play the quarterback and the tailback. Teams have several ways to play this. The first is to do nothing. This technique doesn't harm this offense because of the quick-hitting abilities of the plays. The second is for the tailback to square up his shoulders against this defender and make him wrong. If the defender is trying to read which decision the quarterback is trying to make and the quarterback gives the ball to the tailback, the quarterback will accelerate off the mesh as if he has the ball. The mesh has no end point in this offense, so the quarterback can read and ride as long as he likes. Also, the tailback will square up his shoulders against this defender and change directions. This predicament is shown in Figure 2-32. Unless Lawrence Taylor is playing defensive end (and even he would have problems with this), it's very hard for a defender to sit in the hole, try to read what the quarterback does, and then have an immediate and radical change in angles in which the tailback is attacking the defense.

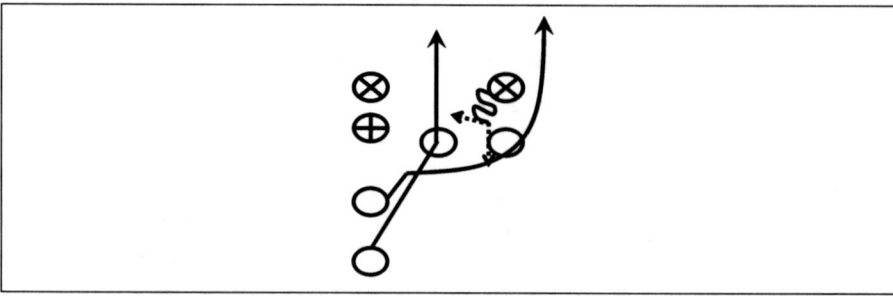

Figure 2-32. Tailback making the "squat" defender wrong

The next situation where the tailback will square up his shoulders will be when the guard is covered and the 2 technique slants into the B gap (Figure 2-33). Again, this will naturally happen and the tailback rarely needs to be reminded about this.

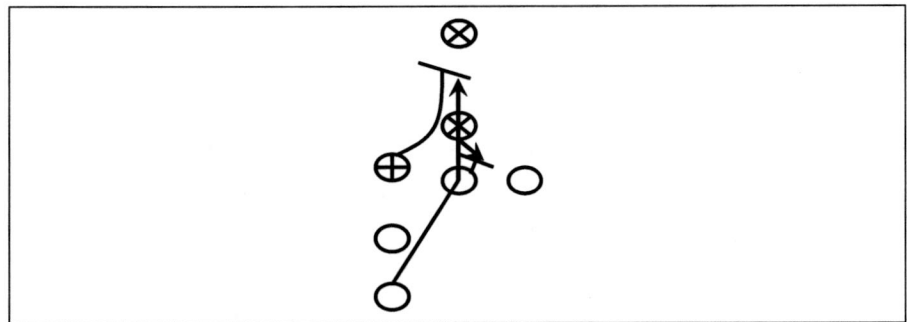

Figure 2-33. Tailback squaring up his shoulders against a slanting defensive tackle

Even against the stunt, where the 2 technique goes B gap and the linebacker blitzes the A gap, this is great for the offense. Because the center is performing his "playside backside" technique, the A gap is protected. Many defenses will try to play the fullback from the outside in, but using the proper techniques makes this rarely a problem.

The last situation where the tailback will square up his shoulders is against a noseguard who's slanting hard into the playside A gap. This is a scenario where having the tailback's aiming point at the inside leg of the guard is a benefit. If he's wider, the nose can destroy the play. However, this scenario isn't used often. Even if a nose slants the A gap, the technique of the center's block will take care of the nose. However, if the goal of the nose is to penetrate the playside A gap with no other responsibility, this tailback technique will happen most of the time without the tailback even knowing it. The tailback must not be afraid to square up his shoulders and make the nose wrong in the way he's heavily slanting (Figure 2-34).

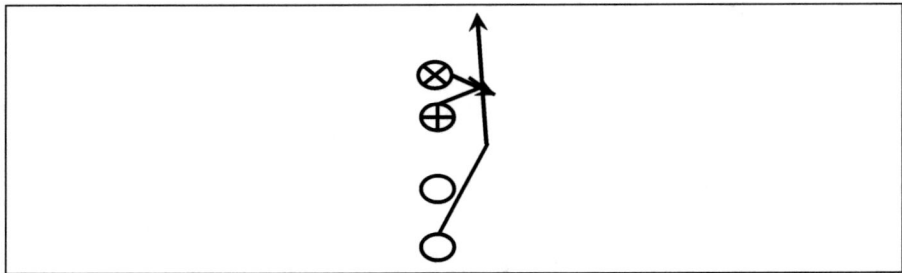

Figure 2-34. Tailback squaring up his shoulders against a slanting nose

The last important point for the tailbacks to understand is that *they can never cut back on triple and midline*. The reasoning behind it is that they'll run into unblocked players. This can be hard to explain to them, but after giving them sound reasoning, they'll understand.

Many football players believe that NFL and collegiate runners cut back all the time. That's not accurate. It's true that they do cut back, but the vast majority of the time, it's not a cutback but rather the offensive line doing its job. When the tailback squares up his shoulders on triple, he must understand that the backside linemen are essentially zone blocking (even though it's a scoop). If the tailback stays on his path, the linemen will magically come into his picture and pick up the unblocked players. On film, to the crowd, to the players, and even to most coaches, it will look like the tailback cut it back. But he didn't. The offensive linemen are just performing their jobs of being on their scoop paths and picking up the first defenders who flashes before them. The difference between cutting back and staying on the path is shown in Figures 2-35 and 2-36.

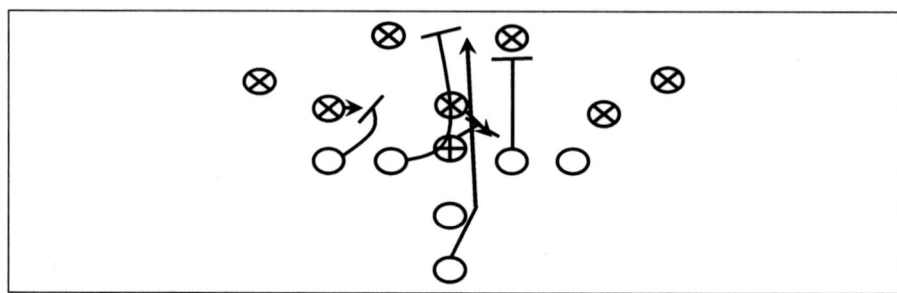

Figure 2-35. How it should look

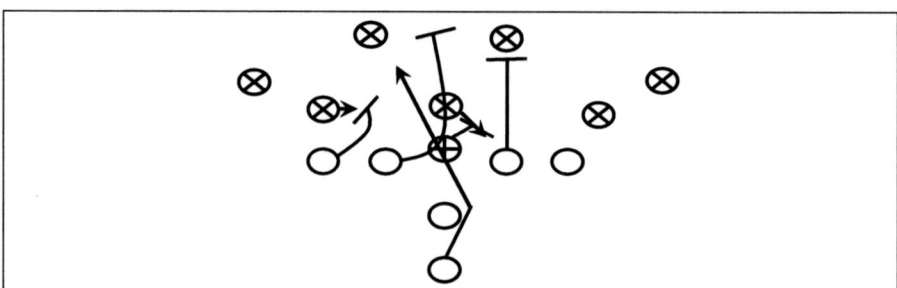

Figure 2-36. How it shouldn't look

It's important to emphasize with the tailbacks that they must trust their path. If they don't, bad things can happen. The blocking scheme takes into account all the basic problems that could happen. Once the tailbacks have been alleviated from their path, the offense is in trouble.

Slotback Play

The slotback's main job in the triple option is to arc block. This is one of the hardest things in football to perform. Blocking in space, along with tackling in space, is hard, which is why arc blocking is the number one priority for an option offense for slotbacks. The second main job is to go in motion and get into pitch relationship with the quarterback, who's pulling and replacing.

Stance and Alignment

The traditional slotback stance isn't used in this offense. This is for one reason and one reason only: the passing game. In this offense, the receivers are vertical threats that the defense must be accountable for. For that reason, the slotback stance will be a modified receiver stance. However, it must be understood that if the offense isn't going to consistently attack the defensive secondary, all advantages of this stance are lost. If the offense is just going to run the ball, the modified receiver stance has no advantages in the running game. It can be said that the nature of the "pistol spread" formation resembles more of the run-and-shoot double slot formation than the traditional flexbone formation.

The slotback will align one yard by one yard off the tackle (Figure 2-37). He has the freedom to slightly widen his stance if he prefers to. However, this gives the offense an advantage in the running game and in the passing game. The slot will have his inside leg up and good knee bend to keep lateral and backward movement possible. His hands need to be up. Having the hands up will encourage the slotback's "rip" on his motion.

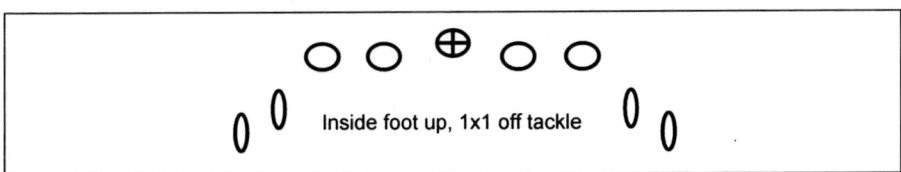

Figure 2-37. Slot's alignment

The first skill a slotback must have in the option offense is to get into proper pitch relationship. This requires repetition and feel as well as a willingness to do the right thing. If a slot is lazy in this procedure, he must be replaced. If a slot isn't in proper pitch relationship all the time, he can't play slot. The first thing a slot must learn is how to go in motion. He'll go in motion when the quarterback barks the beginning of the cadence. His aiming point is the tailback's heel (Figure 2-38). He should be running through the tailback's heels. He can't be too deep and he can't be too shallow. Repetition after repetition will give him the muscle memory needed to become good at this.

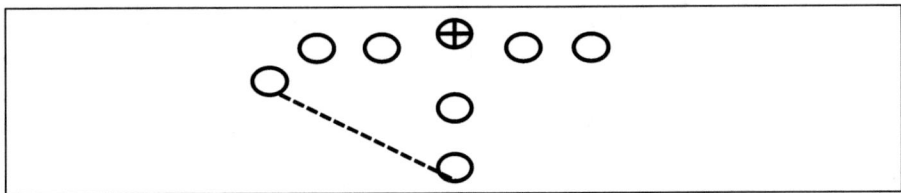

Figure 2-38. Slot's aiming point

Many option offenses teach on motion that the slot can't go past two steps. This attack extends that for one reason: The stance of the slot is different from traditional spread option stances. For this reason, inertia in the ground isn't generated with as much power as traditional spread option stances that require the slot to have his forearms on his thighs and taking a slight instep. However, this is only extended to three steps. The slot can never go past three steps on his motion running this offense (Figure 2-39). Three steps is perfect because the counter game in this offense is off three-step motion. Thus, the basic rule is two to three steps on motion and absolutely no more.

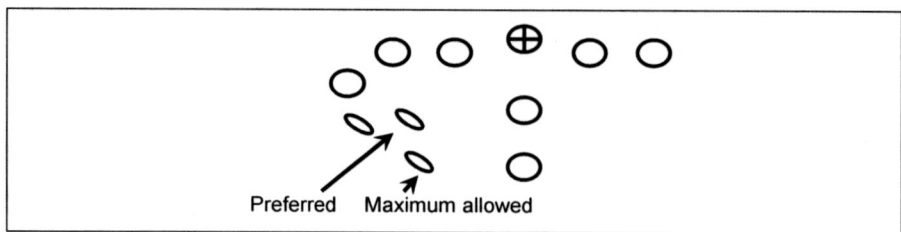

Figure 2-39. Steps during motion

Once the slot has taken his two to three steps in motion, he'll run through the heels of the tailback. Once he clears the tailback's heels, he'll take three to four steps laterally and start coming downhill with the quarterback in pitch relationship. The textbook definition with these two techniques is three lateral steps and turn up with the quarterback in a 5x1 relationship. In a perfect world, this is what would be ideal, but this is subjective depending on who's playing slot. Would a 5x1 or a 4x2 relationship be preferred? Sure, but getting in pitch relationship isn't necessarily textbook and is a feel that the slot must learn through experience. Three steps laterally is the preferred goal (Figure 2-40). The main point to get across to the slot is that he must be headed downhill with the quarterback. The offense needs to be attacking the defense downhill at all positions.

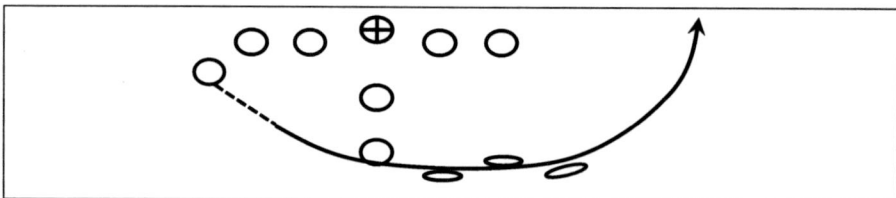

Figure 2-40. Slot's path on the option

Again, the major part of this has to do with the natural feel of the slot playing for this to be effective. The only way to perfect this is repetition after repetition. Another strong point is that it takes many repetitions because the quarterback has to learn to "pull and replace," and if the quarterback is too wide, the option play will be a disaster.

Once the slot has gotten in pitch relationship, his goal is to favor to the outside and run the "option alley," as shown in Figure 2-41. The reason for the option alley is simple: It's the alley where the perimeter blocks set up the pitchman to run. Also, favoring to the outside will make the perimeter block of the slot much easier. The reason is he won't be in the dark about where the ballcarrier is trying to run the ball. The alley is his friend and that's where he needs to run. Sometimes, are there circumstances where it won't be open? Sure, but the vast majority of the time, this is where the slot needs to run the ball once he receives the ball from the triggerman.

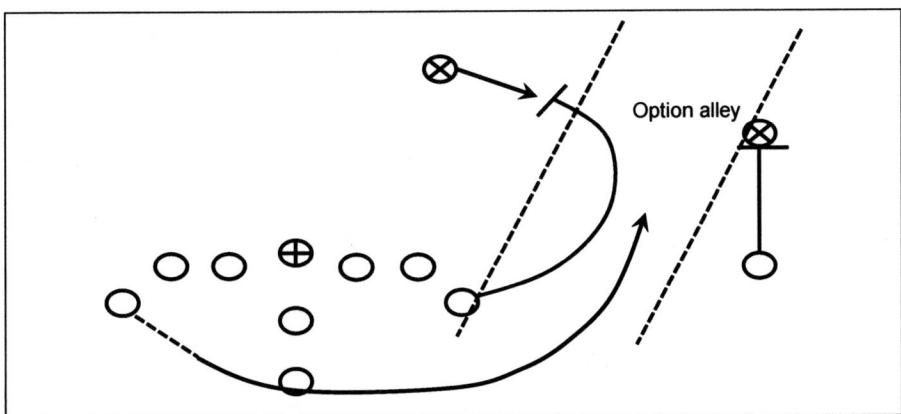

Figure 2-41. Option alley

Catching the Pitch

The last coaching point about being the pitchman is knowing how to catch the pitch. The quarterback is performing a "dead" thumb-under pitch. The slot must *run through the pitch*. He doesn't wait and isn't slow catching the pitch. He must run through the pitch. Also, *the eyes tuck the football away*. The eyes will guide the football to the ball security position that will be explained later. Once this is mastered, the slot will be at full speed after the offense has cancelled out two defenders.

Arc Blocking

As already talked about, the arc block is the toughest skill a slotback must master. It's difficult because he's blocking in space with no knowledge of what the pitchback is going to do with the football.

The slotback needs to master several steps. The first step he must master is his "arc step." This step is the most crucial for the slot to master. It's a 45-degree step with his outside foot. This step is important because it sets his path for his arc block (Figure 2-42). This angle can change depending on the width the slot must work for. The path the slot will stay on is a "curve-shaped path." It will look something like Figure 2-43. The slot will stay on his path and will only leave his path to protect the runner on the inside (Figure 2-44).

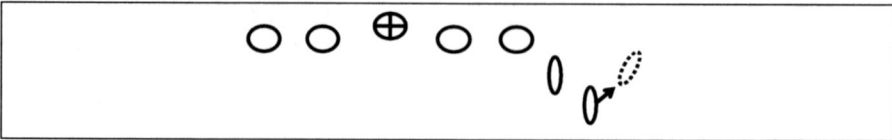

Figure 2-42. Arc block path

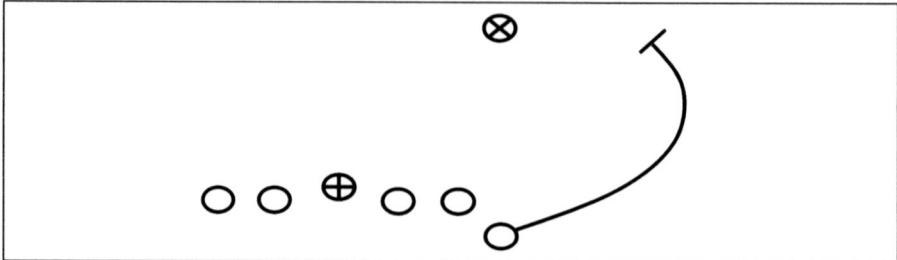

Figure 2-43. Curve-shaped path

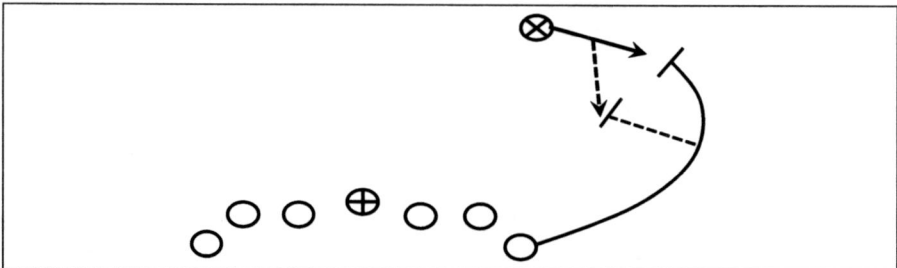

Figure 2-44. Slot protecting the runner

Staying on the path is the most important aspect on this block. The specific reason for the slot starting his path wide is so he can handle any extreme move from #3 to pick him up. If the slot simply went straight toward #3, the safety would outleverage him purely on angles (Figure 2-45). It must be emphasized that if the slot starts on a straightforward path toward his responsibility, he won't have a successful block.

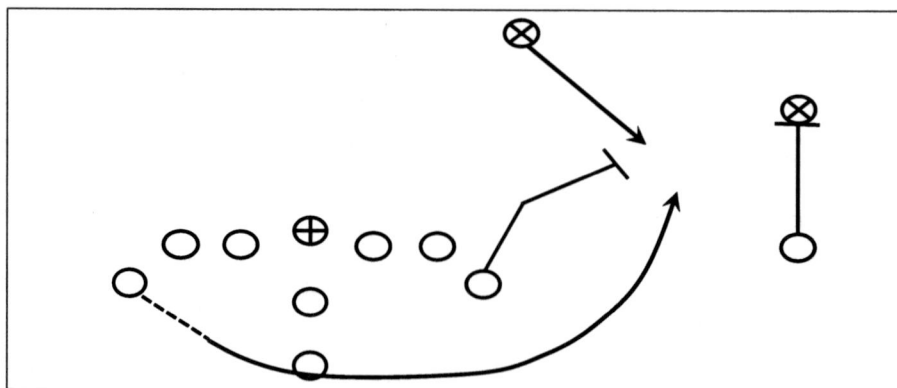

Figure 2-45. Taking the wrong angle

As shown, the slot will have a difficult time redirecting. His redirection will be all for not. The safety will have a kill shot on the pitchback.

Two more attributes help make this block successful. The first is maintaining outside leverage on the defender. The slot should be aiming/mirroring the outside shoulder of the defender. The outside path of the pitch must be protected. It's using this principle that will make a safety try to undercut the slot's block. The slot needs to make the safety travel 15 yards over the top of him. This will take the defender out of the play. Outside leverage is an absolute requirement for this block. The runner will help out the arc block by favoring the outside first and run the option alley, picking the seam that's created by the angles of the wide receiver's and slot's blocks.

The arc block's principles have many of the same principles as the stalk block. The last vital principle of the arc block is "mirroring" the defender. This is a tough skill, which only repetition after repetition will allow the slot to master. The problem with the arc block is this: The slot doesn't want to sprint all the way toward the defender because he'll always make him miss. The slot won't be under control enough to block the defender if he performs a lateral movement. However, if he's too slow, the defender will either run over the top or undercut the block. Thus, a rule of thumb is, if the defender is playing fast, the offense plays fast, but if the defender is playing slow, he comes under control two to three yards before he makes contact. Staying on the path while matching the speed of the defender and keeping outside leverage aimed for the outside shoulder of the defender will give the slots all the tools to succeed.

When it's a single high safety, slight adjustments should be made to the arc block. Instead of having a wide curve-shaped path, the slot will need to make his path skinnier and use the same principles (Figure 2-46). The hard part of blocking a single high safety is a safety that undercuts the arc block. However, that's a symptom of the slot having his path too wide, which makes it hard for the slot to go get the safety who has undercut him. Thus, the solution is to maintain all the principles of the arc block but keep the path skinnier (Figure 2-46). It's especially important on this adjustment to match the speed of the safety. If the slot fails to do this, the safety will run right by him.

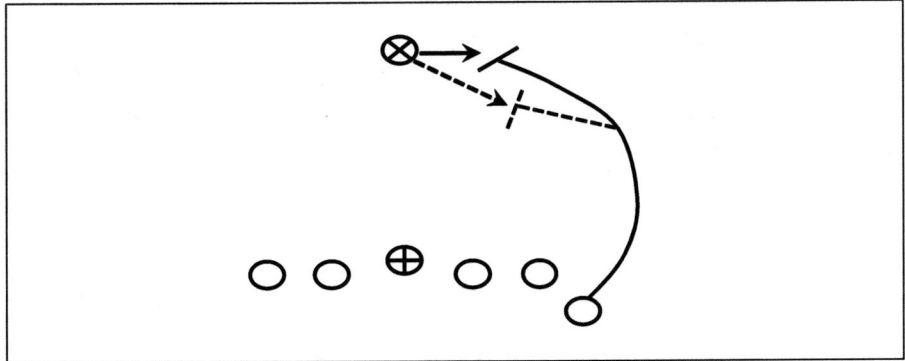

Figure 2-46. Slot's arc vs. one high safety

The arc block can be summarized with an analogy of a pitcher. It doesn't matter if the pitcher throws three balls, has four pitches fouled, or almost has a home run hit against him. If he gets the batter out, he's out. It doesn't matter what he had to do to make that happen. Arc blocking is very similar because it's a block that's unnatural and somewhat blind. If the slot makes the block, no matter how "ugly" it looks, it's good enough. Obviously, the offense wants devastating blocks on the perimeter, which is the difference between a first down and a touchdown. It's important to note that the principles of this block aren't new and they're not genius. It's simply going back to the principles of the wishbone arc block. The block and principles are the same. The two differences are the positioning of the back, and from the spread, it has to be inverted because of the vertical passing game.

Switch Block

The switch block is performed for several reasons. The first is to deal with a rolled corner. Cover 2 (cloud) teams can be tough to block the perimeter. It's true that under option theory that it's difficult for a team to play cover 2 because of runoff principles. (See Chapter 3.) Even though it will get burned through the air, the offense will eventually have to run against it. Running against it can be just fine. However, to maximize the offense's dominance of cover 2, the offense will switch block the defense.

The slot on this block won't take an arc step. Instead, he'll take a "picture step." The picture step will be a lateral step, setting him on course with his shoulders parallel to the sideline (Figure 2-47).

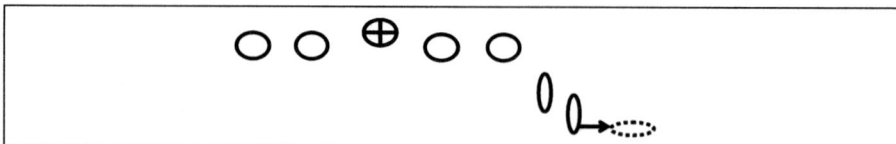

Figure 2-47. Picture step

A general rule of thumb is that the slot will attack the cornerback inside out. He'll attack the cornerback inside out because he's already playing out wide with the wide receiver. The slot will work laterally first, except on this block, he won't necessarily mirror the corner. His goal is to kick him out as fast as possible. However, the slot must stay under control. Once a slot is moving so fast he can't control a block, he's in trouble. The path is shown in Figure 2-48.

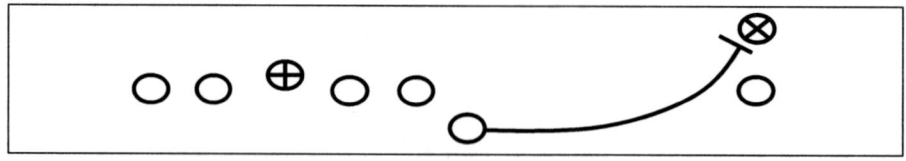

Figure 2-48. Slot's switch block

Again, the key is to work laterally first for four or five steps. Like the arc block, this has to be a feel developed by every individual player. It's not practical to have slots block the perimeter like a robot. Guidelines exist that must be ingrained in them so blocking becomes a feel and not a robotic move.

This block is somewhat different when it's performed against a corner trying to squeeze the pitch lane for the option. When the defense is playing like this instead of kicking out the corner, the slot wants to work to reach him. The reason for reaching him is twofold. The first is the monster trying to compress the "option alley." The second is that he's the contain/force player, so when he's trying to be "reached," he'll widen with the angle of the slot. He's taught that nobody can be outside of him, so the idea is to influence him to stay outside and then kick him out (Figure 2-49).

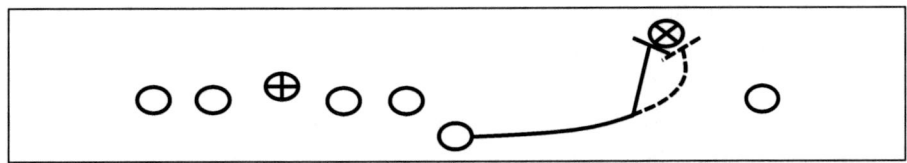

Figure 2-49. Vs. a compressed corner

Ball-Carrying Techniques

It's imperative for an option team to limit turnovers. The only way for an option football team to be beat is twofold. The first is that the opponent is simply better. The second is turnovers, which is most prominent. An option football team must take pride in taking care of the football. If care isn't taken with the football, this offense can be a disaster waiting to happen. Although this doesn't necessarily correlate with running the triple option specifically, this is added to this section to emphasize the importance of taking care of the football.

Several techniques are employed in order to reaffirm good ball security. The first one is hand placement over the football. To have the best and most equitable leverage on the football, the ballcarrier should "eagle claw" the top of the football. That means having his middle finger over the tip of the football. If a runner can put more than his finger over the ball, that's fantastic, but many high school football players have small hands. In this case, it's good enough to only have the middle finger over the football.

The second important coaching point is keeping the football high and tight. Saying high and tight is a good phrase. However, explaining high and tight to players doesn't mean anything. Coaches automatically know what that means, but remember, it's not what the coaches know—it's what the players can know and comprehend. A better way to connect with players is to emphasize having *their wrists above their elbows*. That directly tells a player what's needed to be done. Having his middle finger over the top of the football and having the wrist above the elbow tightly gives the ballcarrier a great advantage of running the football.

The next step is that the ball must be tight on the chest. Thus, the ball is high and tight, the wrist is above the elbow, the grip is an eagle claw, and the ball is pushed to the offender's chest. A way to check if a player has good ball security is this: If a coach is standing behind the player and he can see any part of the ball, ball security isn't good enough. The ball must be hidden if a defender is trying to chase down a ballcarrier. The culmination of those first three steps can be summarized as the ballcarrier having four points of contact with the football to his body. The four points of contact are hand, forearm, bicep, and chest.

The next technique is when a player is about to have contact with a defender. Many coaches teach that both palms are opposite of the ball's points and the two arms shield the ball. That's a good way to teach, but that has one fundamental problem. When a ballcarrier is carrying the football in the manner described here, if the ballcarrier goes from having four points of pressure on the football to having it pressed with the wrist above the elbow, this can be a disaster. Thus, the emphasis of this is to simply add a fifth pressure point, with the opposite arm slapping the ball to cover it. Is having two hands opposite of each other probably the best way for contact? Yes and no. Yes if the runner is running inside and no if the runner is running outside. But the most practical way to teach two hands on the ball by using the techniques described is to simply have the other arm slap the ball on its exposed area.

When running with the football, a ballcarrier has two more demands he must meet to ensure great ball security. The first is that the ball is in the outside arm at all times. The reason is twofold and obvious. The first reason is that if the ballcarrier fumbles (which he better not), the ball will go out of bounds. The second and the actual reason for this is that it gets the football away from the defense. If a runner is running down the sideline and the ball is in the inside arm, the defender has a better chance of knocking the ball loose. The goal of this is to keep the ballcarrier's body between the football and the defender.

In order for a running back to keep the ball in his outside arm effectively, he must be able to "switch" the football on a dime. Having the instincts to immediately place the ball in the outside arm is very important. The technique for switching the ball is simple: The ballcarrier will slap his opposite bicep and accept the ball going into the other hand. The hard part of this is to maintain the middle finger over the top of the football. This requires repetition after repetition every day in practice.

Turnovers have a direct connection with the coaching staff's effort not to fumble the football. If a team has a fumble problem, it's the coaches' fault. No brand of football—whether it's option football, wing-T, or run-and-shoot—can survive if an emphasis of holding onto the football isn't held to the highest standards. That's why it's a good idea to have any skill position hold onto the football as much as possible during practice. Every second of offensive practice, the skill positions should have a football in their hands, switching the ball, keeping it in the outside arm, having a wrist above the elbow, keeping a middle finger over the tip, and pressing so nobody behind the player can see the football.

This is a demand for winning. More games today in football are lost rather than won. If a team has a bad turnover ratio, it's more likely to be at the bottom of the standings.

Wide Receiver Play

In the triple option, the wide receiver has two responsibilities: stalk block and run a flash route. The stalk block in this offense is a little bit harder because of the theory of running the option.

Stalk Blocking

One of the main theories of the triple option was the idea of attacking the deep third of the field. This principle helps running the option for reasons that will be discussed later. Thus, the stalk block in this offense is a bit harder because the receiver must threaten the deep third of the field and then commit his block.

The technique for stalk blocking isn't hard. The stalk block he performs is the difference between a first down and a touchdown. The first emphasis to put on a wide receiver is he must make everything initially look like a vertical route. He'll come off the line of scrimmage making it look like he's going to run past the corner in a pass route. He needs to make it look like he's running vertical because that will make the corner respect the deep pass that will force him to backpedal deeper than normal. Once the corner reads run, the receiver will pick a spot three to four yards away from the man and "stalk" the corner's every move (Figure 2-50). The wide receiver shouldn't engage fully until the corner gets into him. However, once the receiver engages the corner, he'll have his hands inside, forklifting the defender to the outside.

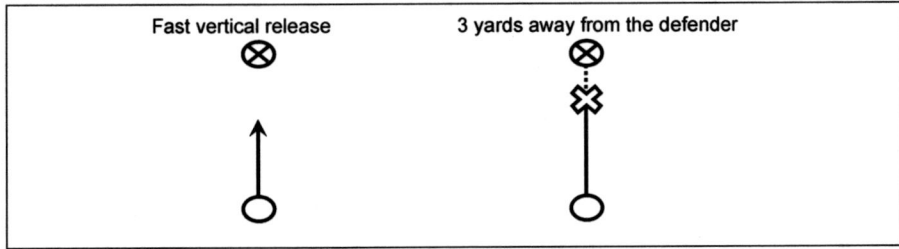

Figure 2-50. Wide receiver's stalk progression

The receiver needs to have a good feel for when he has a ballcarrier behind him pressing his block. Once the receiver feels the pressure of a runner pressing his stalk block, the harder he must engage into his target.

The second perimeter block the wide receiver will have to perform is his part of the switch block. On this block, he'll start the exact same way as he did normally, but he'll press vertical as far as possible. Against hard cover 2 corners, he'll essentially run by the corner right off the line of scrimmage. The receiver will keep pressing vertically while keeping an eye on the safety. Once he sees the safety commit to the run, the receiver will run to where the safety will be at—not necessarily where he is (Figure 2-51).

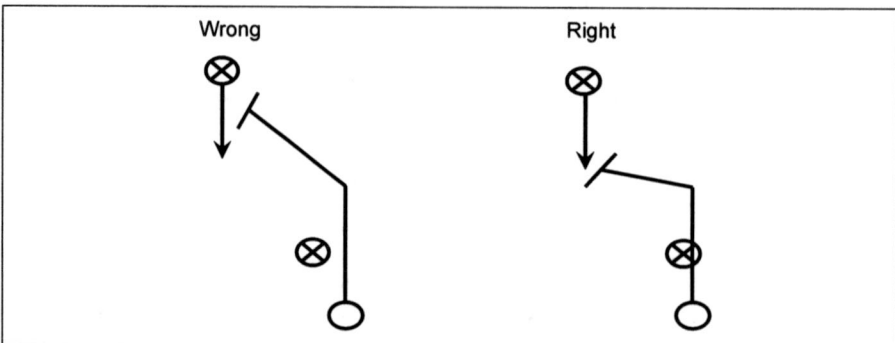

Figure 2-51. Wide receiver's path

The last receiver technique for blocking is against man coverage. This is simple: If the receiver feels the corner's eyes and body attached to him, he'll run him off. A good saying is to take him to the locker room. It must be emphasized that against man coverage, the wideout must take him as far away from the play as possible.

The Flash

This is a technique used by the backside receiver on triple. If the corner is playing seven yards off the ball, it's an automatic flash throw to the receiver. The technique for the flash isn't difficult. He simply runs two steps at the corner and looks at the quarterback for the ball. Once he receives the ball, he becomes an athlete and is out in space one-on-one.

A theoretical reason for adding this portion of the play to the triple is that this route theoretically takes out a "roll" cover 3 look from the defense. Some defenses against the option will start in a seven-man front and roll to a cover 3 to the motion side. This route takes this defense out of the equation (Figure 2-52). If the defense plays like this, an athlete has many ways to take advantage of a corner one-on-one in the open field.

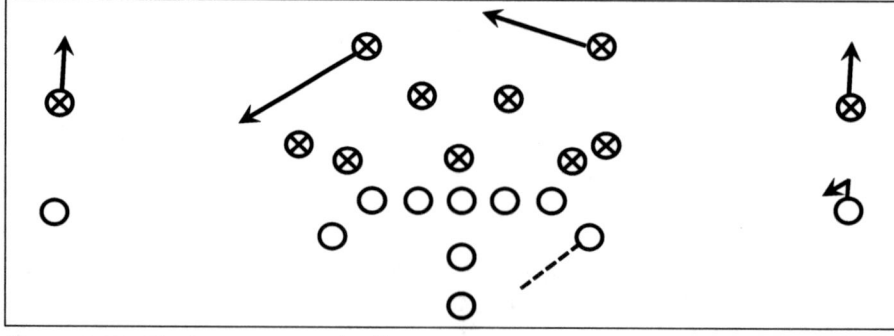

Figure 2-52. Flash vs. cover 3 "roll"

Offensive Line Play

Games are won on the offensive and defensive lines. Football is that simple. Priority for any offense should always be on the offensive line. One of the reasons for running the option is that it takes the burden off the idea of five big, strong, agile offensive linemen dominating the defensive line every play.

Offensive Line Stance

Option offensive linemen have a three-point stance. Some option offenses have their linemen in a four-point stance. However, that stance is detrimental to the fundamentals of pass protection. Next, most offensive linemen's stances start with a wide base. This isn't the case with an option offensive lineman. Option offensive linemen want to have narrow starting bases. This base will help them explode off the football (Figure 2-53). Their feet should be a little less than shoulder width apart. This helps them fly off the football.

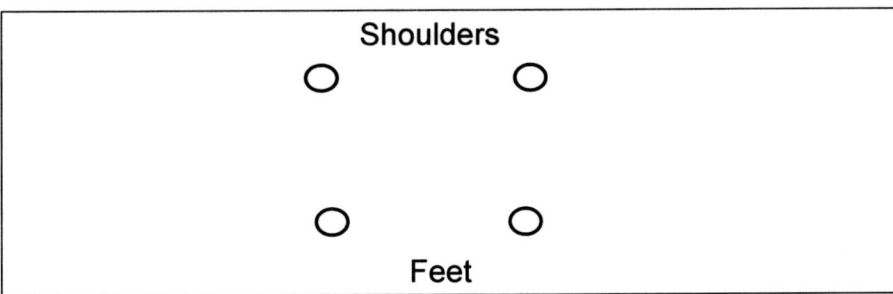

Figure 2-53. Offensive lineman stance

Another key point of emphasis is the starting position of the linemen's toes. In order to get off the football, the offensive linemen will want to slightly pigeon their toes inward. This helps them get off the football by being able to push off their big toes.

Splits and Alignment

Since the evolution of the option with the split-T offense, large splits and option football are married together. When Don Faurot took the idea of "splitting" defenders to create running lanes, it was radical and an instant success. It's important to understand the marriage of splits and option football. Widening the hole for the tailback/fullback is a must.

The initial split for the offensive line will be three feet across the board. The guards have the freedom to split as far out as five feet. The tackles have the freedom to split out to seven feet (Figure 2-54). Rarely any situations call for tightening splits. Option football is much more difficult to defend when putting the handoff key farther away from the quarterback. Versus stack defenses, all linemen will take their maximum split to create running lanes.

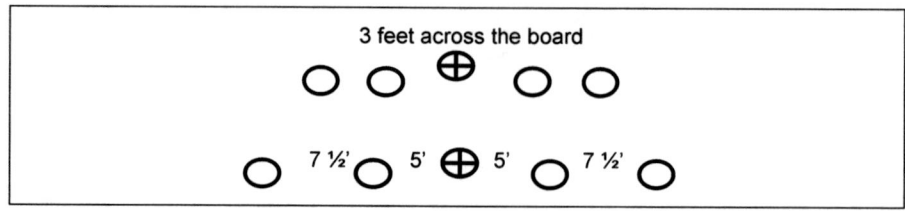

Figure 2-54. Normal splits and maximum splits

Theory Concerning Line Splits

The reasons for using splits for the run game are the same now as they were in the days of Bud Wilkinson, when the split-T dominated college football. One purpose behind line splits in this offense is to create space. Another purpose is that if a defender widens out, much more room is created for the backfield to operate. However, if the defender doesn't split out, blocking angles are now created for the linemen, especially for the guards (Figure 2-55).

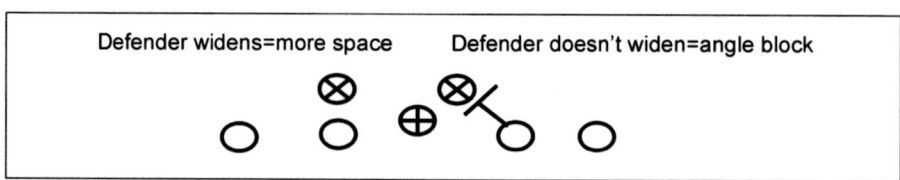

Figure 2-55. Spreading the defense and creating angles

It must be stressed that this must be viewed as widening to create space and not widening to create angles. If the trend becomes reversed, this can cause problems for the offense. Thus, the goal is to widen to create space, and if the defender doesn't widen out, angles occur because of his refusal to widen out.

The last part of line splits to acknowledge is that 98 percent of the time, tightening splits isn't a solution. Most problems in this offense are caused by linemen cheating their splits against the defense. It's true that a lineman will naturally tighten his split during the course of a game. However, the big boys up front must understand that the coaching staff knows and understands it's difficult to base block a defender out in open space. Don't worry about that. If a defender cheats either inside or outside and no one gets a great piece of him, the offensive design will take care of that problem. Creating space maximizes the potential for an option offense.

Alignment is the next issue to deal with. The offensive linemen want to be as deep as legally possible. A rule of thumb is that they must be deep, but their helmets must break the belt buckle of the center. They must be deep for several reasons. The first is that it gives them the best angle to scoop block. They must be able to cut off defenders and lining up deeper than normal gives them an advantage with scoop blocking. The second is that it puts the "veering" tackle farther away from the defender who might be trying to squeeze his inside release. This gives the tackle more of a fundamental chance to get away from the defender. The third reason is that it gives the tailback a great aiming point, a great angle of departure, and great running the wall possibilities when he's aiming for the guard's inside leg. Fourth, it allows an offensive lineman to get his first two steps into the ground to create torque, power, and a base in order to perform a substantial drive block. One of the goals of a drive block is being able to get his first two steps into the ground as quickly as possible before initiating contact with the defender. If the offensive linemen are crowding the ball, they'll only get one foot into the ground before they make contact. When that happens, the party is over for an offensive lineman's chance of having a dominate drive block. Fifth and last, it gives an offensive lineman ample time to read the charge of a defender if needed. This helps offensive linemen who are playing against defenders who are stunting and penetrating.

General Fundamentals

Because the feet are much narrower than the traditional lineman's stance, the first step must gain ground and widen the lineman's base. The line wants to start off with narrow feet, but when a lineman engages a defender, he must have a wide base. Once engaged, the lineman's base on a run block can almost never be too wide. Thus, emphasizing a wide base after the initial stance is important.

The goal of a block from an offensive lineman is *to create lift.* The line doesn't want to push the defender. It wants to lift him. Once a lineman gets into a mode of trying to push the defender, a well-coached defender will have a field day on that lineman. What's required to create lift? First and foremost, once the linemen have taken their first step, both hands should be cocked with their thumbs up on the beltline. This puts their hips in a great position to roll on contact. The lineman strikes the defender going upward on a 45-degree plane. The reason for the hand being shot from the beltline is that it naturally rolls the lineman's hips. A coach can yell and scream "Hip roll" all he wants, but if linemen aren't doing the correct technique, it won't happen. When the lineman strikes, his elbows are tight and his hands are inside. This is important for biomechanical reasons. The first is that having tight elbows makes his hands stronger. The ability of having his elbows being able to be squeezed on the rib cage gives the lineman a hand strength advantage. The next reason for having tight elbows is the lineman lats become activated in the block. Without having tight elbows, the lats are a wasted muscle group in the body. Keeping tight elbows and striking with tight elbows gets his lats involved in the block.

Once the strike has occurred, if the fundamentals are correct, the hips should roll on contact. Once the hips roll, the defender should be able to be lifted by the lineman. However, the lineman must accelerate his feet so they can catch up to his hips. If his feet aren't accelerated, the hip roll will be limited and not affected. Once the lineman has struck the defender with great fundamentals, he shouldn't stop pounding the defender until he's in the ground. Emphasizing a wide base is critical. Many times, a lineman will have a great block for two to three seconds and then all of a sudden, he corkscrews off the block. He corkscrews because his base becomes narrow, so he naturally falls off the defender. Keeping a wide base on contact is a must for a lineman to consistently stay on his blocks.

Although many more details to great offensive line play exist, these are just general characteristics. A more comprehensive lineman book should be consulted to get more into the subject of general offensive line play.

Center Play

The center will employ two techniques when running the triple option. The first is his "playside backside" technique he'll use when he's uncovered. The second is his 0-scoop technique he'll use when he's covered.

Playside Backside Technique

The "playside backside" technique will be employed when the center is uncovered. The first thing the center will perform once he snaps the football is step with an aggressive six-inch, 45-degree step. The center is first looking for a linebacker run-through in the playside A gap. If a linebacker runs through the playside A gap, the center will pick him up (Figure 2-56).

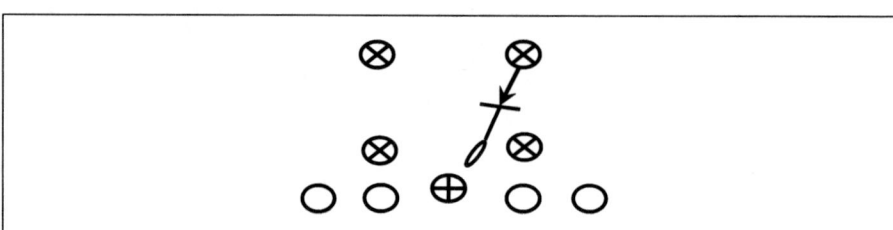

Figure 2-56. Center's first step

If the center takes two steps playside and sees the linebacker attack the B gap or runs over the top, the center will immediately work to the backside linebacker (Figure 2-57).

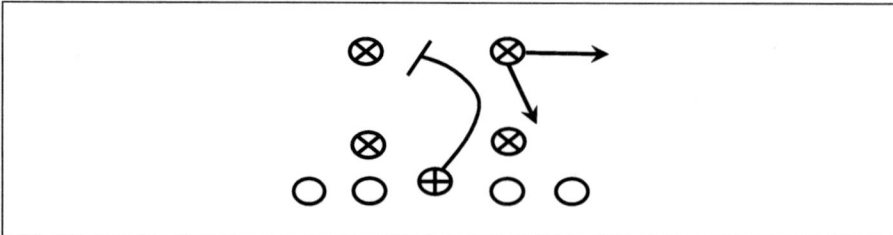

Figure 2-57. Center working backside

When the offense is playing against a 4-3, the center's responsibility is simple. He'll perform his playside backside technique, except now with only one middle linebacker, he needs to take a good angle in order to stop a scraping Mike over the top (Figure 2-58).

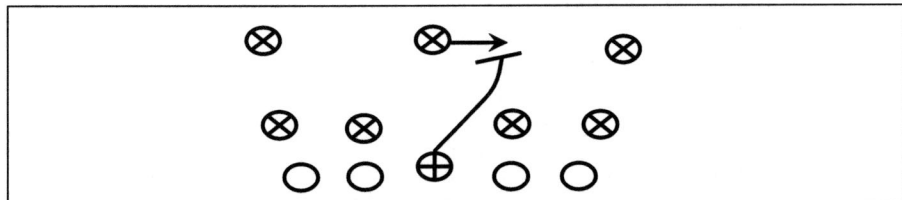

Figure 2-58. Center vs. one middle linebacker

0-Scoop Technique

The 0-scoop technique is an integral part of blocking the triple option. This gives the offense a numbers advantage by being able to zone block the defensive front. In essence, this is a zone block, except he must cut off the defenders at all costs. When the center is covered, he and the backside guard are responsible for the nose and the backside linebacker. The guard's techniques will be covered later, but it must be understood that these two linemen must take care of those two defenders.

The first step the center will take is another aggressive six-inch, 45-degree step (Figure 2-59). The aiming point for the center is to get his playside arm across the defender to his playside number. That aiming point is very important. It must be understood that two techniques can be performed to achieve this. The first is that the center will use his hands against the nose and the other is that he shoulder blocks the nose. Regardless of which technique the center uses, his steps and thought process stay the same.

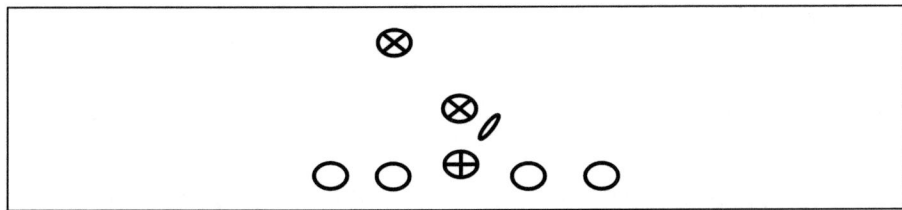

Figure 2-59. Center's first step vs. a nose

The nose can react in one of three ways. The first way he can react is by trying to bull-rush the center. When that's the case, the center will take an aggressive 90-degree step with his backside foot, maintain playside leverage, and drive the defender out. The aggressive 45-degree step is important because he must maintain leverage in the playside A gap. The nose getting across the face of the center will destroy the play (Figure 2-60).

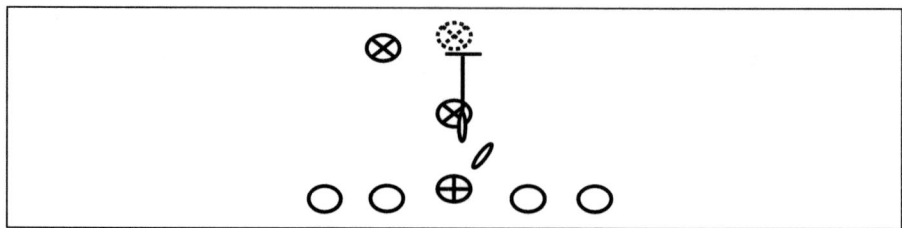

Figure 2-60. 45-degree angle to a 90-degree angle

An effective way to perform this block when the defender is bull-rushing is simply to shoulder block him. This ensures that the nose won't get underneath the center. If the center's pad is under the noseguard's pad, he'll be in pretty good shape.

The next scenario is when the noseguard slants in the playside A gap. The center will simply stay on the 45-degree track that his first step puts him on. He should keep on performing 45-degree steps (Figure 2-61). It's imperative for him to control the playside A gap without swinging his hips into the hole. Normally, swinging hips into the hole to protect that gap is fine, but because the nose is so close to the mesh point, the swinging of the hips will cause the center to lose ground fighting the nose. The goal remains to protect the playside A gap by not swinging his hips and maintaining the aiming point of his backside hand to the defender's playside number. Again, if the center is having trouble maintain the playside A gap without swinging his hips, shoulder blocking can be a lethal advantage.

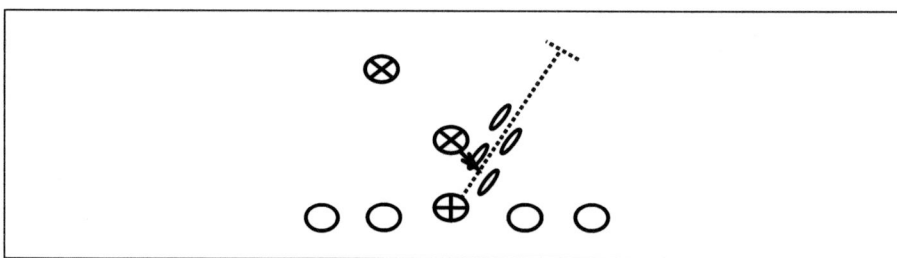

Figure 2-61. 45-degree angle to a 45-degree angle to a 45-degree angle—stay on line

The last technique used is against a noseguard who goes backside of the center. This is simple: The center will simply perform a 45-degree step to a 90-degree step and block the linebacker. Once the nose has shot backside of the play, the center's head, eyes, hands, and feet will relate to the backside linebacker (Figure 2-62).

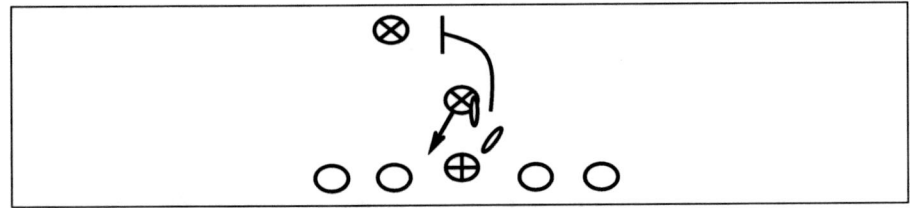

Figure 2-62. 45-degree angle to a 90-degree angle to the backside linebacker

If the noseguard is slanting hard to the playside A gap and the center can't keep him on his 45-degree line, the center will simply throw his backside arm across the nose and drive out of the path. The tailback will read this and react accordingly.

Guard Play

The playside guard has the rule of base. He'll base the defender over him. Whether that's a linebacker or a defensive tackle, he'll block him. The easiest way to demonstrate is when the guard is covered, he'll simply base block him by using the techniques that have been talked about earlier (Figure 2-63).

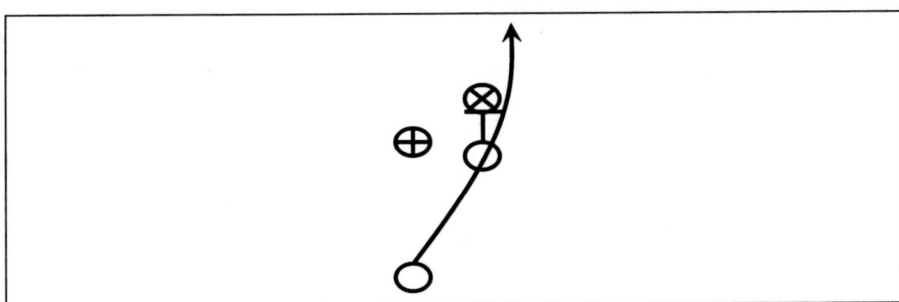

Figure 2-63. Guard base blocks

It doesn't matter whether the defensive lineman is in a 1 technique or a 3 technique—the guard will base block him. If the defender is in a 1 technique, the guard will simply down block him.

When the defender is a linebacker, the playside guard will base the linebacker (Figure 2-64). It's important to know that when blocking an "Okie" front, the guard has inside leverage on the playside linebacker. If the linebacker runs over the top, then the guard will simply block the backside linebacker or whoever threatens him to the inside (Figure 2-65).

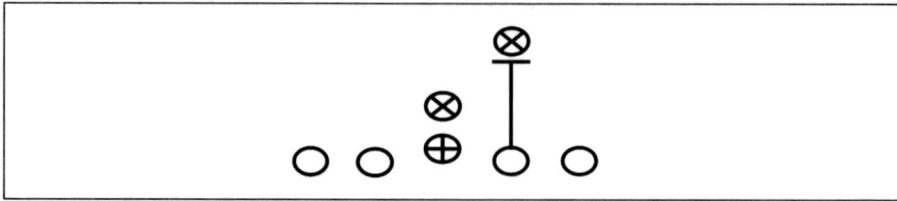

Figure 2-64. Guard blocks linebacker

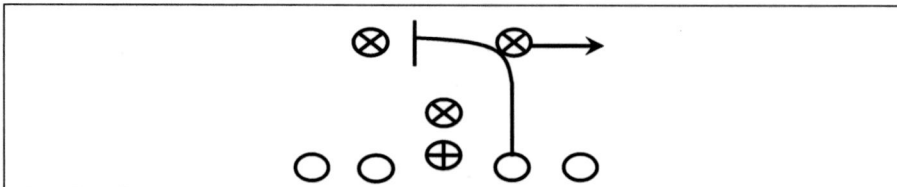

Figure 2-65. Guard works to the backside linebacker

The guard will only go to the backside linebacker if it's clear the playside linebacker is running over the top. The reason why the guard needs to go to the backside linebacker is just in case the 0-scoop performed by the center and backside guard fails (Figure 2-66).

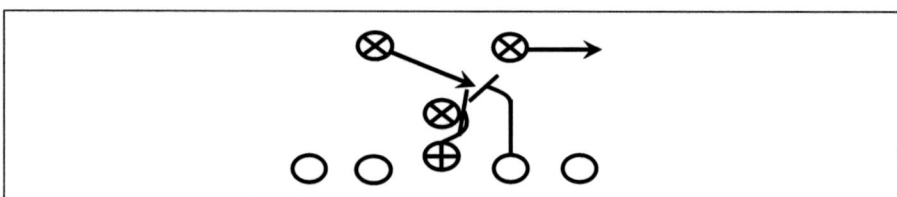

Figure 2-66. Guard accounting for cheating linebacker

The backside guard will perform a scoop. This is most important when he's performing his 0-scoop technique with the playside center. His first step will be a 30-degree step with his playside foot. It needs to be a shallow 30-degree step that gains ground. His second step will be a 45-degree step. By his second and third step, the guard has enough information to make his decision about what to do. He'll be eyeballing the noseguard while performing his steps. If by his second step he sees that nose slant the opposite way, he'll then aggressively stay on his path and block the backside linebacker (Figure 2-67).

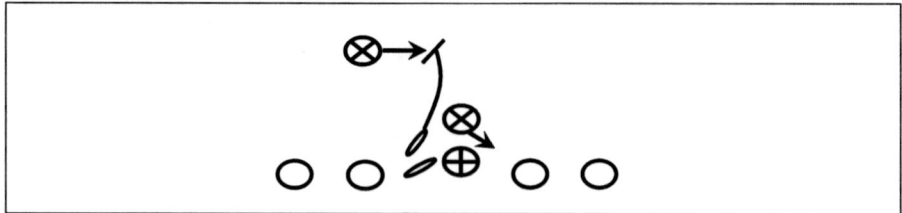

Figure 2-67. 30-degree angle to a 45-degree angle

If the noseguard slow-plays backside of the center's block, the guard will simply stay on his 45-degree path and get outside leverage on the noseguard (Figure 2-68). He can't let the nose play the backside of the center and come in untouched.

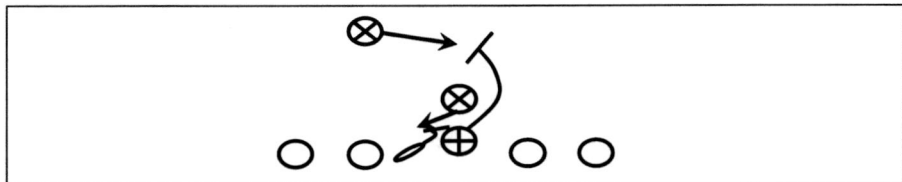

Figure 2-68. Guard taking the nose

If the guard senses the nose is slanting hard through the backside A gap, the guard has the freedom to take his first step and cut the nose (Figure 2-69).

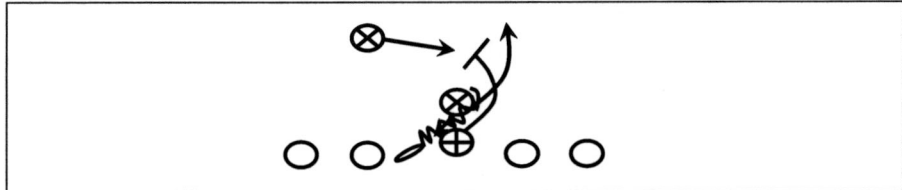

Figure 2-69. Guard cutting the nose shooting the backside A gap

It's important to note that when performing a cut block in this offense, the offender obviously wants to cut down the defender. However, as soon as he's made contact, the guard needs to bear crawl back to his feet and continue on his path.

Tackle Play

The playside tackle's rule: When he's covered, he'll loop, but when he's uncovered, he'll veer release to the middle linebacker. The tackle being covered must understand that when he's covered, he has outside leverage on the middle linebacker. The middle linebacker in the "Okie" defense has to be dealt with in case he either blitzes inside or scrapes outside. The tackle is looping so that as the middle linebacker runs over the top, the tackle will be able to get him. Figure 2-70 is a scenario where the tackle inside releases against a scraping linebacker.

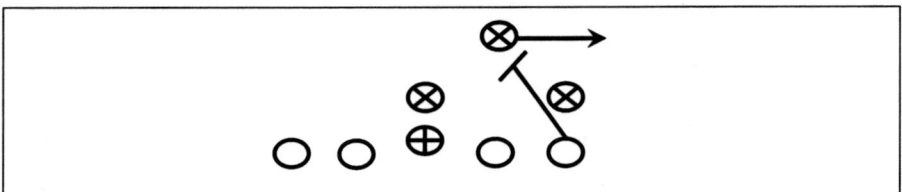

Figure 2-70. Tackle veering against a scrapping linebacker

It's virtually impossible for the veering tackle to get to the scraping linebacker. Thus, to help with the situation, he'll outside release in order to get to the scraping linebacker (Figure 2-71).

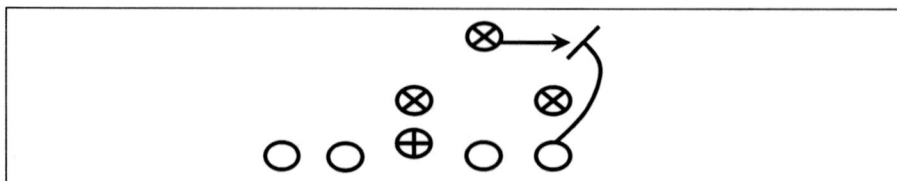

Figure 2-71. Tackle looping against a scrapping linebacker

If the linebacker blitzes inside, the tackle looks for the backside linebacker to safety. He'll cut off the one threatening him first (Figure 2-72).

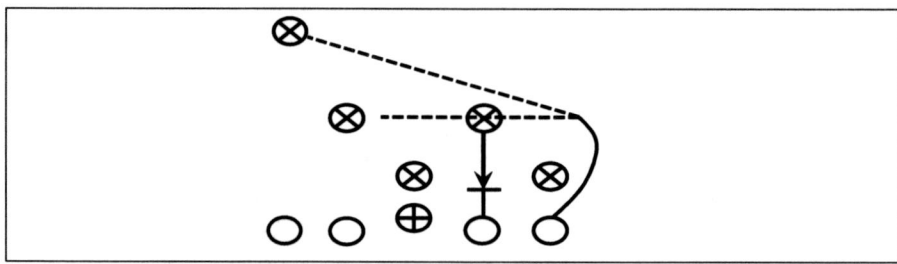

Figure 2-72. Tackle looking for first threat

The next technique the tackle will perform is a veer release. When the tackle is uncovered, he'll inside release to the middle linebacker. The tackle will perform a technique in order to protect him with a squeeze technique performed by a 5 technique. The tackle will dip his outside shoulder, grab grass, and become skinny. It's important to note that the initial goal of this block is to not initiate any contact with the defensive end. If the tackle can't escape a squeezing 5 technique, the middle linebacker will be running free all game long. Once he's avoided contact with the 5 technique, he'll read the steps of the playside linebacker. The reason why he doesn't specifically read the first step of the linebacker is because more often than not, the first step performed by the middle linebacker is a read step, so that can be deceptive.

If the tackle reads the linebacker's feet going downhill, he'll meet him where his body is taking him. If the middle linebacker's feet are lateral, he'll make his path straight upfield in order to meet him on the path he's taken. Both situations are shown in Figure 2-73.

The backside tackle will perform a scoop block. Because the tackles are athletic, they must be able to cut down any defender near them. The tackle will perform a 30-degree step, to a 45, to a 90. He must take an angle that will allow him to "gain

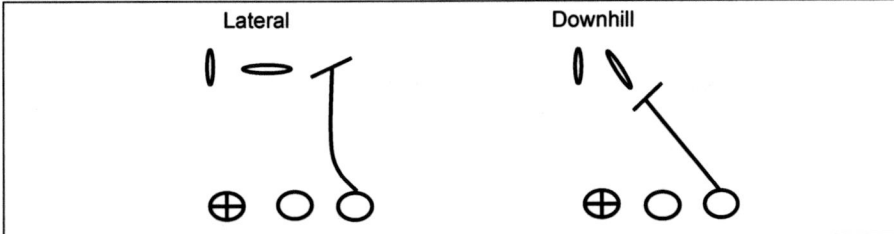

Figure 2-73. Different foot paths by the linebacker

ground" and cut off defenders. If the tackle can't scoop a defender because he's too fast or is too far inside, the tackle has the freedom to "superman cut" in order to reach the defender. He must understand that he must bear crawl back to his feet and stay on his path and block the nearest defender.

Double-Teaming the Noseguard

Sometimes, an offense will play against a defender that's very difficult to block. In this case, the center can communicate for a double-team. Some general characteristics are important to go over when a center calls for a double-team. The first is that the center won't step directionally but straight ahead instead. His goal is to give the nose everything he's got. The guard will then step toward the center and double-team the nose. The goal for these two linemen is to bury the nose in the ground (Figure 2-74).

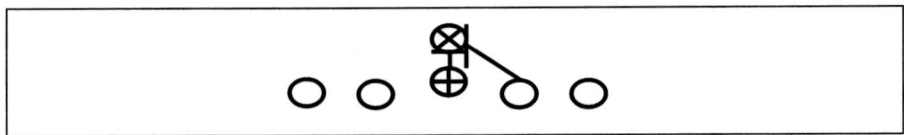

Figure 2-74. Double-team

The next characteristic of this block is what happens if the nose slants the opposite way of the double-team. It's simple: If he slants in the opposite direction, the guard will simply block the backside linebacker and the center will throw his backside arm across the nose and drive him backside of the play (Figure 2-75).

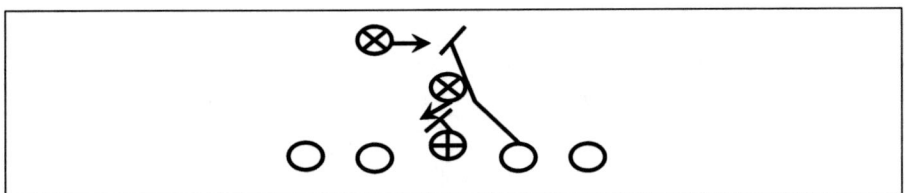

Figure 2-75. Double-team—guard works backside

The last part of double-teaming the nose is what the tackle will do. Because the guard and center are responsible for the nose, the tackle must veer release inside in order to protect the B gap. If he doesn't, the backer can blitz through the playside B gap and destroy the play. Because of that, a double-team between the center and guard is an automatic veer release. Both scenarios are shown in Figures 2-76 and 2-77.

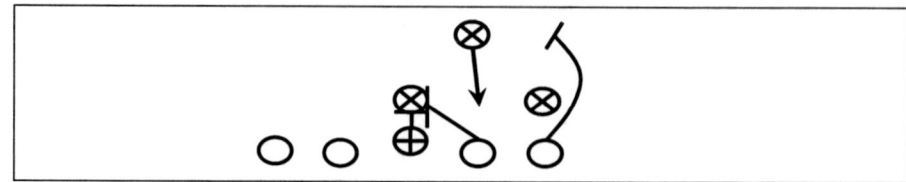
Figure 2-76. Tackle loops—B gap not protected

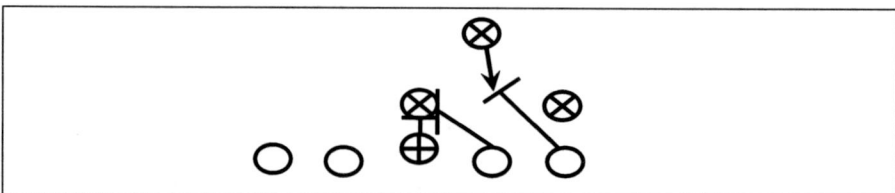
Figure 2-77. Tackle veers—B gap protected

Double-teaming should be used sparingly because if a double-team is used, a backer can scrape over the top and be the fifth perimeter defender, therefore defeating the theoretical realm of running the option.

Other Variations of the Triple

With the use of two slotbacks and a wide-open formation, an offense has different ways in which it can run the option. It's also true that if a defense is locked into the basic way to run the triple and the core plays of the spread option offense that a change-up option look can catch the defense off-guard. However, the variations should be used scarcely, as a change-up and with a purpose. Adding a variation just for the sake of having a variation distorts the original thinking of this offense. The variations of the triple option won't be covered because the subject of this book is the base plan of a pistol spread option offense. The truth is, out of the spread, coaches can devise up to 10 to 20 variations of triple options that can be used in different situations. Throwing a change-up at the defense has some merit, but do it wisely and not recklessly.

3

The Pistol Spread Option Passing Game

As explained, the reason for the pistol spread formation is to enhance pass protection. The advantages lost in the option game are directly transferred to the passing game. Expressing four verticals to the defense enhances the option game and the passing game. In all offenses, passing the football isn't a suggestion. It's a demand. Even in the wishbone formation, the ball must be effectively placed in the passing game. The pistol spread activates all areas of the field that the defense must defend against.

Many critics of the offense will say the passing game from an option set isn't effective because of its limitability. They're correct in their assertion that the passing game from whatever option set is limited. However, option football coaches shouldn't take that as an insult because the truth is that it's a compliment. To be proficient at running the option, a team must spend 50 percent of practice time dedicated to perfecting that phase of the offense. That leaves 50 percent to the passing game. Of course, in theory, this is nothing different compared with other offenses. However, the limitability is an added bonus for the simple fact that most football coaches add too many concepts in their passing game. If a team is running 20 passing concepts, how can it master all the routes, reads, blitzes, and adjustments to all defenses? Unless the team is Stanford, that's very difficult even for the collegiate level.

Obviously, the passing game from an option set is much different from passing in a pro-style offense or a 2x2 offense. The reason is simple: A broad summary of the option attack is that the triple option attacks the width of the defense. The option is the best tool invented to fully utilize the 53.3-yard width of the field. Stretching the defense horizontally is one of the goals of the running game. Common sense would then say the passing game is the vertical stretch that stresses the defense. In theory, it's difficult to soundly play the option horizontally and vertically. Stretching the defense horizontally controls perimeter defenders. The threat of the pitchman and the threat of the receiver attacking the deep third of the field puts the defense in a place that it must designate defenders to defend those specific areas. This makes the passing game explosive out of an option set. Dictating the way perimeter defenders play by running the option makes the defense vulnerable to the vertical passing game.

Two Principles Established by the Wishbone

Several advantages come with running the option against pass defenses. The first and obvious reason is that the option attack will hardly ever see tough pass defenses. The reason? The triple option dictates to the defense how to play its perimeter defenders. The old theory of option football states that one defender can't play the quarterback and the pitchman and one defender can't defend the playside deep third of the field and take the pitchman to stop the regular option play. Instead, it takes four perimeter defenders. To stop the triple option play, it takes five perimeter defenders. This advantage is huge because in option theory because defenses can't run the toughest defense to throw against: cover 2. The corner can't stop the pitch and stop the fade route by the wide receiver. This principle was established by Emory Bellard out of the wishbone (Figure 3-1). The wishbone rarely saw tough pass defenses because if it did, it would be shredded. This is also significant to the shape of the wishbone formation. The wishbone had one split end to control the rotation of the secondary. This evolution of the passing game is very important to understand. The wishbone was created partly because the split-T option pitch phase was destroyed by outside rotation with two tight ends on the formation. That's the reason why the wishbone formation has a split end in its formation: Send a receiver downfield to attack the deep third of the defense so outside rotation from corners becomes difficult (Figure 3-2).

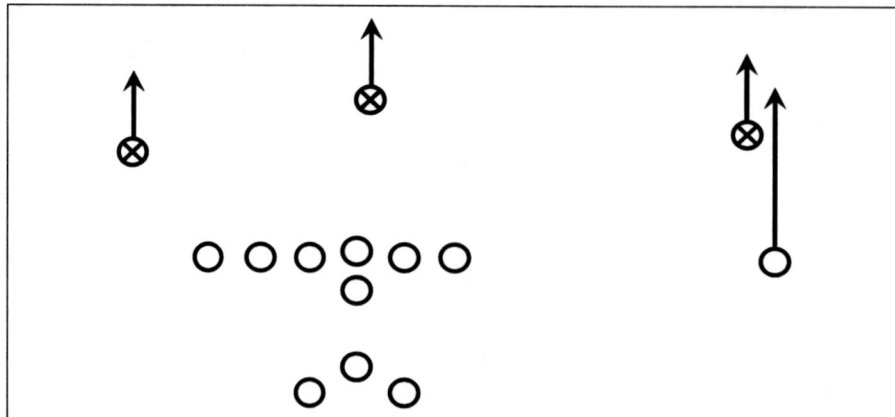

Figure 3-1. Wishbone attacking the deep third

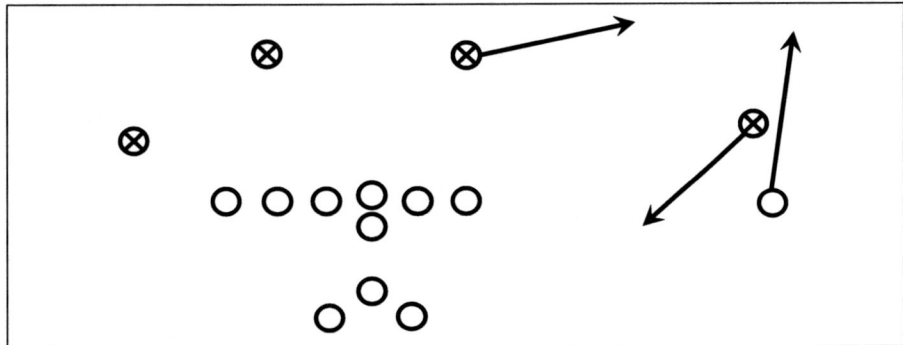

Figure 3-2. Wishbone defeating outside rotation

The principle that the wishbone established was a focal point for the success of the triple option attack. Dictating what perimeter defenders can and can't do is a huge advantage to the offense because it takes the best pass defenses out of the defensive playbook. Defenses are forced to play man, three deep, or four deep (umbrella). The spread enhances the control of perimeter defenders. If the defense plays a cover 2 shell and defends the option like it does in Figure 3-3, it will be a touchdown by the inside slotback every snap.

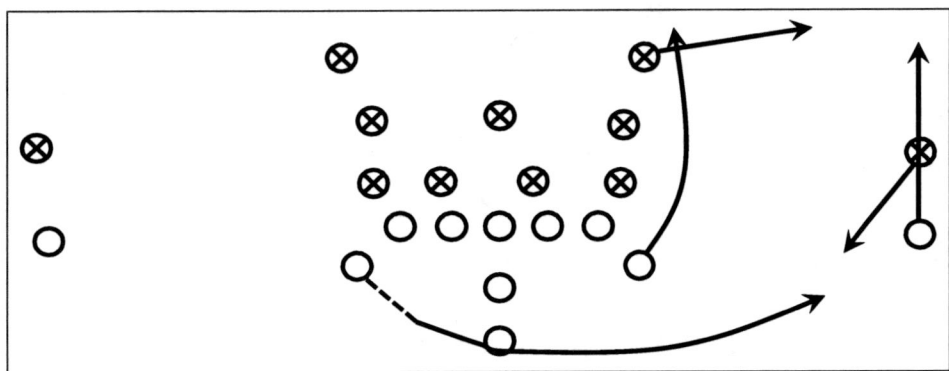

Figure 3-3. Outside rotation vs. the option

As shown and demonstrated, outside rotation defending the option is impractical because of the basic principles established by the wishbone. This forces defenses to invert its rotation against the option, which the offense will exploit through huge gains in the option game. Defenses can choose to pick their poison by challenging the offense to attack the outside deep third of the field and take chances—and some defenses get away with it. Defenses get away with it because modern option coaches don't use the idea of attacking the deep third with their wideouts. Understanding and attacking this defense is a must because the spread formation will fall into the trap that took the split-T out of college football. Just because the offense aligns in the spread or the wishbone doesn't mean this problem will go away. However, using this principle will destroy defenses that use outside rotation.

The wishbone having a wide receiver wasn't only there to disrupt the design of a cover 2 defense. Having a wide receiver in an option attack also controls three-deep secondaries. One problem a double-tight formation would have running the option is having a three-deep secondary rotating and outnumbering the triple. Having a receiver split out takes the numbers game away from three-deep secondaries. Also, if a three-deep secondary still tries to rotate toward the option side, the defense is playing with fire. The defense has now conceded to the offense that the receiver has the entire field to work with against the corner (Figure 3-4). This enhances a basic principle of football: Offensive teams want a lot of field to work with and few defenders. The defense wants little space and a lot of numbers. Option football is the most proven way to enhance that basic principle of football.

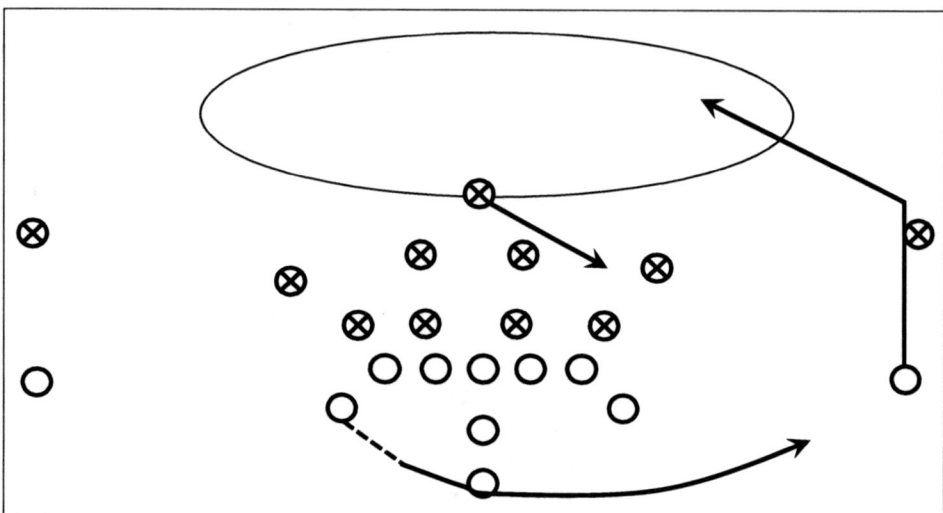

Figure 3-4. Three-deep secondaries inverted rotation vs. the option

The Bottom Line With Wishbone Principles

The bottom line with an option team is that if they do not adhere to the principles first established out of the wishbone, *they will see the toughest pass defenses and run defenses*. An option football team must be cognizant of when teams are utilizing outside rotation and an inverting safety against the option. Although throwing might not completely stop it, it will discourage it. Attacking these areas will make secondary players hesitant to fully commit to the option.

Simplified Coverages

One reason why the passing game is as exciting through an option offense as compared with any other offense is that the offense will immediately know what coverage the defense is playing. Many offenses can be easily confused by defenses disguising their coverage schemes. This rarely happens to the option. Because the option dictates what the perimeter defenders can do, the defense has to immediately declare what coverage it's in. Also, because the option is run out of a balance formation and it's the base formation for the offense 80 percent of the time, anybody in the stands can figure out what coverage the defense is utilizing against the option. Brilliant coaching manuals have phenomenal blitzes and secondary coverages that are designed to disguise and confuse offenses. Many of them are very excellent tactics and can force offenses into problems because they're being baited into running certain plays or making certain adjustments. This rarely happens to the option. A defense may catch the option once or even twice into a trap, but the vast majority of the time, the offense will bust open the defense for overthinking itself. As the run-and-shoot offense welcomes all-out blitzes, the option offense welcomes exotic secondary schemes from the defense. It will result in a win for the offense.

In practice, the pistol spread option offense has few passing concepts, a quick game, and rollouts. The point of the concepts and quick game is simple: Attack coverages. Running routes for the sake of running a route is a waste of time. Attacking coverages and making defensive rules wrong are essentials of the pistol spread passing game. Beating man, cover 2, cover 3, cover 4, cover 6, and cover 10 is the main priority of the offense. The option principle of beating defenses that play outside rotation is the first pass pattern to put in (stretch). If the defense is playing the option that way, stretch can be called every snap. However, coverage beaters are the rest of the passing game. They can have the backfield play-action or they can be a simple dropback game. However, the goal still remains the same: *Attacking coverages is the priority of this offense.*

The Benefits of the Passing Game Through the Pistol

The main reason for the spread and the pistol to be married together is pass protection. Pass protection with wide splits under center is very difficult. Being in the pistol benefits the quarterback, with him having depth beyond the line of scrimmage, and it benefits the offensive line by giving it extra space that it wouldn't have if the quarterback is under center. Other than that, it must be understood that the option game is affected because speed is affected. These areas of this offense are where the depth actually helps the offense (speed option, counter speed, slot iso). However, when the triple and midline options are considered, they're not as effective as they are under center. However, other benefits do come along with the pistol in the passing game. These aren't the reasons to go to the pistol, but they're benefits that naturally come with the pistol.

The first extra benefit in the passing game is the simplicity of the drops needed to be perfected for the quarterback. Under center, drops can vary from a three-step drop to a five-step drop to a quick five to a five and a hitch to a seven-step drop to a half roll. The pistol spread offense requires one drop for the quarterback: a three-step. When running quick game, no quarterback drop is required. The quarterback is already armed with the necessary footwork needed to make this offense thrive. He can focus on what's going on downfield rather than asking himself if his footwork's good. This is also significant in the early part of the season or spring football. The quarterback can immediately dive into his reads and progressions without having to think about his quarterback footwork.

The next benefit is significant for the actual game itself. Limiting the offense to only a three-step drop, how can a defense decipher what kind of passing concept is going to be thrown? It's much more difficult. Well-coached defensive backs are taught to key drops by the quarterback. If they read a three-step drop, they know quick game is coming right at them and they react accordingly. If they read a five- or seven-step drop, they know that a medium- to long-range passing concept is coming at them. The pistol gives the defensive backs a gray area of decision. Seeing a three-step drop only and having the receivers give the illusion that they're going vertical every play puts their defensive instincts in a bind.

The last benefit of being in the pistol is that it immediately gives the quarterback space in order to operate. Many young quarterbacks will naturally freak out when they see defenses trying to blitz when they're under center. When a quarterback automatically operates out of a three-yard pistol, this doesn't happen as often. Depth away from the line of scrimmage naturally gives the quarterback a sense of relief. The vision given to the quarterback is also much easier than under center. That's the reason why football in the past decade has moved from under center to the shotgun. Because most offenses have become pass happy, the shotgun has become more popular.

Those are benefits that are added to running the pistol. But the main goal of being in the pistol is to enhance pass protection first. Without that, teams have no reason to go to the pistol. The benefits of the under-center option game and throwing out of the gun are married together as much as possible.

How Simple the Passing Game Is

The passing game can be as simple or as complicated as a coach wants to make it. The truth of the matter is, only several principles are needed to beat coverages. The rest are techniques that enhance beating coverages. Running the triple option requires a simple passing game. This isn't a suggestion. It's a demand. Running a complicating passing game with many facets to each play won't work. For example, it's believe that the run-and-shoot offense is one of the best passing offenses ever invented. However, it doesn't fit into the realm of running the triple option. They're separate entities. It would be a mistake to try to combine them. The run-and-shoot passing game practically requires 85 percent of practice time every day to master the passing aspect. That doesn't coincide with the triple option. Making the passing game coexist with the option is the goal of the option offense.

Teams can employ several tactics to attack the defense in the passing game. One way is to attack field coverage markers. Another way is to directly attack a defender, which is done in one of two ways: Get a lateral stretch or a vertical stretch on a defender. This makes whatever defender is isolated wrong. The simplest way to do this is to get a lateral stretch on an outside linebacker. Running a slant/arrow concept creates a lateral stretch on the linebacker. If he goes out to defend the arrow, the slant is thrown. If the defender takes the slant, the arrow is thrown (Figure 3-5).

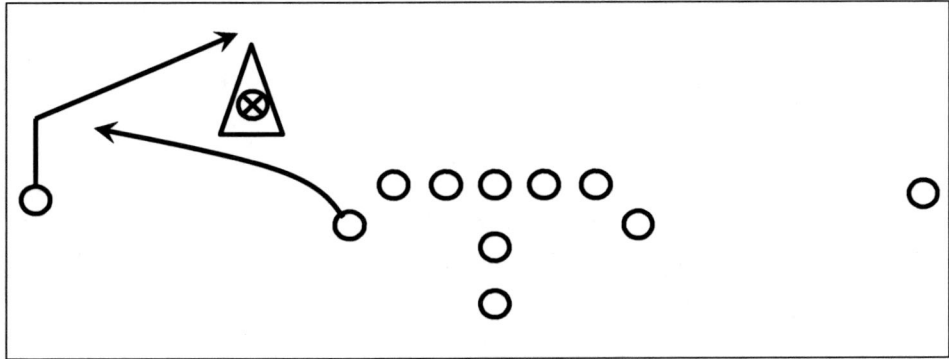

Figure 3-5. Horizontal stretch on defender

The next way to attack coverages is to get a vertical stretch on a defender (Figure 3-6). This is the exact same principle, except in reverse. Whatever the top of the coverage chooses to defend, the opposite is thrown.

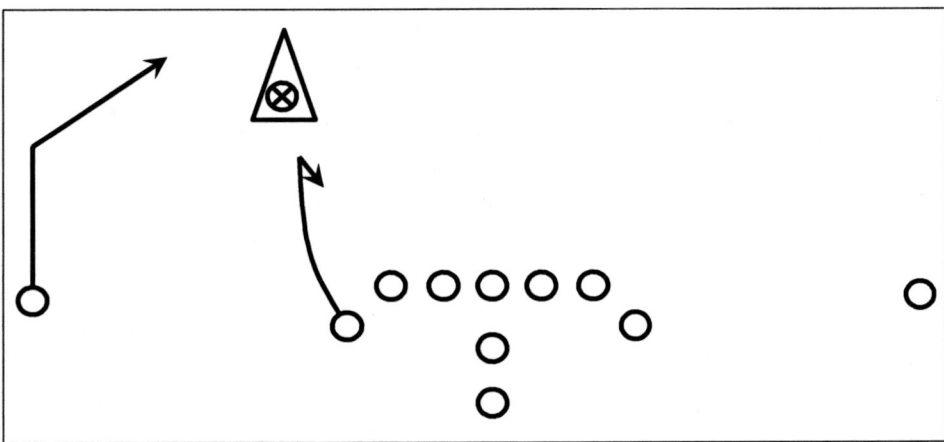

Figure 3-6. Vertical stretch on defender

The passing game can be that simple. If the offense knows the coverage scheme being used by the defense, isolating the bottom or top of the coverage is easy.

Progression Passing Game vs. Reading a Defender

To simplify the passing game for an option quarterback, a set progression is used on every pass play. The progression passing game is a set list of receivers the quarterback will look at on every pass play. An example of this is stretch, fade, comeback, checkdown. The advantage of this is it's something that can be drilled into a quarterback's head. Directly reading a defender is the best way to attack a defense. However, it's more difficult and not everyone can do it. For example, Bo Levi Mitchell played at Southern Methodist University. SMU runs the run-and-shoot offense and directly reads defenders and reacts accordingly. Mitchell wasn't able to do that. It's not a knock on the quarterback's ability. It's simply something he couldn't do. Most NFL quarterbacks don't read defenders. Mitchell then transferred to Eastern Washington, where they did not directly read defenders, and won the 2010 FCS championship. Some quarterbacks can directly read a defender, but others can't. Because the option takes a large chunk of practice time away from the passing game, a progression read is used. To be clear, using a progression passing game still means reading defenders. Instead of telling a quarterback to directly react to a defender's reaction, the progression is used to defeat the defender instead.

Becoming a Vertical Threat

On 95 percent of all passing routes, wide receivers and slots should understand that they must have a vertical stem. The offender must make the defender believe he's going deep on every route he's running. The offense has two advantages that every offensive coach and player must understand. One of them is that they know what the play is. It must be understood that in nature, offense is a dictatorial process and defense is a reactionary process. Defenses must react, which is why most defensive players aren't as knowledgeable in a "book smart" way as offenses are. Defensive players are no doubt smarter than offensive players. However, that's "street smarts" and "instincts." Offenses must be "book smart." Offenses must make the defenders believe they're going to the house every play. All receivers and slots must adhere to a specific technique when selling a defender deep on every play. The wording used is "vertical eyes, vertical hands, vertical feet."

It must first be explained why this is significant. A receiver—whether a wide or a slot—must take into consideration the thought process of a defensive back. The number one rule for a defensive back is to not get beat deep. The defensive back will play percentages on certain downs and will use every small advantage at his disposal in order to get an advantage on the offense. If the offensive player can always make the defender believe he's going deep on every route, the offense will win the majority of snaps in the passing game. If the receiver forces the defender to turn his hip to cover deep, the receiver can simply sit or cut right and left. He'll be open if he makes the defender believe he's going deep. Defenders must react because offenders are the dictators of a football play. Becoming a vertical threat gives the offense an advantage in the passing game.

The phrase "vertical eyes, vertical hands, vertical feet" must be explained in its entirety to coaches and directly to the players in order for them to understand why this is important. Having "vertical eyes" is very important. The offender's eyes must be vertical, as if he's going to score a touchdown. The reason? If the inside slot is running a choice route and his eyes are staring at his eight-yard decision point, the defender who's covering him already knows he's not a vertical threat. This technique must be employed and trained into an athlete. Coaches must recognize when their players aren't doing this. If a defender can immediately pick up that the receiver's eyes aren't in the end zone, the physiological effect will be that the defensive back will push his weight forward instead of backward, thus not forcing the defense to defend 30 to 40 yards vertically down the field.

Vertical hands is another important technique to sell the defender that the receiver is going deep. Using vertical hands goes hand in hand with vertical eyes. However, the physics of vertical hands must be explained. When a receiver is going deep, his head is slightly down and his arms are pumping hard. When a receiver is going short, his head is up and his arms aren't pumping as hard. Keeping the head down slightly with the posture of a receiver going forward sells the defender that the receiver is going deep (which goes with vertical eyes). Pumping the arms as hard and as fast as the offender can physically do so will tell the defender he's going deep.

Vertical feet is something that doesn't need to be explained because it's common sense. Run as fast as possible from point A to point B. Some players run faster with short, choppy steps, whereas other players run hard by using long strides. Changing that would be absurd, but the point is obvious. The saying "vertical eyes, vertical hands, and vertical feet" is a catchy phrase that players will immediately understand when it's implemented and explained. When a receiver does the wrong thing, using this phrase will have his mind reset and help him know what he was doing wrong.

Why is it worth explaining "vertical eyes, vertical hands, vertical feet" in detail? Because the option offense must sell the defense that it's going deep on every play. *Without selling the defense on this idea, the option will see the toughest pass defenses and toughest perimeter defenses.* Before the idea of a passing concept is even introduced to the players, explaining to the receivers that offense is a dictatorial process and that having a touchdown-scoring vertical stem on every passing route/stalk block will keep the defender guessing all game long.

Pass Protection Schemes

The base pass protection scheme in this offense is a seven-man protection. In the passing game, the absolute first priority is protecting the passer. That's why the base protection scheme is a seven-man protection. The offense can still attack all coverages with only three men in players' routes. But attacking coverages is worthless unless the offensive line can protect the passer.

Seven-Man Protection—Dropback Game

The seven-man protection has a tenant attached to it: Whatever system is being used to call it, the call should go to the side where the slot is running his route. The basic rule for the playside is big on big to fan for the playside and the backside will be big on big. The backside slot will check bubble off the outside linebacker or the 9 technique and the tailback will check release off the playside middle linebacker. Base pass protection would look like Figure 3-7.

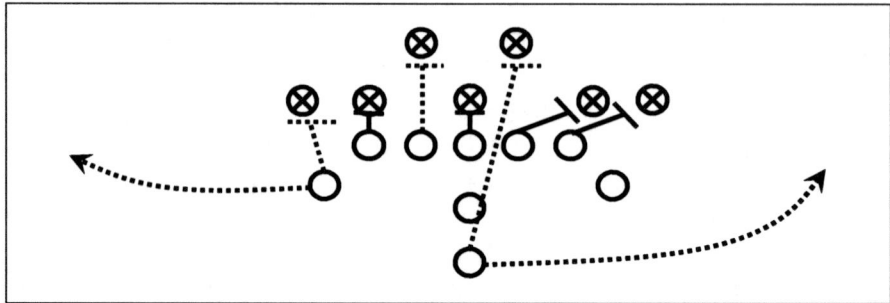

Figure 3-7. Seven-man pass protection scheme

Specific coaching points must be immediately addressed. The first is the tailback's check release. The tailback must understand that if the playside middle linebacker blitzes, *he must meet the linebacker on the line of scrimmage!* It does the offense no good if he meets the linebacker two feet in front of the quarterback. When the slot and tailback check release/bubble, they must recognize that they work laterally until the football is thrown to them. Once the football is released, the ball will lead them forward. Keep working laterally until the ball is thrown in front of them (Figure 3-8).

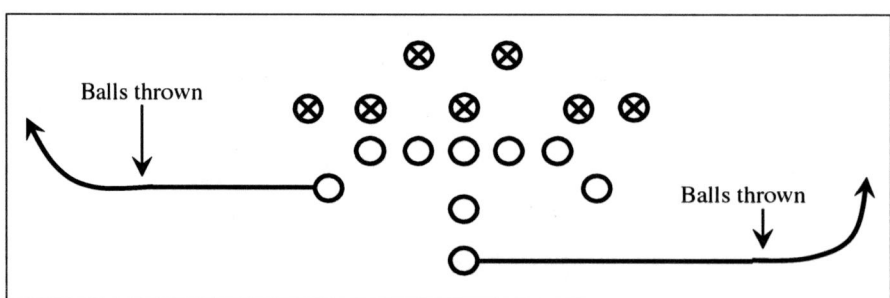

Figure 3-8. Checkdown path

The slot and tailback must stay under control while they're working laterally. If they're sprinting to the sideline, they won't be under control to catch the football while accelerating. Both positions must understand they'll catch the football many times while being a checkdown. Many skill players only go all out when they know they're getting the ball. These positions must understand they'll get the ball in the passing game.

The seven-man pass protection scheme will be examined against an eight-man front with four down linemen (Figure 3-9). The offensive line will block the "four down and the Mike" against four down linemen. However, against a 4-4 with two middle linebackers, the Mike backer they'll account for will be the backside linebacker.

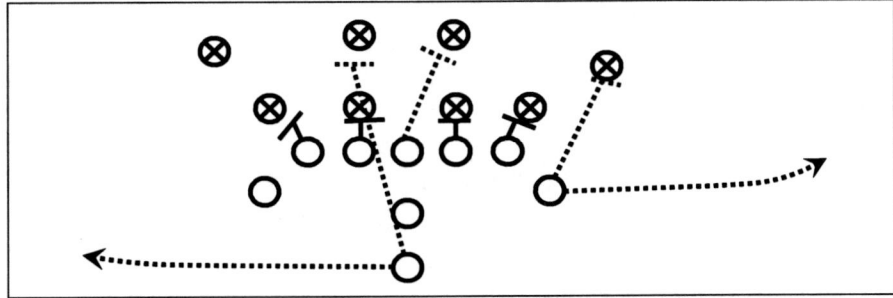

Figure 3-9. Pass protection scheme vs. eight-man front

Built-In Hot Routes

One of the beauties of this system is that "hot" receivers are automatically built in without the players even knowing it. Many times, the only defender the offense can't account for is the linebacker who's playing over the slot the offense is calling a route for. That's why the slot is always the first progression read by the quarterback. If the defender vacates his area, the quarterback will automatically throw hot without even knowing it (Figure 3-10).

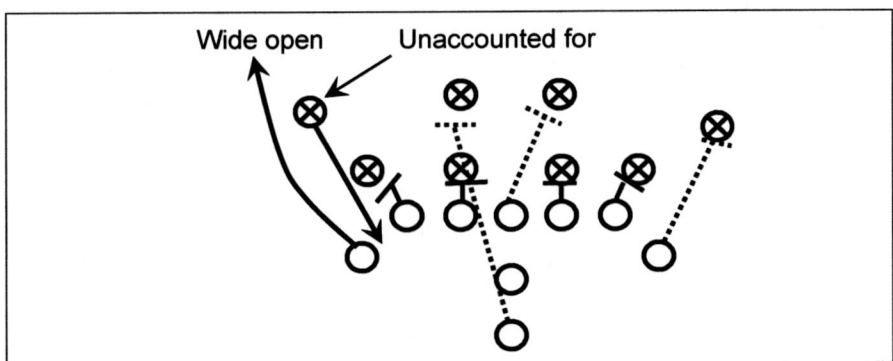

Figure 3-10. Built-in hot routes

A flaw within the West Coast system is that "hots" are used against every defense on every pass play. This offense has built-in "hots" that don't even need to be addressed with the players. The scheme takes account for what the defense is trying to do. A 30-minute blitz pickup period doesn't need to occur for the offense to see thousands of radical defensive stunts. Running the option puts an automatic constraint on the defense's stunting. If the defense stunts against the option, it's committing suicide and this indirectly helps pass protection. An offense running the option has three advantages in the passing game. The first is vanilla pass defenses, the second is that the scheme has taken out the best defensive coverage in football, and third is that pass protection is easier because the defense won't stunt.

Play-Action Pass Protection

A lot of carryover occurs from the seven-man pass protection to the play-action pass protection (Figure 3-11). Throwing the ball off play-action is a priority of this offense. One of the slots will be in motion, so there must be accountability for having one less blocker backside of the passing concept. This is why the backside of the line will turnback protect. Turnback protection starts with the first uncovered lineman on the backside. If the center is uncovered, he'll start it. If the guard is uncovered, he'll start it. If both are covered, they'll big on big protect.

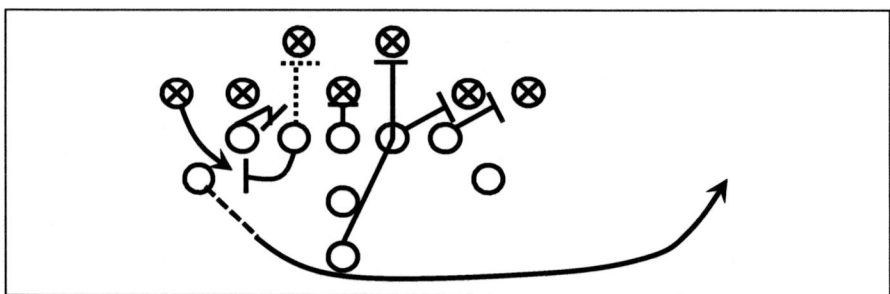

Figure 3-11. Play-action pass protection scheme

The first uncovered lineman must block the linebacker in front of him if he blitzes. If he drops into coverage, the lineman will "molly" in order to pick up anything coming backside. It will be noted that backside protection of the passer is very thin, so he must get the ball off as fast as possible (Figure 3-12).

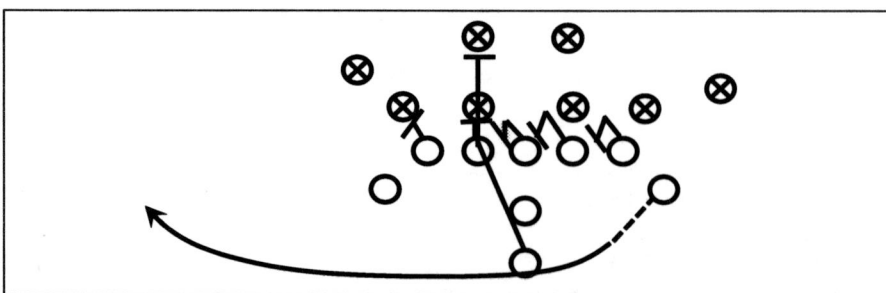

Figure 3-12. Play-action pass protection scheme vs. 4-4

Pass protection is everyone's responsibilities, including the quarterback and receivers. Even though most people blame the offensive line, the ball must be gone and receivers must be open.

Quick Game Protection

Quick game protection uses a slide protection scheme (Figure 3-13). The reason is simple: The ball is going to be gone quickly. Second, a bootleg is tagged on the backside of the quick game. If the quarterback deems a cloudy read on the quick game, he'll immediately bootleg to the backside and have flood routes set up.

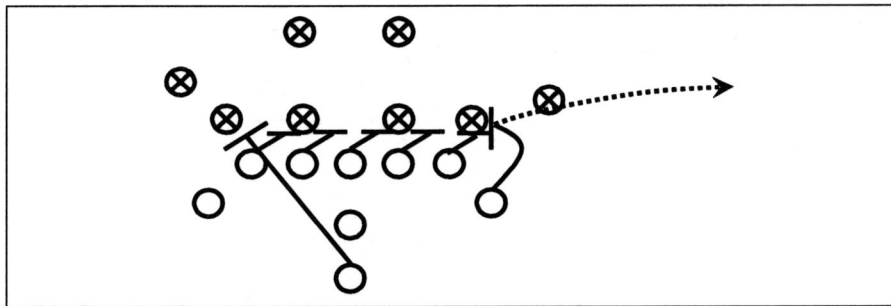

Figure 3-13. Quick game pass protection scheme

Two important coaching points need mentioning. The first is that the tailback will fit directly off the tackle's rear end. The tailback will sit and punch and then work the end man on the line of scrimmage inside out. The backside slot will slam-release the end man on the line of scrimmage. Once the tackle overtakes the 5 technique, the slot will work for a shallow route, aiming two yards out of bounds beyond the line of scrimmage. He needs to be shallow so the drag route and post corner route have proper spacing between them.

Passing Concepts

Stretch Concept

The stretch concept is the first and most important concept to install in this offense (Figure 3-14 and Table 3-1). If defenses aren't playing vertically sound, this play will destroy the coverage. Stretching the defense vertically is the goal of this passing game. Teaching the slots to run proper seam routes will put the defense in a bind.

The important route technique must be employed by the slotback running the stretch route. Versus one high safety, he wants to split the difference between the corner and the free safety. Ideally, he wants to be running up on the high school hash that perfectly divides the football field into thirds. If the safety works horizontally, the slot needs to work for more width. Once the slot has passed the under coverage, he should immediately bring his eyes to the quarterback and expect the football. The inside slot must arc into the seam. If the slot simply runs straight to get open, he'll end up in the hospital because the free safety will take his head off (Figure 3-15).

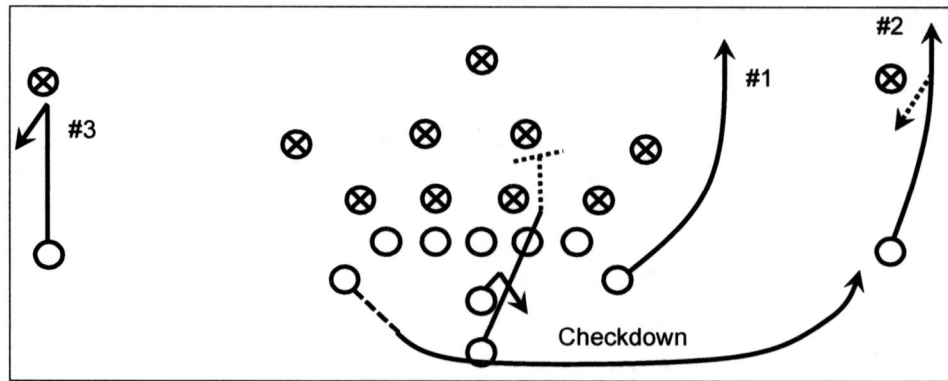

Figure 3-14. Stretch concept

QB	Three-step drop or play-action; progression: stretch, fade, comeback, checkdown
TB	Seven-man protection: check release; play-action; blocks the Mike
PS Slot	Stretch route
BS Slot	Seven-man protection: check bubble; play-action: option route; stays flat
PS WR	Fade, converts to comeback at 12 to 15 yards
BS WR	Comeback

Table 3-1. Assignments for the stretch concept

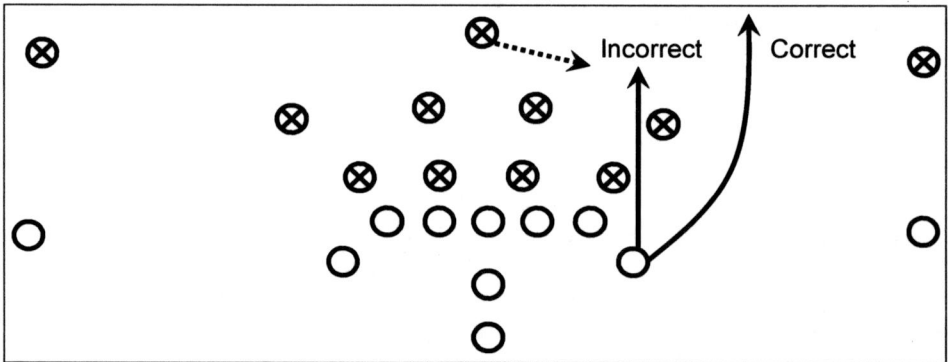

Figure 3-15. Correct and incorrect way to run stretch

The playside receiver will be running a "fade unless." A good portion of the triple option is based on the idea that the wide receiver aggressively attacks the deep third of the field. This is what makes the option go. The playside wide receiver will catch a good number of balls on this play. If the receiver is even with the defender, he's leavin'. If the defender opens his hips and runs aggressively against the fade route, the receiver simply converts his fade into a comeback. The receiver must at all costs be thinking touchdown. He must get a vertical stretch on the cornerback for this play to work.

The reason for the backside wide receiver to run a comeback is to stress the defense if it's flowing everybody to motion. Once the defense is overloaded to the playside, *the backside comeback is always open.* Most of the time, he won't see the ball, but every once in a while, the ball will be thrown to him for a good gain.

The next coaching point is against a cover 2 shell (Figure 3-16). Against this defense, if properly run, the slot or wide receiver will be open. Having two receivers running vertical routes will defeat/discourage outside rotation against the option.

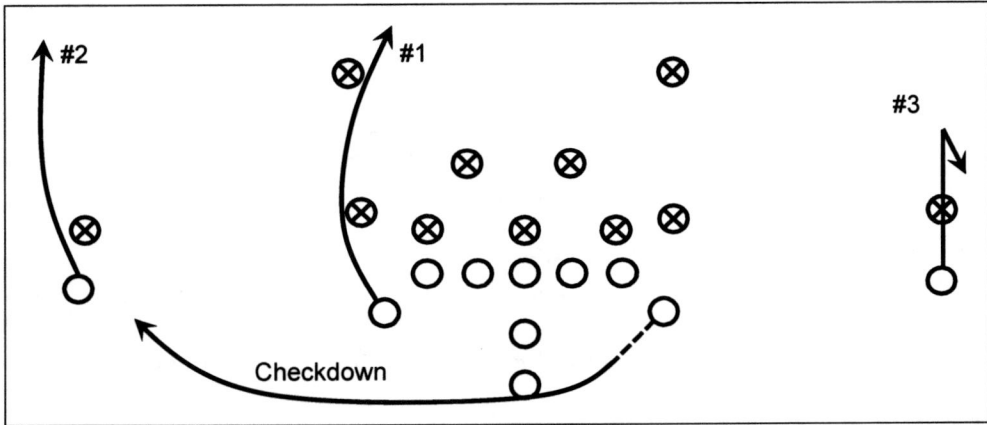

Figure 3-16. Stretch vs. cover 2

The route the slot must run now is different from what he runs against one high safety. The slot will arc to the outside shoulder of the playside safety. Once he gets into range of being able to touch him, the slot aggressively runs through the inside shoulder of the safety. It's important to note that *the slot runs through the inside shoulder of the safety.* If the slot is simply told to split the safeties, it will be a hospital ball thrown to the backside safety (Figure 3-17).

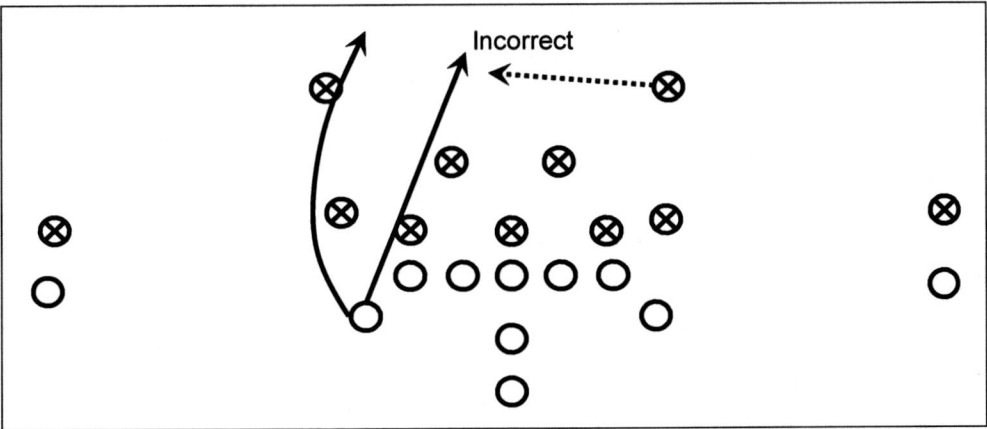

Figure 3-17. Different slot paths vs. cover 2

93

A specific reason to call this play exists, but generally, out of the spread, the opposite will occur. The play caller wants to call this play when he's getting outside rotation by the corner, so the reason to call this play is actually to hit the wide receiver running a fade route, but the material benefit of this play out of the spread will make the inside slot open. The problem with only calling this play to "split the safeties" is that if this play is called versus cover 4, the play will be adequately defended if the safety can recover from his run support. Thus, calling this play against the splitting two safeties is a falsehood. Calling this play in order to hit the receiver running a fade is the point. The material benefit of having the inside slot running the seam route will come as a result.

Choice Concept

This is the second route to install in this offense and feeds off the success of the "stretch" play. To adequately defend stretch, the defense must be vertically conscious. If the defense is vertically conscious, the choice route will be wide open (Figure 3-18 and Table 3-2).

As already discussed, option theory requires the defense to invert its rotation against the option, which is what the offense wants. This leaves the defense vulnerable to the choice concept. Choice can be run versus various coverages in certain situations. However, it's the #1 cover 4 beater in this offense. To understand why this play is so

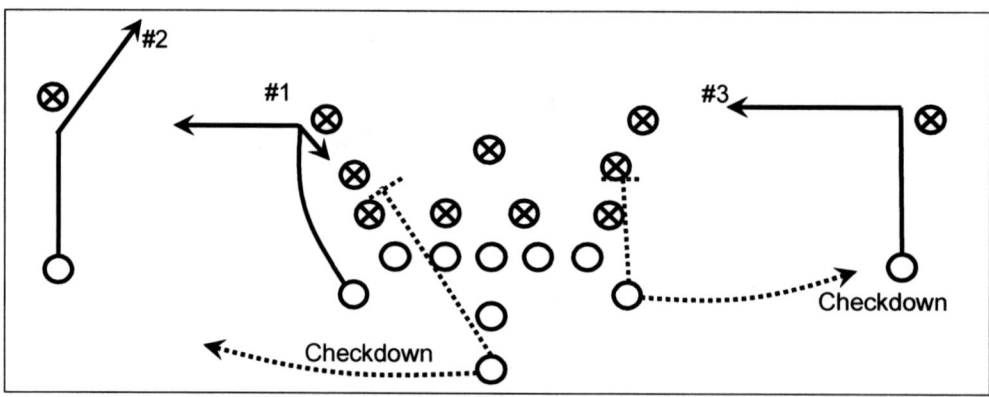

Figure 3-18. Choice concept

QB	Three-step drop or play-action; progression: choice, post, dig, checkdown
TB	Seven-man protection: check release; play-action; blocks the Mike
PS Slot	Choice route, runs vertically to eight yards. If the backer expands, sits inside, but if the backer is inside, converts to an out pattern. The stem must be eight yards!
BS Slot	Seven-man protection: check bubble; play-action: option route; stays flat
PS WR	Eight-yard post/skinny post. The stem must be eight yards!
BS WR	12-yard dig

Table 3-2. Assignments for the choice concept

deadly, understanding the coverage aspect of cover 4 must be explained. Cover 4 has distinct run support using the safeties (Figure 3-19). The corners play man over the #1 receiver and the safeties are man on the #2 receiver. Knowing and understanding this, the offense must attack the area where the safety vacates on run support.

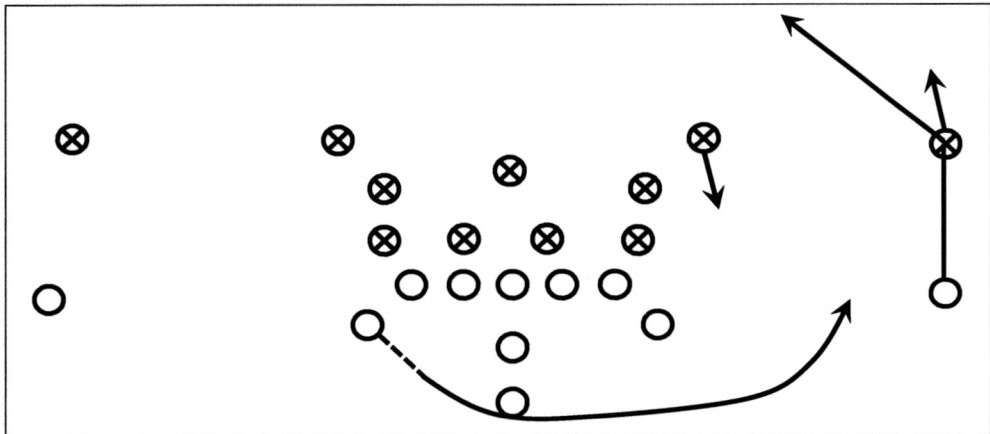

Figure 3-19. Cover 4 run support

Although many ways exist to attack cover 4, this is just one of them. However, being an option football team, this is all that's needed. Many West Coast teams attack cover 4 by simply sitting their #2 receiver down on a curl route. That's fine and is potentially a big play. However, it stresses the defense more and gives the quarterback a much clearer picture to have the slot run an out than to just sit down on a curl.

The most important aspect of this concept to know and understand is the yard marker that both playside receivers must hit before they make their cuts. They must make their cuts at eight yards. The reason why they must make their decisions at eight yards is because at eight yards, cover 4 becomes pure man coverage (Figure 3-20). Once that point has been hit, both secondary defenders are locked on their men and this play is going to make their rules wrong.

The slot has the choice to turn and sit at eight yards or turn out at eight yards. He makes his read off the outside linebacker. Whatever the backer does, the slot does the opposite (Figure 3-21). If the linebacker expands, he sits inside. If the linebacker sits inside, the slot turns it out. Essentially, if the safety plays this concept correctly, the defense is still wrong. The offense will still win because the slot is reacting off the linebacker.

Choice isn't just good against cover 4. It can also be an excellent cover 3 and man coverage beater (Figure 3-22). The reason it can be good against cover 3 is the alley player against the option in cover 3 is the safety, so the post route over the top is a check against him like it would be against the playside safety in cover 4. Having this play in the spread option weaponry makes the idea of three-deep rotation against the option dangerous because the defense is giving the offense the majority of the field to toy with the corner.

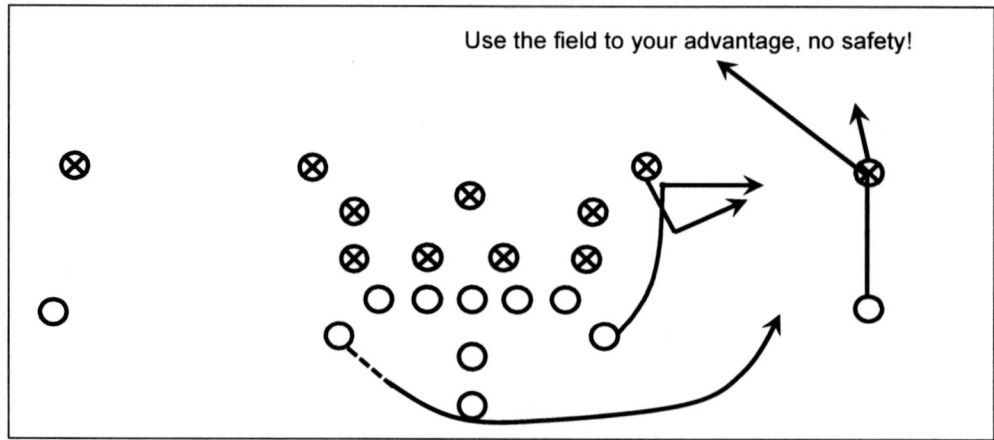

Figure 3-20. Cover 4 covering the choice concept

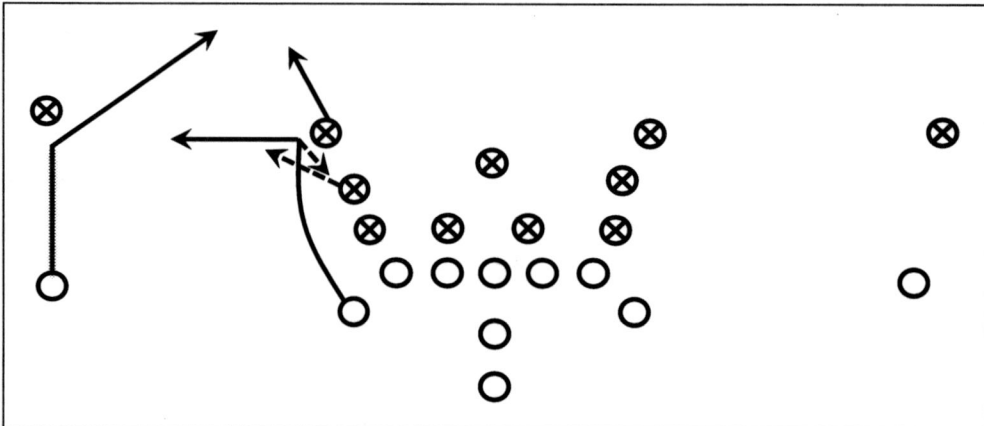

Figure 3-21. Slot running his choice route

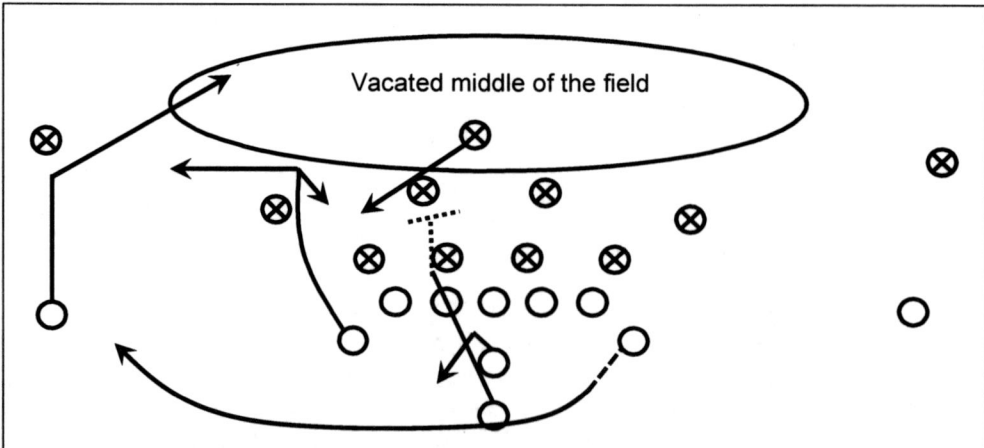

Figure 3-22. Defeating three-deep secondaries inverting

The great part about this play is that even if the offense doesn't score over the top because the safety plays "true" quarters coverage, the offense still wins with a 10-yard gain. This play adds an explosive dimension to the option offense for two more reasons. The first is that option theory forces defenses to run inverted rotation versus the outside dimension of the play, which means the offense can take full advantage of that with the choice route. The second is that this play is made more effective by the fact that "stretch" is the number one passing concept in this offense. Because the defense is worried about the vertical threats by the wide receiver and slots, the defenders play into the offense's hands. The receivers will be given plenty of room to run over the top of the safety because the corner will be worried about being beat in the deep third of the field. The safety is also baited into the idea that he's protecting his deep part of the field, but once he sees the slot sit or run out, he'll jump to cover the slot. This leaves the wide receiver wide open.

The last coverage that this play is great against is man for the simple reason that the receivers are getting a vertical stretch with their stems (Figure 3-23). This physiologically forces the defense to protect against the long ball over the top. Once the vertical stem has been established, the slot running the out or curl pattern will be open.

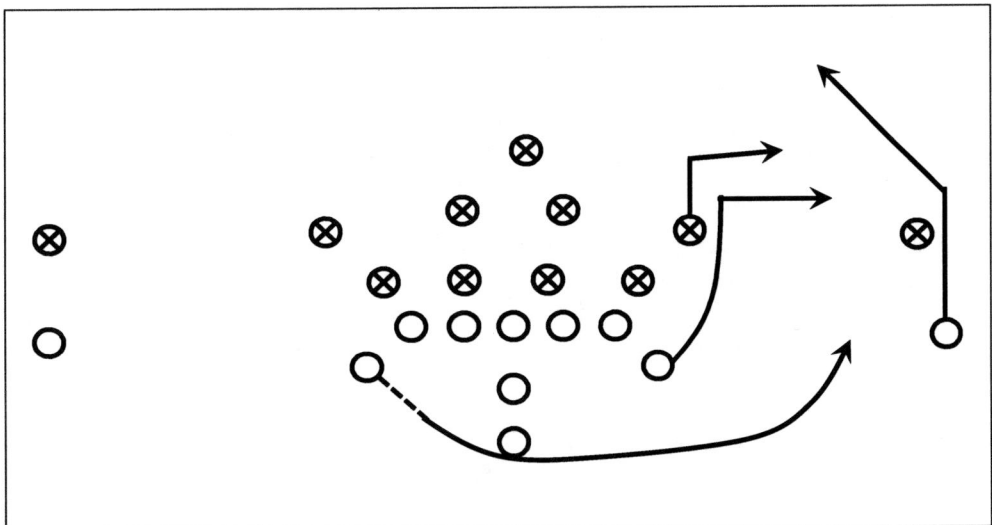

Figure 3-23. Choice vs. man

Switch Concept

In the world of option football today, this is the number one passing concept. In the pistol spread attack, this is the third concept installed (Figure 3-24 and Table 3-3). However, if this passing play is open, it's a deadly weapon versus most coverages for various reasons. It's also important to explain that this route is a field marker route combination. Landmarks are used in order to get proper spacing around the defense.

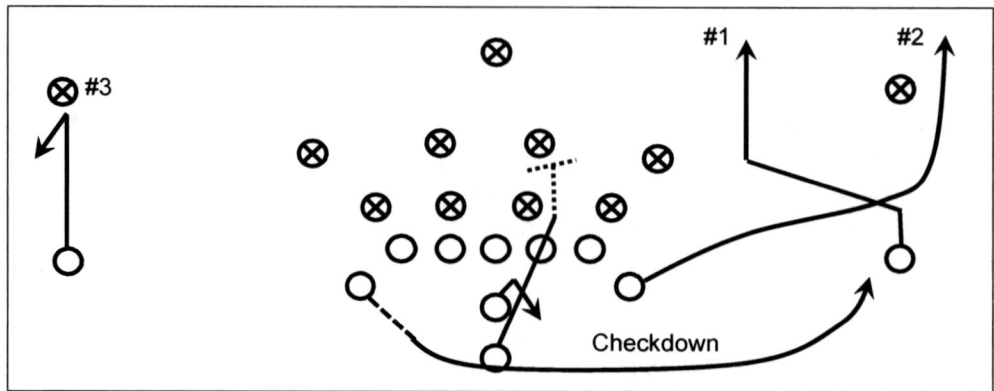

Figure 3-24. Switch concept

QB	Three-step drop or play-action; progression: wide receiver, slot, backside comeback
TB	Seven-man protection: check release; play-action; blocks the Mike
PS Slot	Runs flat initially; once he reaches the numbers, explodes vertically and up on the numbers
BS Slot	Seven-man protection: check bubble; play-action: option route; stays flat
PS WR	Pushes vertical three steps, then runs at a 45-degree angle to the hash; once he's hit the hash, gets vertical on his route
BS WR	12-yard comeback

Table 3-3. Assignments for the switch concept

In the textbook world of the spread option offense, the "switch" route would actually be post/wheel. However, an obvious problem occurs when running this route that way. If the defense is playing one high, the post route is taking the wide receiver into the free safety. It's an obvious fallacy that most people don't talk about (Figure 3-25).

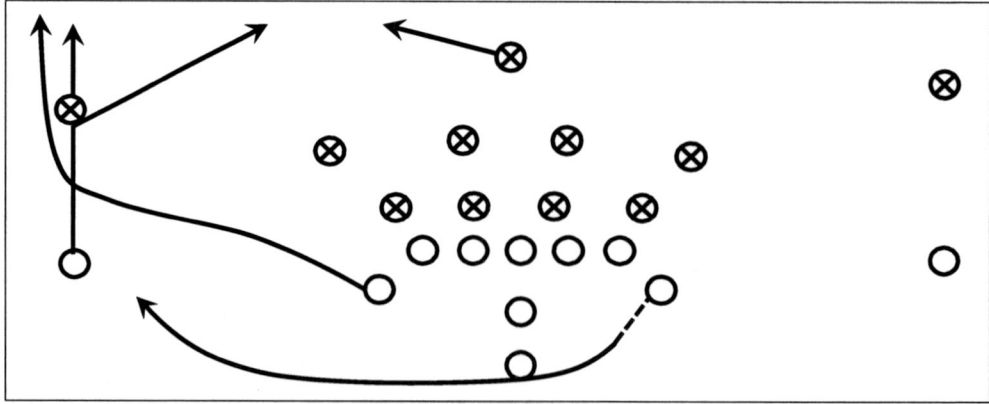

Figure 3-25. Traditional spread option post/wheel concept

The textbook spread option world would counter and say that the purpose to run play-action post/wheel against a one high/two high look is to take advantage of a safety on run support, which is true and works out great if run properly. However, this offense attacks that differently. If one high safety is active in run support, "stretch" or "choice" will be called, taking advantage of an active safety. That's the reason this is the third route installed in this offense.

Three specific situations exist where the "switch" route will be called. The first and foremost is to attack man coverage. Normally, this wouldn't be difficult for a defense to defend against when the defense is playing man coverage (Figure 3-26). However, against the option, it puts the defense in a bind. The outside linebacker has to play the quarterback or pitch and then directly run with the wheel route down the sidelines. Especially when the offense has been pounding the defense, the wheel route will be open.

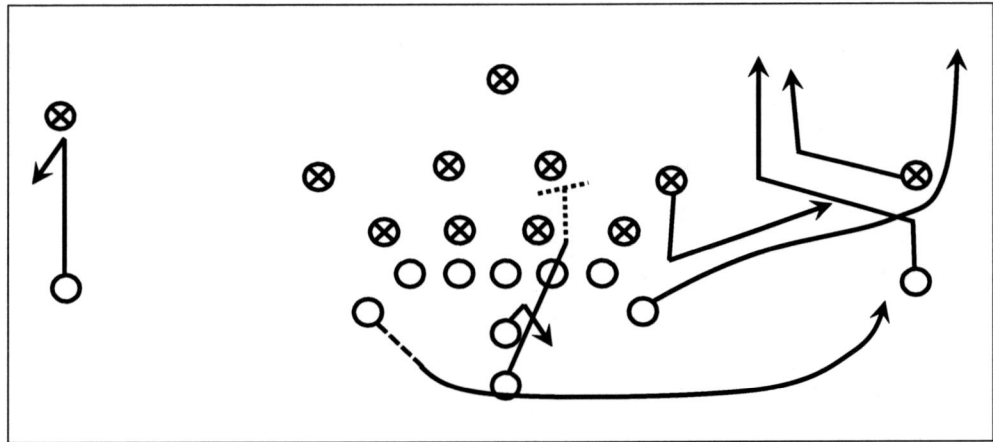

Figure 3-26. Switch vs. man

An important coaching point should be made in case against man coverage the defender plays it correctly and runs with the wheel route. If the slotback feels attached to the defender, he wants to build up his route and flash his hands to the quarterback. After he's built it up and has made the defender believe he's running a shallow route, then he turns it up. The goal here is to make the defender undercut his route and then turn it up for a touchdown. This is shown in Figure 3-27.

The next situation that switch can be run against is a cover 2 front that the offense has been "switch" blocking (Figure 3-28). The reason for this is simple: When a switch block is performed against a front that has outside rotation, switch looks the same and is hard for the corner to decipher whether it's option (Figure 3-29). For most well-coached corners, this is seldom a problem, which is why "stretch" is the most important route rather than switch. But it's still difficult to play down in and down out. This play is out to manipulate the corner's actions on run support.

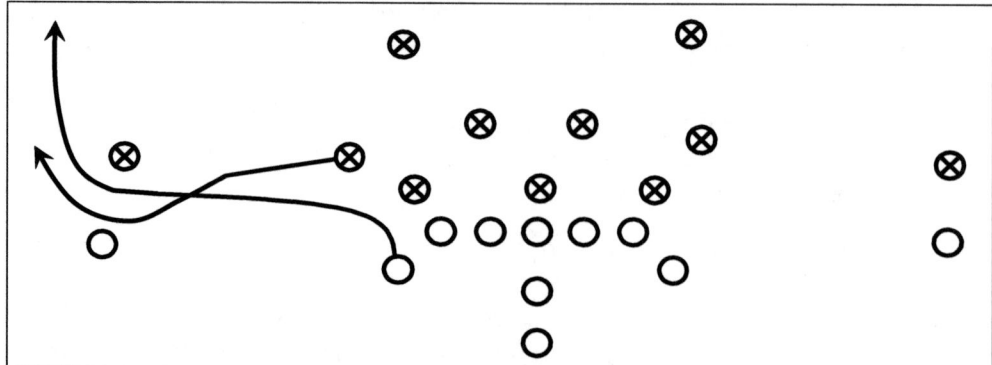
Figure 3-27. Slot technique vs. tight man

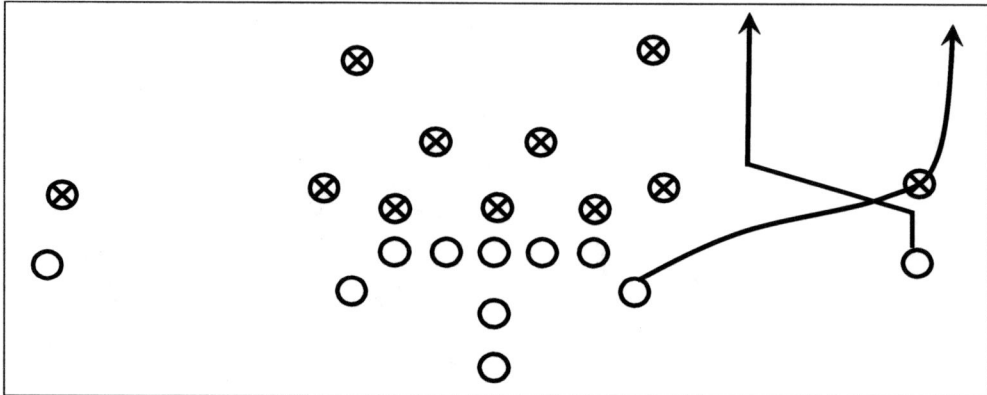
Figure 3-28. Switch vs. cover 2

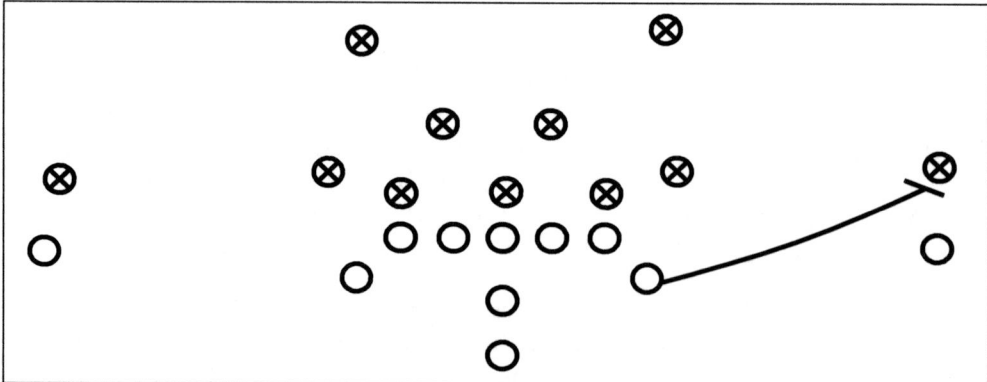
Figure 3-29. Switch block path

The next situation where switch can be a very effective play is running it against a seven-man front that rolls its safety down. Most of the time, the safety will be rolled to the wideside of the field. Being an option team that has a balanced formation, the defense has no choice but to roll its safety to the wideside of the field or it would be an extra guy short in the most important area of the field. The strategic way to attack this is frontside of the motion. Because the backside safety has to come all the way to the middle of the field, this leaves the wide receiver route on the hash wide open. As shown in Figure 3-30, when the backside safety runs to the wideside of the field, he's in a bind getting over and covering the wide receiver's route.

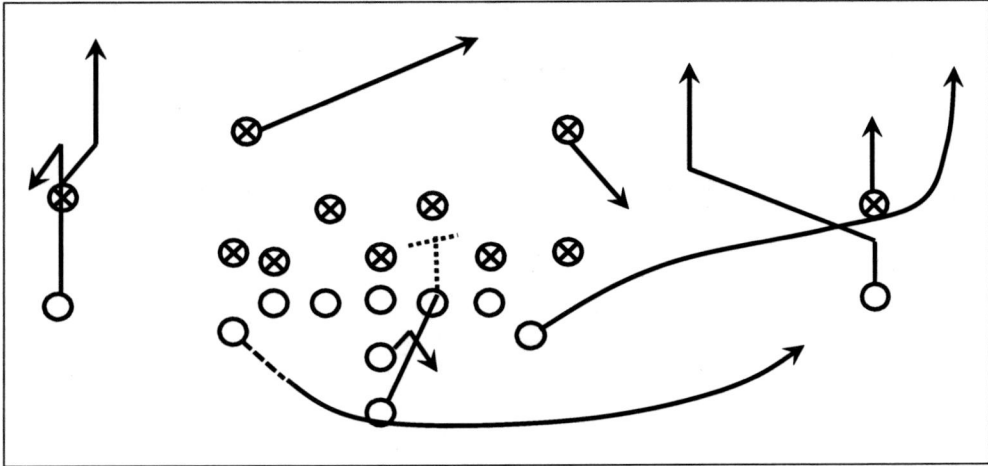

Figure 3-30. Cover 3 roll

Scat Concept

The scat concept is different in the sense that it doesn't particularly attack perimeter defenders per se (Figure 3-31 and Table 3-4). But it's a dropback concept that attacks one high defense and directly attacks two players on the defense simultaneously.

The genius of this play is how it attacks two defenders with two different types of stretches on those defenders. The first stretch is on the outside linebacker/flat defender. First in the quarterback's progression is the scat route run by the slot. The slot wants to arc to four yards, somewhat chip the outside linebacker, and then turn inside directly at the sideline. He needs to be at four yards in order to give good spacing to the wide receiver running the dig behind him. If the backer stays inside, the scat route is thrown. If the backer expands, the dig is thrown (Figure 3-32).

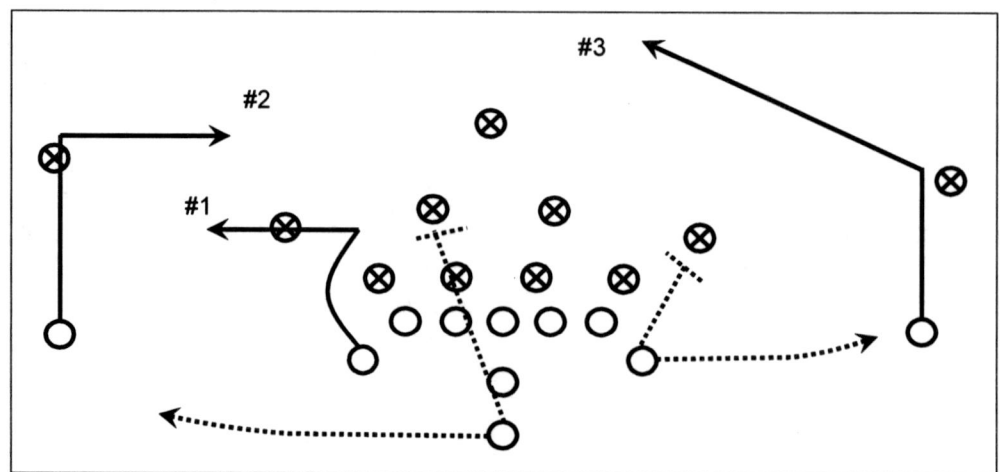

Figure 3-31. Scat concept

QB	Three-step drop or play-action; progression: scat, dig, post, checkdown
TB	Seven-man protection: check release; play-action; blocks the Mike
PS Slot	Arc to four yards, slam on the linebacker, inside pivot to the sidelines
BS Slot	Seven-man protection: check bubble; play-action: option route; stays flat
PS WR	12-yard dig
BS WR	Post

Table 3-4. Assignments for the scat concept

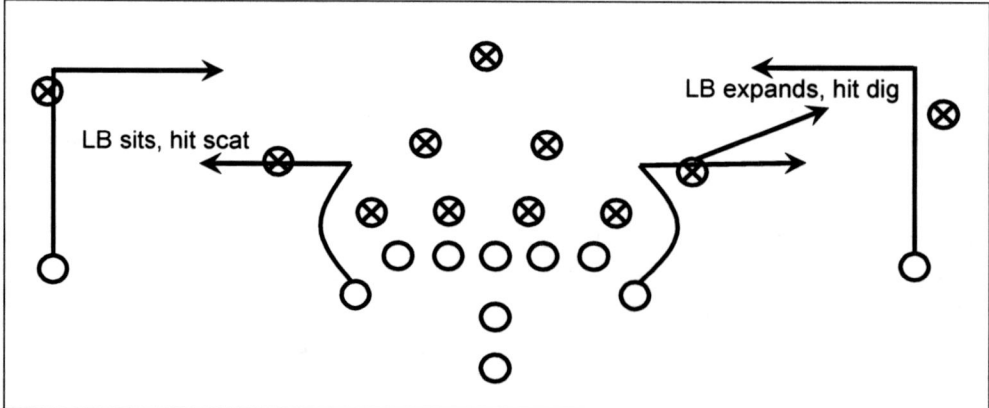

Figure 3-32. Linebacker is wrong

That part of the play puts a horizontal stretch on the outside linebacker. The next part of the play is the fun part because it puts a vertical stretch on the free safety. The only way for the defense to soundly defeat this play is to have the free safety drive the dig once the linebacker expands. Once the safety has committed to destroy the dig, the post is open over the top for a touchdown (Figure 3-33).

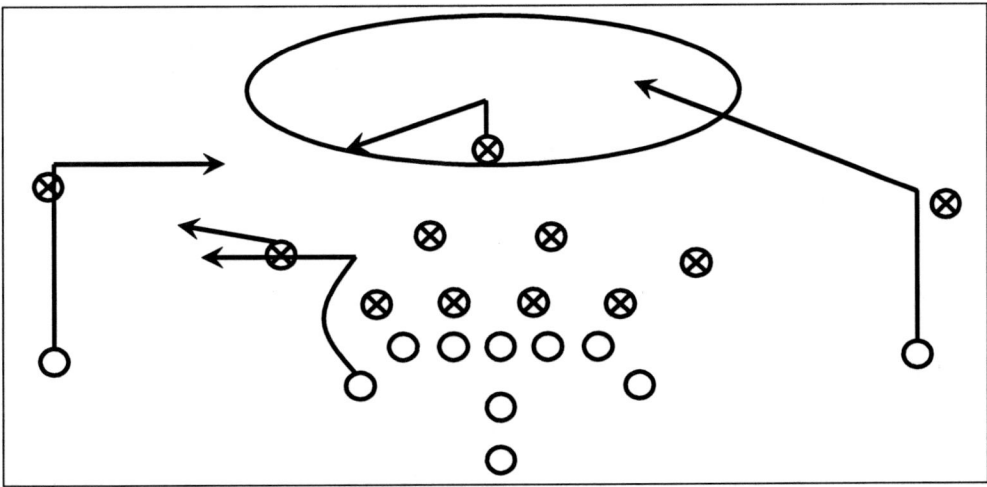

Figure 3-33. Safety jumps dig—post is wide open

If the safety drives the dig, it's six points for the offense. One more coaching point to this play needs mentioning: It's imperative that the offense runs this play without play-action. The reason is simple: The easiest way to stop this play is for the inside linebacker to expand enough to cover the dig (Figure 3-34). What motion does is influence him to move lateral. Thus, if lateral movement occurs from the linebackers, this play in essence becomes dead. As shown in Figure 3-34, the defense has this play adequately covered, so the goal is to run this play purely as a dropback play in order for the defense to fall into the offense's hands.

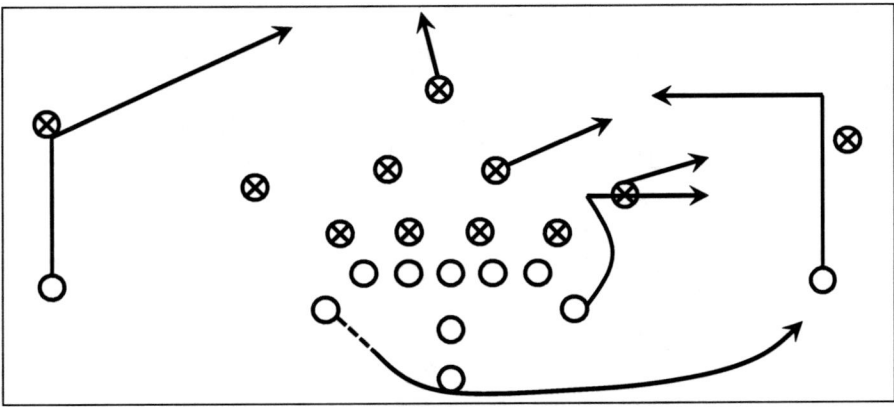

Figure 3-34. Inside linebacker getting in the throwing window

Mesh Concept

The mesh concept is another concept that doesn't attack perimeter defenders but is a dropback concept (Figure 3-35 and Table 3-5). This concept was made famous by the air raid system and isn't a huge part of this attack, but offenses can establish some good ways to attack a defense by using this concept.

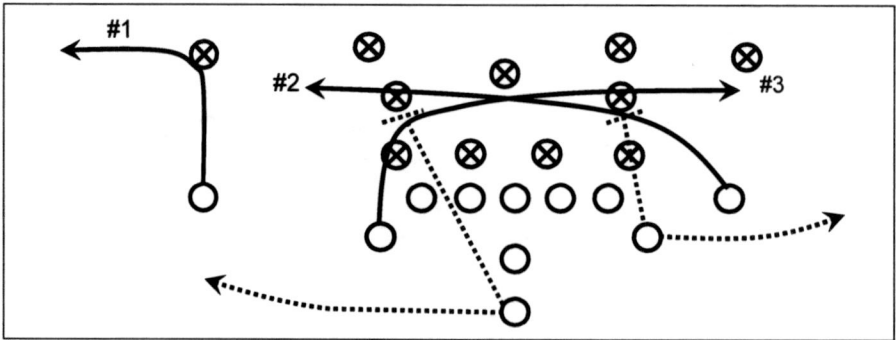

Figure 3-35. Mesh concept

QB	Three-step drop or play-action; progression: out, wide receiver drag, slotback drag
TB	Seven-man protection: check release; play-action; blocks the Mike
PS Slot	Drag route, crosses center at six yards
BS Slot	Seven-man protection: check bubble; play-action: option route; stays flat
PS WR	Eight-yard speed out
BS WR	Drag route, crosses center at six yards

Table 3-5. Assignments for the mesh concept

This concept attacks two coverages. The first is man or off zone. The reason for this is because the first progression for the quarterback is the eight-yard out by the wide receiver. The wide receiver on this route performs a speed cut. The reason is simple: If he performs a regular out route, his hips will drop before he makes his cut. A defensive back keys the eyes and the hips of the receiver. Once the wide receiver's hips drop, the defensive back will drive and possibly undercut the route. Against cover 3 and cover 4, this route will be open every time. The goal of the wide receiver is to push the corner vertical. If the wide receiver pushes him vertical, the corner is in a difficult position to flip his hips around and cover the out pattern (Figure 3-36).

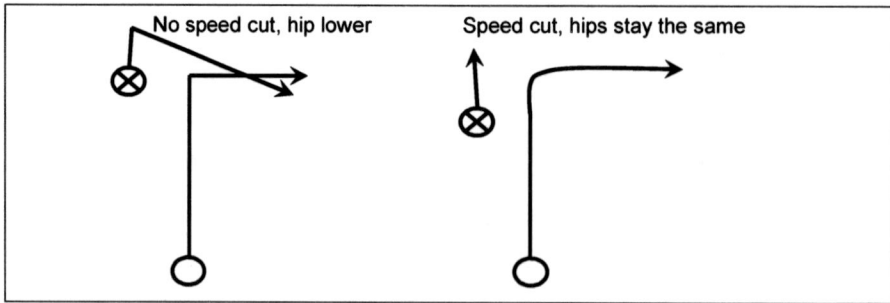

Figure 3-36. No speed cut vs. speed cut

When performing the speed cut, the wide receiver wants to run over his outside foot. This allows him to perform an out without having a sharp angle, thus giving the corner a false key on whether he should push deep or drive the route. No matter how good the corner is, if the wide receiver can push him deep and force the corner to open his hips to defend against the vertical route, this is as simple as playing backyard football.

The next phase of the play is the actual mesh itself. The next phase is good against man coverage. The slot and the wide receiver cross six yards over the center. The goal of the route is to get a natural pick on the defenders playing man coverage. The slot will come right underneath the wide receiver and the receiver will be over the slot. They almost need to lightly strike each other at full speed in order for this play to achieve maximum potential (Figure 3-37).

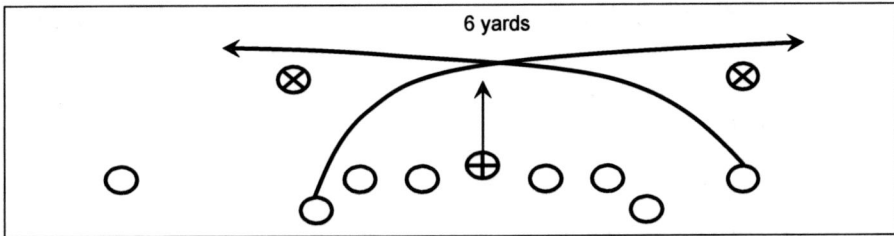

Figure 3-37. Mesh crossing point

The quarterback will look at the wide receiver first to see if he's open. If not, he'll work back to the slot. If run properly, one of them will be wide open. It's almost impossible to play man coverage correctly against the mesh concept if the receivers run by each other the correct way.

Running this play with play-action will distort man coverage. Play-actioning to this will leave the slot running across the formation wide open. However, he has to sneak over there. If he successfully sneaks over there, it will operate like the run-and-shoot offense (Figure 3-38).

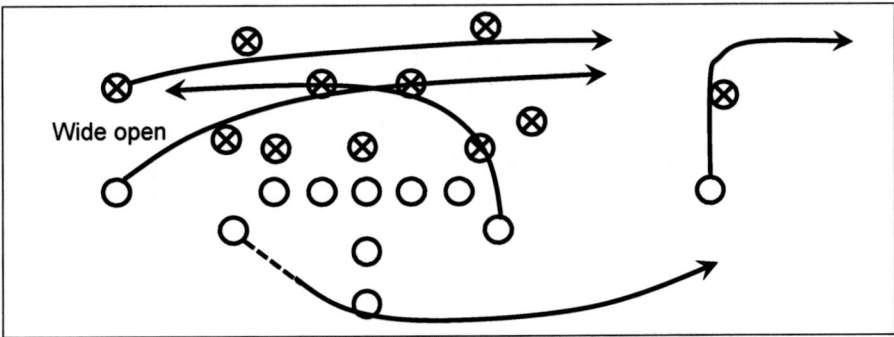

Figure 3-38. Mesh with play-action

Quick Game

Three simple quick game concepts exist. The quick game in this offense is here for one reason: to have high-percentage throws. Sometimes, it's necessary to throw in a change-up for the defense. When a team runs the option, quick game is a nice change of pace to have. It's not complicated, but it's added to the offensive attack. It's believed that it's a fallacy to hang the offense's success on quick game concepts game in and game out. Many high school teams have their entire passing game predicated on quick game. It's difficult because the truth is, quick game looks unstoppable on the chalkboard, but in reality, it's very difficult to continually have success on short completions drive after drive.

A facet of the quick game in this offense that's different from other quick games is that it has a built-in bootleg in case the route called isn't open. Many spread option teams run mirrored routes concepts, which in most cases is good. However, what happens if the defense covers the concept to whatever side the quarterback has decided to go to? The honest answer is the play is dead (Figure 3-39).

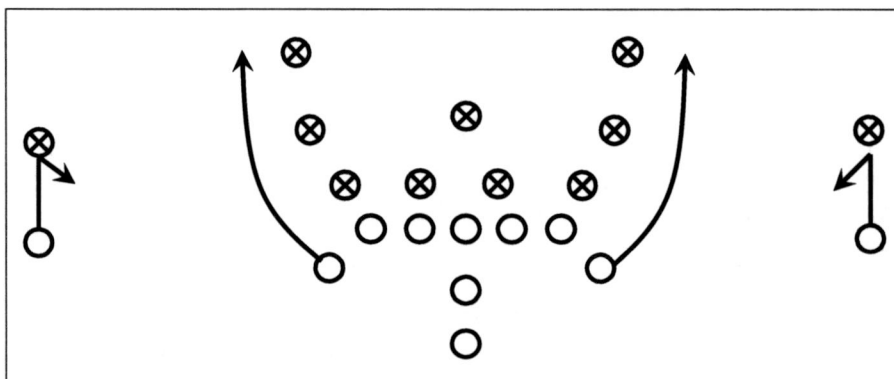

Figure 3-39. Mirrored routes

Running hitch/seem, this play is dead. Thus, it's the goal that in case a bad play is call by the play caller that an answer exists, which is why a bootleg is attached to the backside of whatever route is called—just in case the play called is the wrong one.

The backside of quick game will run the same route no matter what's called. The backside wide receiver will run a post corner. The backside slot will slam-release the end man on the line of scrimmage and wait for the tackle to overtake him. Once the tackle has overtaken him, the slot will run a route heading two yards to the line of scrimmage (Figure 3-40).

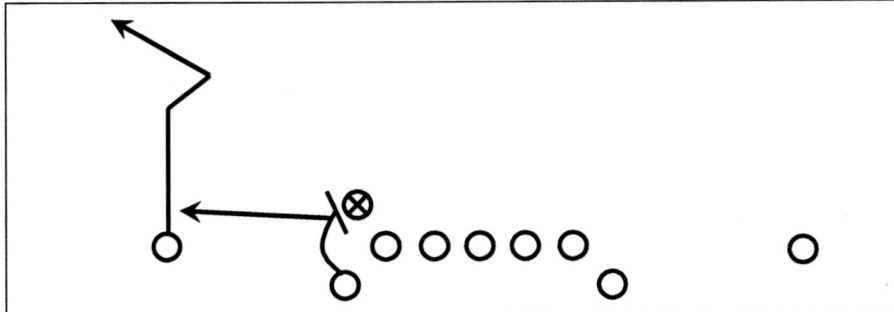

Figure 3-40. Backside slam release

Hitch

This is the easiest throw in football (Figure 3-41 and Table 3-6). This is run versus any off coverage defense—whether zone or man. Anytime the coach simply wants to have a completion, this is always in his back pocket.

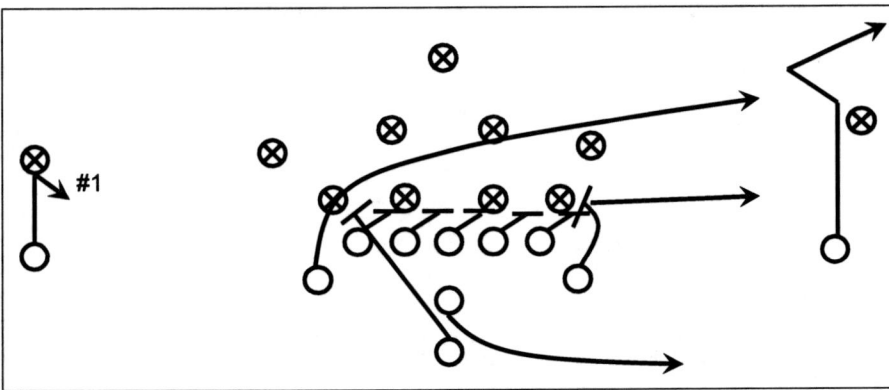

Figure 3-41. Hitch

QB	Catches, steps, throws; #1 slant, #2 arrow; if quick game isn't there, boots
TB	Attacks the end man on the line inside out, meets at the line of scrimmage
PS Slot	Drag route, runs to the opposite sidelines 18 yards from the line of scrimmage
BS Slot	Slam release, runs to the sidelines two yards above the line of scrimmage
PS WR	Three-step hitch
BS WR	Post corner

Table 3-6. Assignments for the hitch

The quarterback can read the bootleg from the top down or the bottom up. The point of this play is to have answers in case of a rapid change from the defense. It's important to note that the slot doesn't release until the tackle has overtaken. Protection is first priority. If the quarterback can't get the edge, then this play has a less likely chance of working.

Slant

Again, this play is simple to run and every team has it in its playbook (Figure 3-42 and Table 3-7). The slant throw is high percentage against non–cover 2 teams, which means against most defenses, it's a good concept.

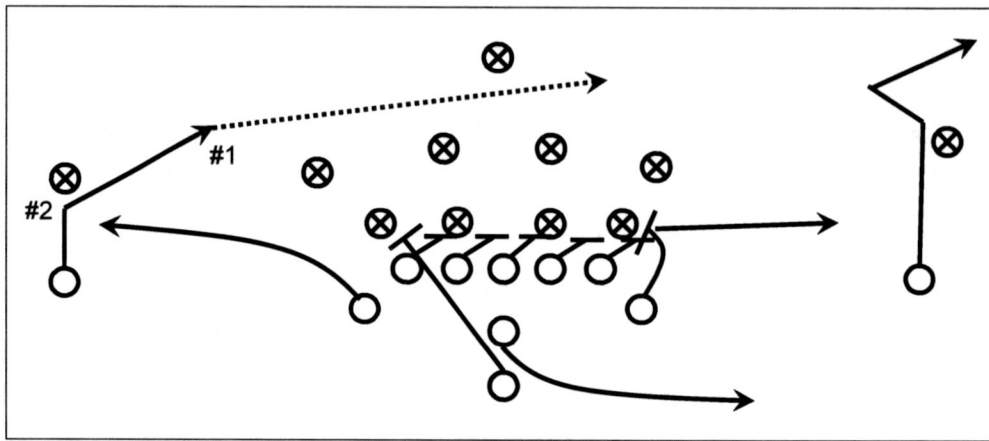

Figure 3-42. Slant

QB	Catches, steps, throws; if quick game isn't there, boots
TB	Attacks the end man on the line inside out, meets at the line of scrimmage
PS Slot	One-step arrow, runs immediately toward the sidelines, aiming two yards above the line of scrimmage
BS Slot	Slam release, runs to the sidelines two yards above the line of scrimmage
PS WR	Three-step slant; if no throw, becomes the 18-yard drag
BS WR	Post corner

Table 3-7. Assignments for the slant

As shown in Figure 3-42, if the slant isn't thrown, the wide receiver becomes the dragger. It also shows that the slot receiver needs to immediately run toward the sideline. The goal is to get an immediate horizontal stretch on the outside linebacker. The horizontal stretch will influence the linebacker to run to the arrow and the quarterback can hit the slant with a clear and precise picture.

Fade

The quarterback will initially look at the fade (Figure 3-43 and Table 3-8). If the fade is covered, the out should be open. If the out by the slotback isn't open, then the quarterback will go to the boot phase of the play. Figure 3-44 shows this play against a cover 2 defense.

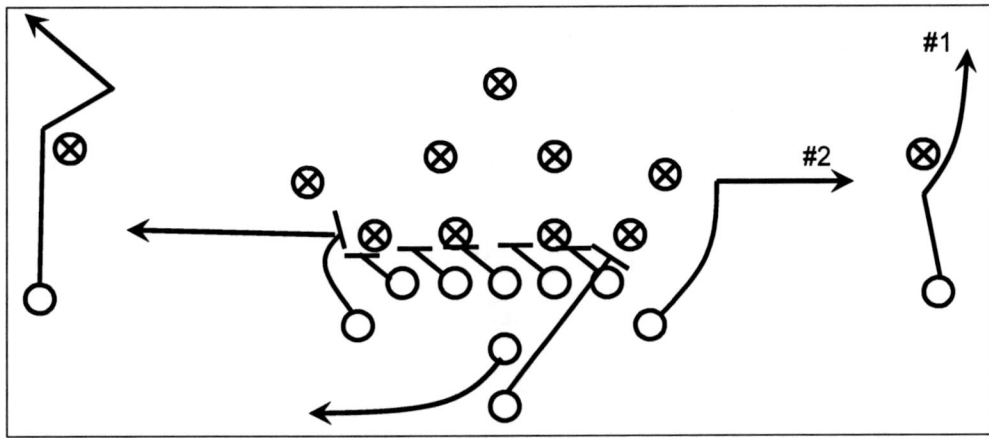

Figure 3-43. Fade

QB	Catches, steps, throws; if quick game isn't there, boots
TB	Attacks the end man on the line inside out, meets at the line of scrimmage
PS Slot	Five-yard out
BS Slot	Slam release, runs to the sidelines two yards above the line of scrimmage
PS WR	Fade
BS WR	Post corner

Table 3-8. Assignments for the fade

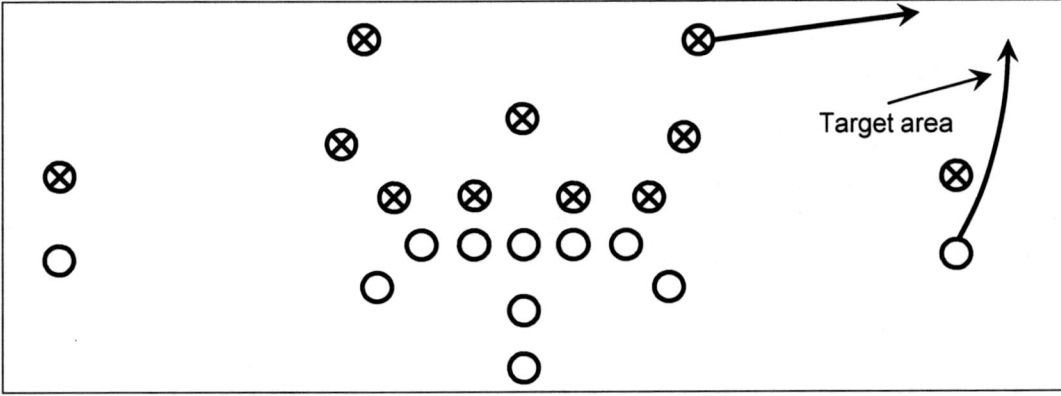

Figure 3-44. Cover 2 target area

Running a cover 2 fade is something that's much different from a regular fade and needs to be practiced every day in practice. The ball must be placed over the corner but placed before the safety coming over the top. Ideally, this throw should be a back shoulder throw, stopping the wide receiver from running into the safety. It must also be understood that if the corner successfully reroutes the wide receiver, he must get back on his line immediately—whether he inside releases or outside releases (Figure 3-45).

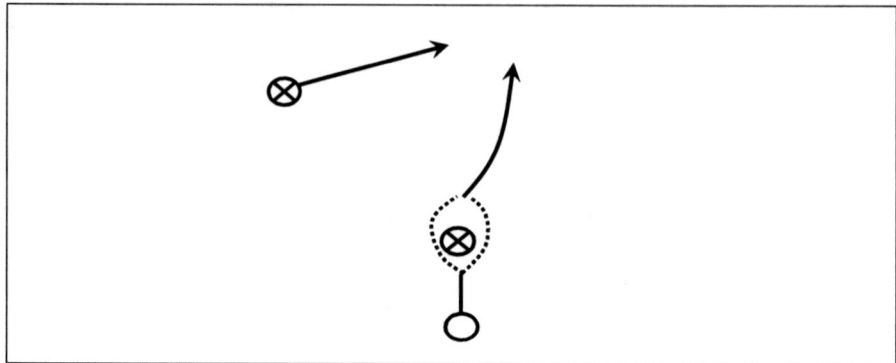

Figure 3-45. Wide receiver getting back on stem

This is definitely an advanced throw. However, this is probably the most effective way to throw against a cover 2 defense, especially being an option football team.

Rollout Game

Since the inception of option football, especially back in the 1960s and 1970s, considerable debate took place regarding whether an option quarterback should be allowed to drop back or if he was strictly a move/sprint-out/rollout passer. Many option quarterbacks are selected because of their ability to move, so having a rollout passing series simply makes sense to have in the package. The sprint-out game operates out of the offense's "trips" set. The first and most crucial item to talk about is rollout pass protection.

Turnback protection is used for any rollout passing plays. The reasoning is simple: Because so much time is spent perfecting specifics of offensive line play, it's unreasonable to expect the offensive line to be able to learn anything complex for a rollout. Another reason: The technique is great and is simple to perform. All it takes is the linemen to perform the correct steps and simply get in the way. If a sprint-out is called to the right, each lineman will step forward with his right foot and then slide his body position to a 45-degree angle and block the first defensive lineman in his path (Figure 3-46).

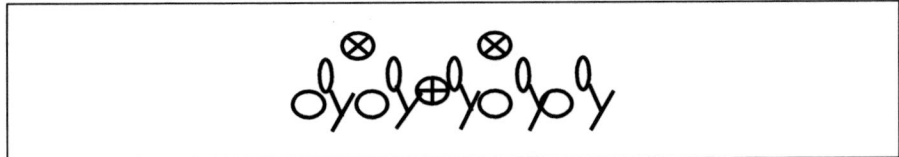

Figure 3-46. Offensive line's first steps on turnback

The next part of the protection is how the backs fit in conjunction with the turnback performed by the line. The inside slotback will step and destroy the first defender inside of him. This is an aggressive block on the perimeter, not a lazy block. The slot must understand that if he doesn't set the edge, the play is doomed. The tailback won't take a direct angle to fit off the slot's block. He'll curve his path just a little bit in case a force player is taking an extreme angle off the edge. If that occurs and the tailback simply fits right off the slot's rear end, the quarterback won't be allowed to reach the edge (Figure 3-47).

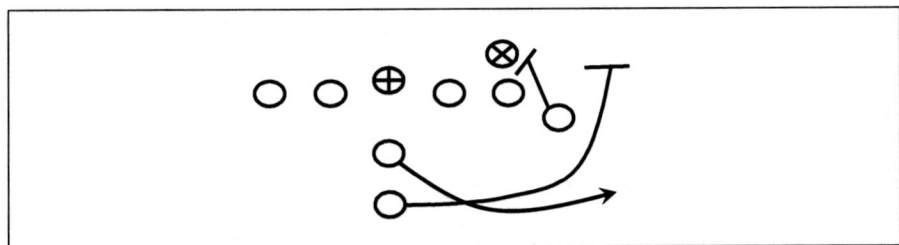

Figure 3-47. Running back's sprint-out protection

Something quarterbacks should always know running a rollout concept is that they always have the option of running. That's part of the reason the protection is the way it is. If the defense floats its hinge player to the closest route to the quarterback, the quarterback will be free to run with a lead blocker in front of him. Believe it or not, sometimes the best play is to have the quarterback run the ball on the rollout. Especially when a defense drops eight into coverage, it's good to encourage the defenders to get depth and then have the quarterback run with a lead blocker in front of him.

Smash

This concept is in every playbook in America (Figure 3-48 and Table 3-9). The West Coast offense refers to this as a "china concept" because the wide receiver and slot are hi-lowing the corner. However, some nuances exist to running this play that are more preferred than the traditional way.

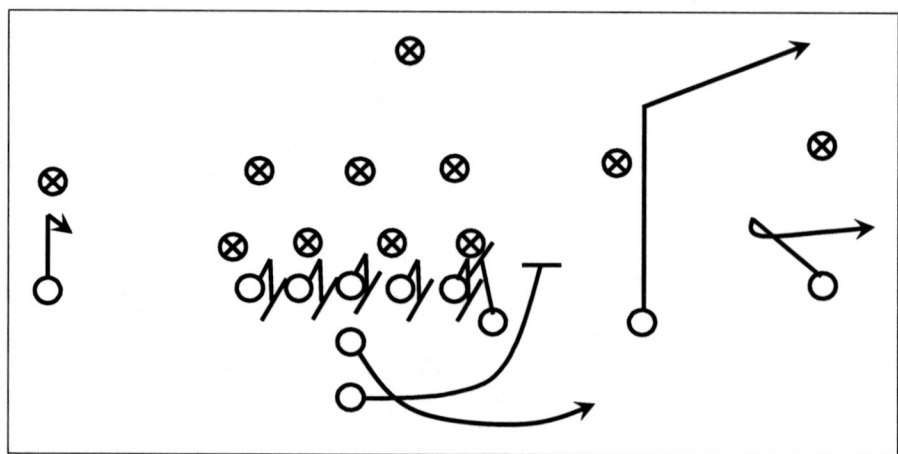

Figure 3-48. Smash concept

QB	Rollout to the right, hi-lows the corner
TB	Rollout pass protection
IS Slot	Rollout pass protection
OS Slot	12-yard corner route
PS WR	Whip route
BS WR	Hitch

Table 3-9. Assignments for the smash concept

The key difference with the way this offense runs this route is having a whip route instead of a regular hitch route (Figure 3-49). A good reason exists for the change. An easy way to defeat smash is to simply have the overhang player drift to take away the hitch route. Thus, if the offense decides to run a whip route instead, it's influencing that linebacker to protect his inside. Once the offense has successfully attacked that linebacker by influencing him, the wide receiver will be wide open. Also, another advantage is that the wide receiver will be in full stride when catching the ball as opposed to simply catching a hitch route where he'll be stagnant.

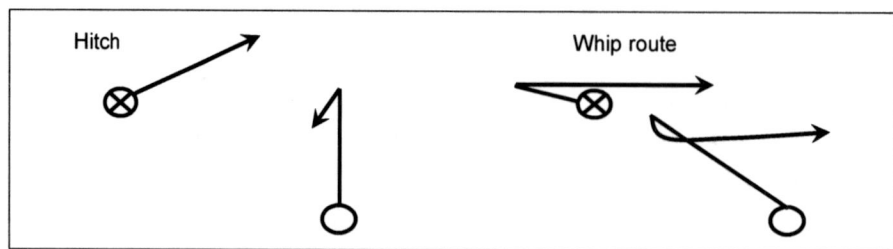

Figure 3-49. Different routes

Combo

This play is another concept that's in every playbook in America (Figure 3-50 and Table 3-10). This simply attacks the flat defender. It's also another way to attack the defense in the rollout game.

The important coaching point on this play is that the slot can't cut it up until the slot reaches the numbers. The slot must understand that this is a curl/flat combination first. It converts to a wheel if the defense adequately defends the play.

Many other rollouts can be run in this offense. The possibilities are endless. These are two simple ones to run. The offense needs to be careful in how many rollouts it installs. If it becomes too much, every play's technical effectiveness in this offense gets watered down.

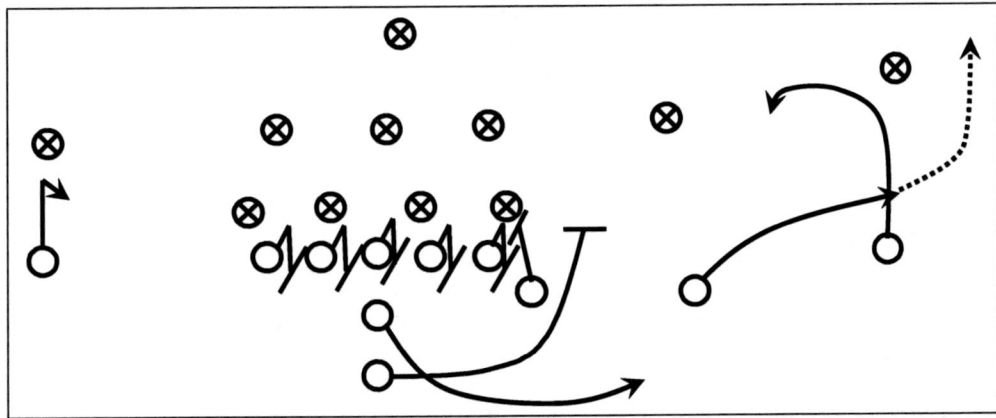

Figure 3-50. Combo concept

QB	Rollout to the right
TB	Rollout pass protection
IS Slot	Rollout pass protection
OS Slot	Flat route, converts to a go once the numbers are hit
PS WR	Curl route
BS WR	Hitch

Table 3-10. Assignments for the combo concept

4

Complementary Plays

Under sound conditions, the triple option is unstoppable. This is the single most explosive play ever invented in football history. However, the key phrase is "under sound conditions." If the defense is playing unsound in theory, gap control, secondary rotation, or blitzing, it's true it can give the triple option play some trouble. In most "unsound" situations, the triple option is still good to go, yet the goal is to keep the defense defending the offense soundly. In order for a wishbone or spread option team to operate consistently and functionally, the football field must be 53.3 yards wide and 30 to 40 yards deep. The passing game constrains the defense to lengthen the field 30 to 40 yards vertically. The triple option and the companion run game plays are there in order to help stretch the defense 53.3 yards.

Something that has been lost in folklore in option football is maintaining all points of attack on the defense (Figure 4-1). It's true to say that if the offense only runs the triple option, the defense can simply send all 11 players in rapid pursuit to the side it believes the play is going to be run. That's true about any football play. One negative about the spread formation is that it naturally and structurally has a pursuit problem. It has a pursuit problem because of its use of quick motion. That's the elephant in the room most spread option coaches don't want to talk about. If an offense only motions to the side where the play is going to be run, the defense can just slant, blitz, secondary rotate, and create erratic pursuit to the football. That's one of the reasons the wishbone is still the gold standard of option football. It's a stagnant formation that the defense has to react to on the snap. That's also why the majority of the wishbone attack is simple blocking adjustments while the offense is still running the triple option. However, the spread doesn't have this luxury. *It's foolish to believe a team can simply motion on every play and believe no negative consequences will occur.* These are the points of attack that must be kept in order to keep a defense sound.

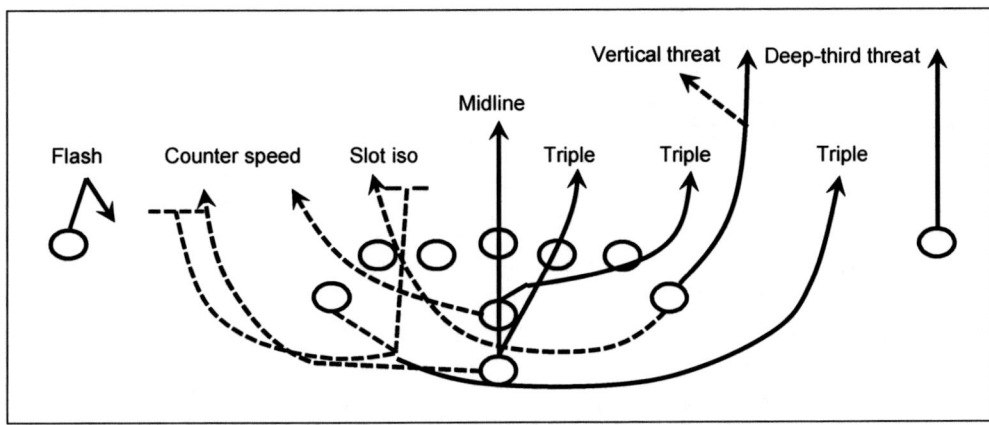

Figure 4-1. Pistol spread option points of attack

The overall goal of any offense is to threaten every part of the field and make a defender not be able to leave his area of responsibility without a huge play happening. That's the goal of the complementary plays. If the linebacker play is unsound, a play will be open. If the secondary play is unsound, a play will be open. The goal is maintain that the defense stays at home and performs its responsibilities. Added to the pressure of the triple option, this will make the defense have a long night defending this offense.

Definition of a Spread Option Play

To emphasize the point even more, it's important to define what the definition of a spread option play is. A spread option play is a play that starts with a two- or three-step motion by the backside slot while the tailback and quarterback start the play as if it were triple (Figure 4-2). This is important because of the endless possibilities a formation with three running backs in the backfield has. Many coaches see the endless possibilities of what an offense can do in a 2x2 set, double slot, wishbone, wing-T, and I formation. But this type of thinking is a negative. It's a negative because once a coach starts searching for all the possibilities he has in a formation, he leaves the entire reason he went to whatever offense the team is in. The spread is no exception. Because motion is used, hundreds of cool-looking plays and "great ideas" can be thought of by coaches. These must be rejected. Every play in this offense is there for a specific reason. Are there a couple plays that will be shown that don't have the definition of a spread option play? Sure, but they're there for a specific purpose and are only used for that specific purpose. Once a play caller has 50 different run plays and variations out of the spread, the original mission statement of the offense is lost.

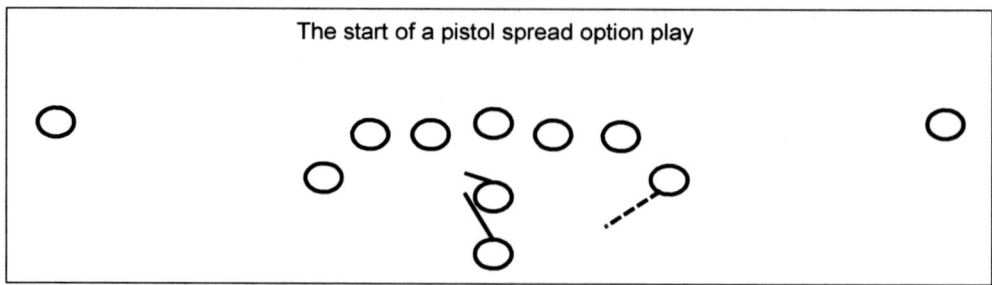

Figure 4-2. Definition of a pistol spread option play

One point to make: The thesis being put here on the definition on a spread option play isn't to discourage a coach to think outside the box (Figure 4-2). One of the many reasons why football took so long to evolve was because football coaches were copycats. As Glenn "Tiger" Ellison once said, coaches need to stimulate their imaginations. Stirring up a coach's imagination can lead to significant changes in football. Such coaches as Ellison, Darrel "Mouse" Davis, Emory Bellard, Dennis Erickson, Mike Martz, and others used their imagination and helped the game of football progress. But the point is that in this offense, everything is done for a reason. If a coach uses his imagination in this type of offense most of the time, it can divert from the philosophical realm of the option. Whether that's good or not is in the eye of the beholder, but the goal is to maintain the original theoretical realm of the option.

Midline Option

The best complementary play ever created in football is the midline option. The midline option in some circumstances is more deadly than the triple. It's important that this is the second run play installed in an option offensive attack. This play has a lot of specific coaching points, but the origins and theoretical realm in which the midline option has evolved give great insights into how to run this option.

As with many football ideas, the specific origin is unknown. However, the practical origin starts with the Syracuse freeze option out of the I formation. This play helped Syracuse destroy defenses in the 1980s, especially because it was the only team running this play. However, the practical reason for having this play in the triple option offense must be understood. The significant reason why midline added an explosive element to the triple option was because of the circumstances that hurt the triple option play. Since the triple's inception in the 1960s, something that has hurt its effectiveness is defensive tackles that line up in a 2 technique or a 3 technique and penetrate the path of the dive back, as shown in Figure 4-3 against the old split-six defense that used to be prevalent in college football.

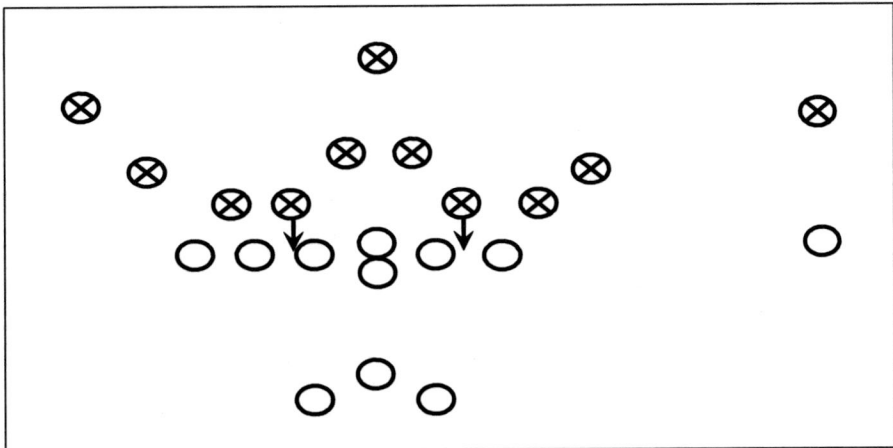
Figure 4-3. Wishbone vs. the split-six defense

The triple option play can still be run. However, it's obviously harder because the defense is directly attacking the dive back's path. This obviously opens up run plays to the outside, but the defense is challenging the offense to strictly run the option outside. Once the midline option evolved to become part of the option attack, penetrating defensive tackles are now constrained to the idea that they'll have the dive back run right by them. This is significant because option offenses now have a smashmouth play against a defense that's just trying to defend the fullback from going off tackle.

Just like everything else in football, the midline option has a truism. The play can be abused and used in scenarios that don't call its use. At option offensive clinics, many coaches say that midline is their number one play. However, this play shouldn't be viewed in that manner. This is strictly a complementary play to the triple option. The reason is simple: The triple puts more of a strain on a defense because it attacks more grass than midline. Obviously, midline can be run a lot during the course of a game. However, that doesn't mean it overtakes the triple in terms of priority. Midline used as a complement to the triple option is the best to consistently attack a defense (Figure 4-4 and Table 4-1). If the offense consistently runs midline over and over again, it runs into the problem of trying to be bigger and better than the opponent. It's great against a penetrating 3 technique. However, the offense still has key blocks it must win in order for the play to be successful. One of the original option theorems is that the offense doesn't want to have to block defenders. With this in mind, blocking fewer players is always the better answer. Run in the right circumstances, the midline option is the best complementary play in football, especially when secondary/linebacker run fits are messed up by the sudden change-up of an option play being run without a perimeter threat.

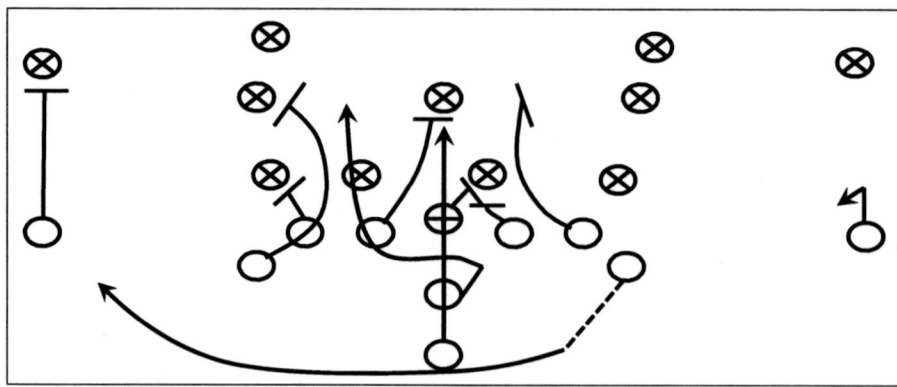

Figure 4-4. Midline option

QB	Midline footwork, reads #1, gives/pulls and replaces
TB	Midline path
PSSB	Runs inside the tackle's out and blocks the playside linebacker
BSSB	Option route
PSWR	Threatens the deep-third defender, then stalks
BSWR	Backside flash, then works to cut off
PST	Out on #2
PSG	Veer
C	Base, midline technique
BSG	Base to scoop
BST	Scoops, cuts if possible

Table 4-1. Assignments for the midline option

Quarterback Play

Much of the fundamentals and concepts of the triple carry over to midline. The quarterback will now read the first defender outside of the A gap instead of the first defender outside of the B gap. He'll still pull and replace regardless of his decision. However, the footwork is different. The footwork concept from the triple option is the same, but now the quarterback will get out of the way of the tailback. The tailback is running right through the center and the quarterback has to get out of the way. Thus, the quarterback will step downhill, except this time, his backside foot will move first rather than his playside foot. He'll step downhill while getting out of the tailback's path. Figure 4-5 illustrates the quarterback's footwork on midline to the right.

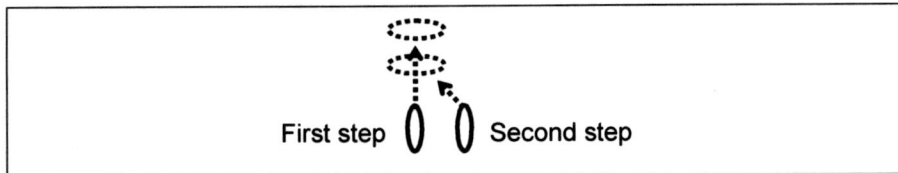

Figure 4-5. Quarterback's first two steps

After the quarterback steps with his first step, the second step will approach rapidly. The second foot will naturally flow with the quarterback's first step because it's unnatural. Because it's unnatural, the body will follow suit to avoid an uncomfortable position. Once the quarterback gets his second foot in the ground, he'll subtly slide downhill with the tailback and read the handoff key. The quarterback is still working the ball back to the tailback. Once he's read the dive key, he'll pull and replace. In the midline option, the quarterback must be conscious of his third step because of the radical angle his foot must make in order for his path to be adequate (Figure 4-6).

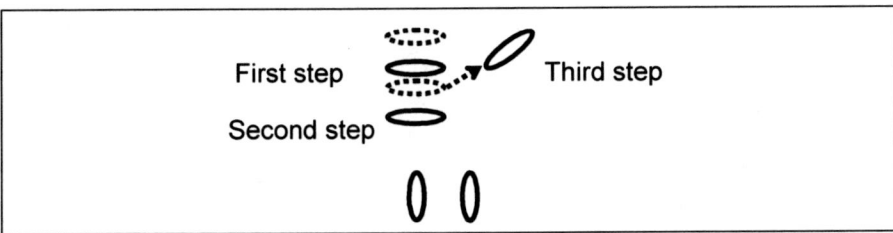

Figure 4-6. Shuffle steps to an aggressive/downhill third step

It's important for the quarterback to understand that he's running inside of the tackle's block. The reason is that the tackle is kicking out the defensive lineman he's blocking. If the quarterback is running outside the block, then the defender will be blocked into the quarterback (Figure 4-7).

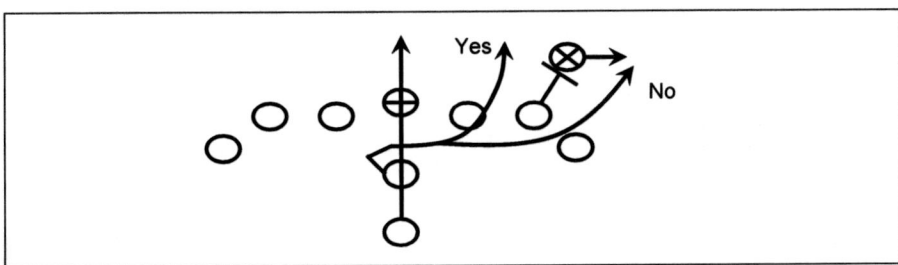

Figure 4-7. Different quarterback paths

It's important for the quarterback to understand that if he doesn't get out of the way, the tailback will run him over. It's solely the quarterback's job to get out of the way, pull and replace, and go score a touchdown.

Tailback Play

As with the quarterback, the tailback play in the midline option has much carryover from the triple (Figure 4-8). The main difference with the tailbacks responsibilities is his path. The aiming point for the tailback is the center's rear end. He's running straight up the midline and is looking to receive the football.

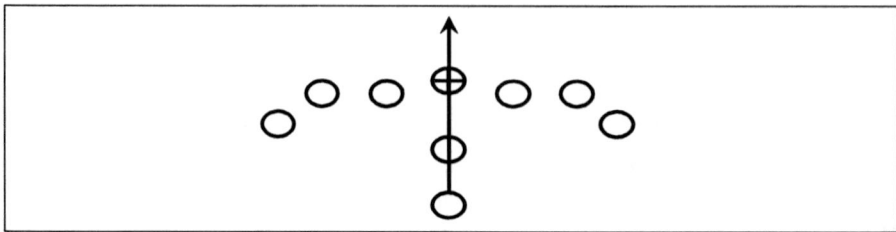

Figure 4-8. Tailback's midline path

The tailback must understand that he must stay on the midline at all costs (Figure 4-9). Very rarely does the dive back on midline ever have to get off his path. The next coaching point comes against a defense with a nose. The tailback's path will change subtly. His aiming point changes. If it's midline to the right, his aiming point is the right thigh of the center. If it's midline to the left, his aiming point is the left thigh. When running this play against a nose, the tailback will cut off the nose. However, it must be understood that once the tailback cuts off the nose, he must get back on the midline. He can't cut back or bend it forward. The midline blocking scheme is built for the tailback to take his path straight up the field.

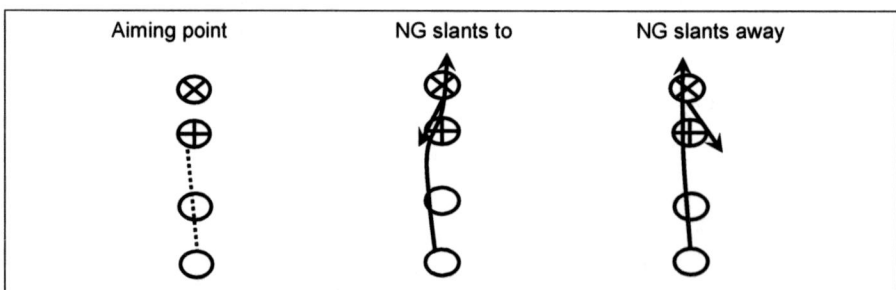

Figure 4-9. Tailback staying on the midline

Slotback Play

Slotbacks must perform two different assignments in the midline option. The first is on the playside. Depending on the front, the slot will block either the middle linebacker or the outside linebacker. Ninety percent of the time, he'll block the middle linebacker. The only time he blocks the outside linebacker is against seven-man fronts without a "lead" call. The slot must understand that a double-team is between him and the playside guard. The guard is blocking for the tailback and the slot is blocking for the quarterback. If the linebacker blitzes the A gap or for some reason disappears, the guard will be blocking him. Thus, the slot must at all costs protect the quarterback's running lane. The aiming point for the block is the outside hip of the linebacker. The slot's goal is to pin him inside. Ideally, the slot should have his inside hand grabbing for the linebacker's heart while his outside hand gets underneath the shoulder pad. This gives the slot leverage to pick the defender up while providing a devastating block for the quarterback to run through (Figure 4-10).

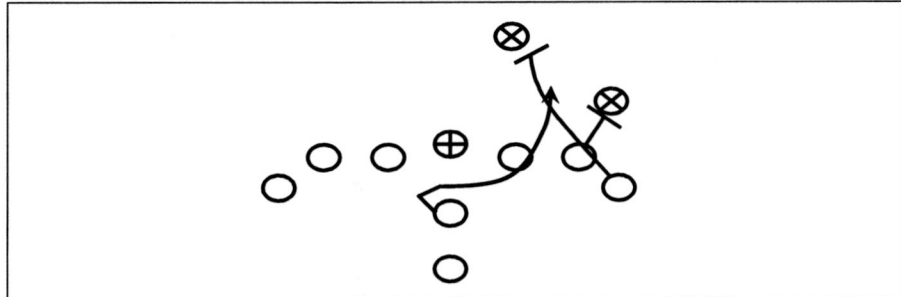

Figure 4-10. Slot blocking for the quarterback

The slot must understand that he must go inside the tackle. It does him no good if he travels to the Mike with an outside release. If that happens, the play will be dead.

Lead

If midline is called without a "lead" call, the backside slot will simply run an option route. However, if a "lead" call is made, the backside slot will motion all the way to the tailback's heels and then he'll come downhill to block the outside linebacker (Figure 4-11). This is used against eight-man fronts that have an extra defender in the box. This variation is deadly, especially against the 4-4 defense.

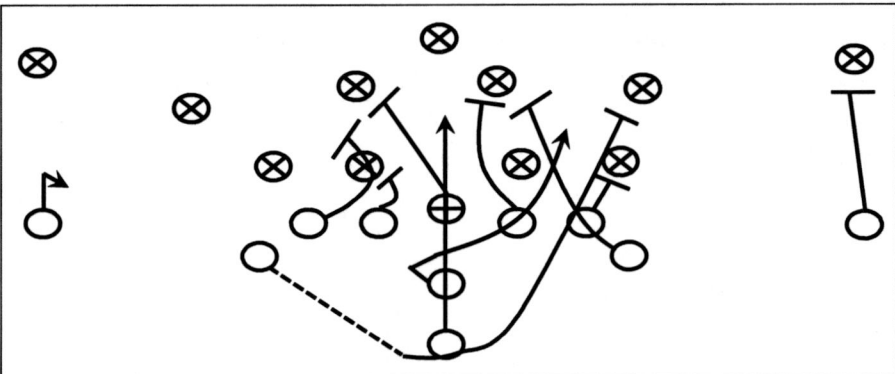

Figure 4-11. Midline "lead"

Kill

When midline is tagged with "kill," that simply means the motion is being killed (Figure 4-12). Having midline installed without motion is important. It's important because the offense must be able to operate without motion. Because of the numerical advantage of midline, motion isn't a necessity. Thus, it's very important that the offense has the ability to run midline without any motion. One more specific technique must be explained. When no motion occurs, the backside slot will now perform a "touchdown block." He'll aggressively arc upfield and try to get a piece of the safety. At first glance, this block seems ridiculous. However, experience has shown that this extra effort given by the slot has boosted a 10-yard gain into 60-yard touchdown run.

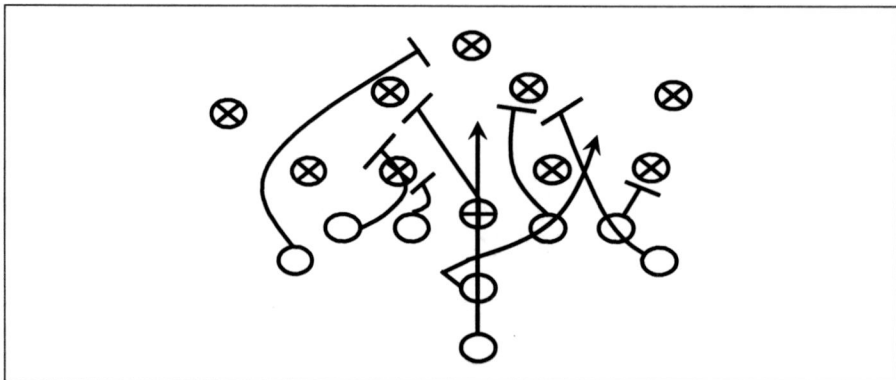

Figure 4-12. Midline "kill"

This block is at its best when the ballcarrier cuts backs after the first level. The touchdown block is pure effort. Anyone can run downfield as fast as possible and simply get in the way. That effort will result in touchdowns.

Offensive Line Play

To start off offensive line play, the tackle's job will be described first. He has the job of kicking out the next defender outside the handoff key against four- and five-man fronts (Figure 4-13). This block is as simple as it looks. As long as the tackle doesn't get completely destroyed, the block is good. His goal is to make sure the defensive end doesn't get inside his block.

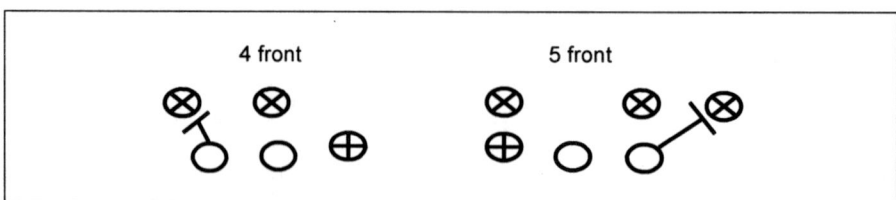

Figure 4-13. Tackle blocking out

The guard has the most important job in this play. He's inside releasing to the playside linebacker. As explained earlier, the slot has outside leverage on this defender. If the defender runs over the top, it would be impossible for the guard to get to him. However, the offense needs inside leverage on the backer. The guard provides this leverage (Figure 4-14).

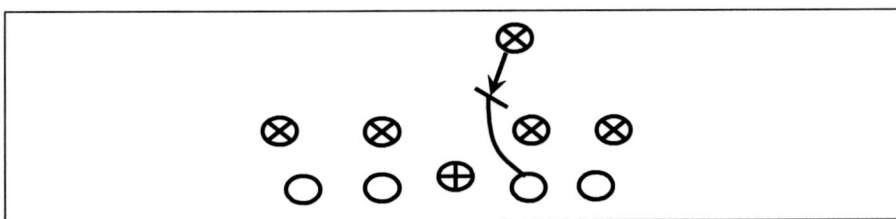

Figure 4-14. Guard veering to the middle linebacker

The next job to discuss is the center's. Unlike in triple, the center must understand that the guard has full leverage on the playside linebacker. That means the center doesn't perform his playside backside technique. Depending on how many linebackers there are determines who he blocks. If two middle linebackers are there, the center will block the backside backer (Figure 4-15).

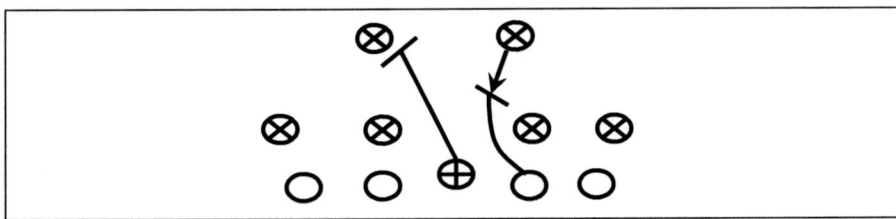

Figure 4-15. Center blocks backside middle linebacker

If the center is uncovered and only has one middle linebacker in his picture, he blocks back on the defensive lineman to the backside. This provides leverage to fully clear the midline for the tailback (Figure 4-16).

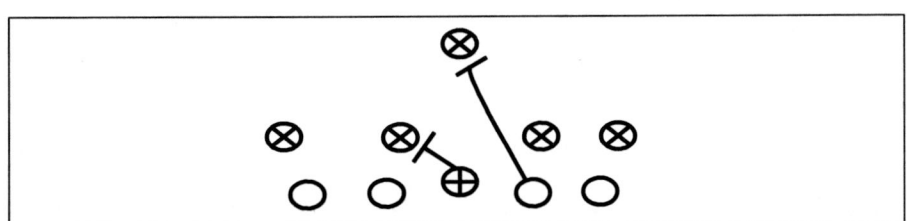

Figure 4-16. Center vs. one middle linebacker

The next technique to talk about with the center is his assignment when he's covered. When the center is covered, the center will come off the football at 100 mph. He'll destroy the noseguard, pick him up, and bury him in the ground. However, if the nose decides to slant a particular way, the center will throw his backside arm across the nose to clear the midline for the tailback. The tailback will subtly cut off the nose. Clearing the midline is important. A lot of coaches say it's not ideal to run midline versus a noseguard. They're correct in the assertion that running midline against an odd front isn't what this play was originally designed for. However, against a slanting nose, this is a phenomenal way to attack him (Figure 4-17).

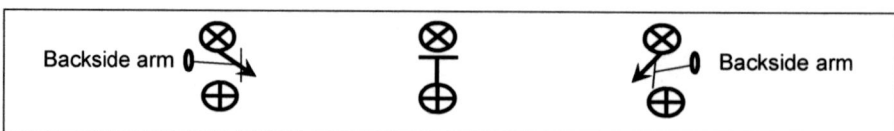

Figure 4-17. Center technique vs. slanting nose

The backside guard has a critical role in making sure the running lanes for the tailback are secured. Unlike most plays in the playbook, the backside guard won't scoop or 0-scoop. His assignment depends on numerous different situations. The first is against an even front. Depending on the shade, most of the time, the backside guard will simply base block whoever is in front of him. He must recognize that he creates and maintains inside leverage on the defender. The other scenario is that only one middle linebacker is there. In this case, the guard will simply double-team the 1 technique (Figure 4-18).

Figure 4-18. Backside guard on midline

Speed Option

Everybody in football is familiar with the speed option (Figure 4-19 and Table 4-2). This is a straight double option to the outside. This is one of the plays that's enhanced by being in the pistol. The reason is that the quarterback is immediately attacking downhill as a natural occurrence of being three yards behind the center. Many reasons exist to add this play to the spread option attack. The first is that it's a simple play that can be run on day one of installing the offense. The "read" is the hard part of executing the triple option, but this play requires no "read." The quarterback simply keeps or pitches the football off leverage. If the motioning slotback has leverage on the pitch key, then the quarterback will pitch the ball. If daylight exists for the quarterback, he'll take it himself and get as many yards as he can.

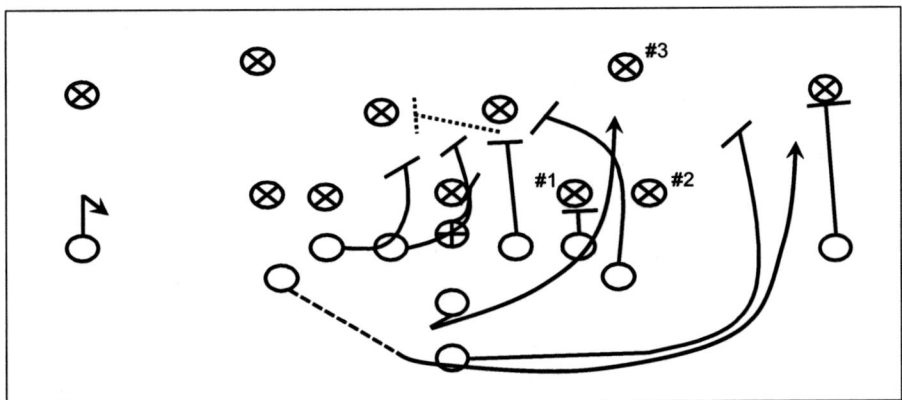

Figure 4-19. Speed option

QB	Steps back for a split second; vs. blood: pitches off #2; vs. normal: pitches off #1
TB	Arc path; vs. blood: blocks #3; vs. normal: blocks #2
PSSB	Vs. blood: blocks inside linebacker; vs. normal: blocks #3
BSSB	Option route
PSWR	Threatens the deep-third defender, then stalks
BSWR	Backside flash, then works to cut off
PST	Veer to the Mike; vs. blood: base #1
PSG	Base
C	Covered: 0-scoop; uncovered: playside backside technique
BSG	Vs. nose: scoops through the nose; vs. no nose: scoops, cuts if possible
BST	Scoops, cuts if possible

Table 4-2. Assignments for the speed option

The second reason for adding the speed option to the offense is to simply run outside when the defense is bringing pressure from the inside. Some defenses like to attack an option offense by blitzing from the inside out. In this case, the speed option will take it to the house. It's true that the downfall of the speed option is when the principle of erratic pursuit comes into play. Pursuit angles immediately change upon the defense receiving full information about the nature of the play. That's why this play is at its best when the defense is blitzing inside.

Third, according to an old school option theory, if the first two defenders outside the center can be blocked, the option without an inside presence has a numbers advantage. This sets a precedence of when it's appropriate to call the speed option. If the first two defenders past the center can't be handled, triple is a much better play call. However, if the opposite is true, this play has the potential for huge gains.

Fourth, it gets the smaller slotbacks in space. One truism of football is that speed kills. Being able to put an athlete in space makes the openfield possibilities endless. In the spread option attack, the smallest players on the field are placed as slotbacks. This inevitably means that the practical nature of being a slot needs to be used to enhance the body types on the field. Using what the players are good at doing is a must for any offensive attack.

Fifth, running the speed option with a lead blocker means the offense will always have a numbers advantage. Unless a defense is dedicating seven defenders to one side, this play can still be run without fear of an unaccounted-for defender making the play.

Sixth, pursuit angles of the defense. Obviously, this point can be a good or bad thing. It all depends on how the defensive pursuit angles change. If the defense has its bodies and minds focused on going forward, running outside on them is a very successful and deadly play to be reckoned with. But if the defense is focused on lateral movement on the option, this play has less of a chance at being successful than it would have otherwise been.

The first thing that must be explained when running speed option is the difference between a blood call and not a blood call. A blood call is made when #1 and #2 are on the line of scrimmage. The blood call means that the quarterback is expecting a quick pull and pitch off the defensive end who's coming off the edge hard. The classic blood stunt is shown in Figure 4-20.

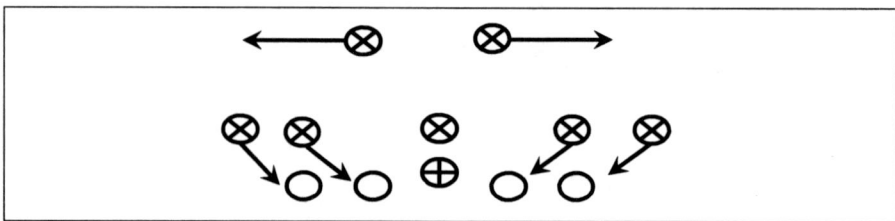

Figure 4-20. Blood stunt

Normally, when a team runs the speed option, the defender who's being optioned is #1. However, with a blood call, that's ridiculous because it's not an option. It will always be pitched. Thus, the logical adjustment to be made for a blood call is to base #1 and option #2. This gives the play an option element while still being sound in the way the defense is being blocked.

Quarterback Play

The quarterback will first take a slight pause backward. The reason being is that it's difficult for the motioning slotback to make up the ground. During the triple option, a ride and decide period occurs, giving the slot time to get into pitch relationship, but during the speed option, such a period doesn't exist. This means the quarterback needs to take a slight step backward to let the tailback get out in open space to block and the slot to get in proper pitch relationship (Figure 4-21).

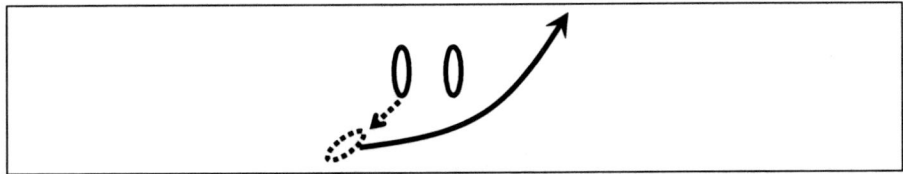

Figure 4-21. Quarterback speed option steps

It's important for the quarterback to know that he's not optioning the defender in the practical sense of attacking him. The rules of replacing and leverage pitching still apply. For example, when the quarterback is running this play against a blood stunt, he'll replace the #1 defender. Obviously, the quarterback has discretion to adjust if the #1 defender suddenly stunts outside. However, in a regular situation, he replaces #1 and leverage pitches off #2.

Tailback Play

The tailback performs his version of the arc block. The principles from the slot arc block remain the same. However, key differences do exist. The tailback's arc block purely resembles the old wishbone arc block, whereas the slot's arc blocking path is a little bit different. The tailback must understand that he must get lateral first and then he must work laterally for five to six steps. Once he's worked laterally long enough, he'll use the same principles of the slot arc block: matching the speed of the defender and focusing his aiming point at the outside shoulder. It must be understood that against a blood call, the tailback will block #3. Against a non–blood call, the tailback will block #2 (Figure 4-22).

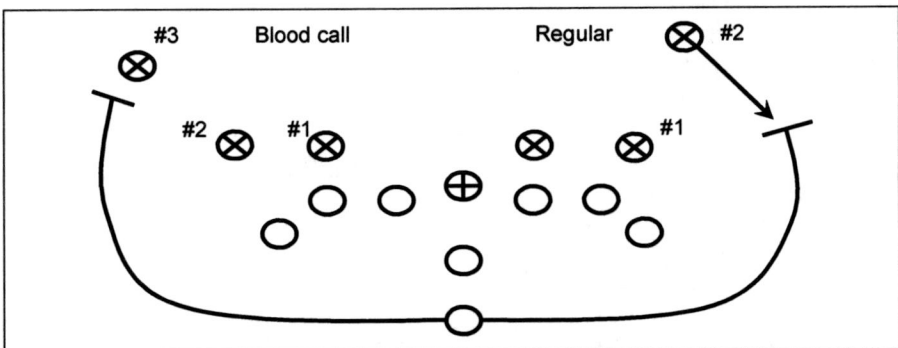

Figure 4-22. Tailback's speed option blocking paths

The same principle applies with the slot's version of the arc block. The tailback will only leave his path to protect the runner on the inside. The slots and tailbacks work for width so they're in a position to handle any extreme movement from the defender they're blocking. If they're too shallow, the defender can handle outside containment. If the arc block starts off wide, the offender will be able to recover and block any sharp movements inside (Figure 4-23).

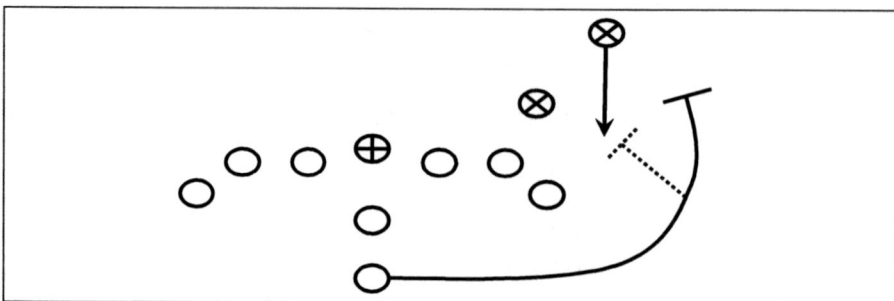

Figure 4-23. Tailback starting to protect the runner to the inside

Why does the tailback block #2 instead of the slot blocking #2? A principle in football states: *The longer a player has to hold onto a block, the more likely the block is destined to fail.* With this predicament, it makes sense that the tailback blocks #2 because the slot would have to hold and maintain outside leverage on that defender for several seconds. The goal is to make it easier on the players. What happens most of the time on speed is that the tailback's block lasts about a second, but that's all that's needed to spring the slot in open space.

Slotback Play

The slot has two different assignments on this play. The first is against a regular defense. In a regular defense, he'll arc #3. However, against a blood defense, he'll load to the playside linebacker. The reason is twofold. First, the tailback is assigned to #3 and the offense has numbers on the defense. Second, the slot is the player who's checking the outside leverage of the playside linebacker. The guard has inside leverage. It's important for everybody on the field to be accounted for. The difference is shown in Figure 4-24.

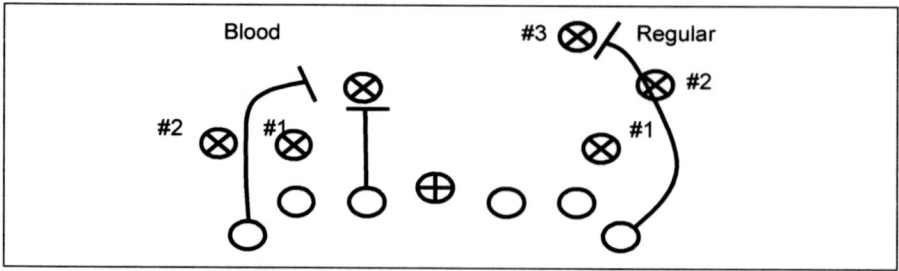

Figure 4-24. Slot's speed option blocking assignments

The slot must understand that if he doesn't have outside leverage on the defender that this play won't work. If the playside inside linebacker is able to run over the top, the play is dead.

Tackle Play

The tackle on speed has two different responsibilities. The first is against a regular defense. He simply veers inside and blocks the playside linebacker just like he does on triple. The second assignment he performs is against a blood front. Against this front, he'll base #1. It's important for him to realize that he must gain outside leverage on the defender. This play shouldn't be called against a blood front if the tackle can't handle his man to the inside (Figure 4-25).

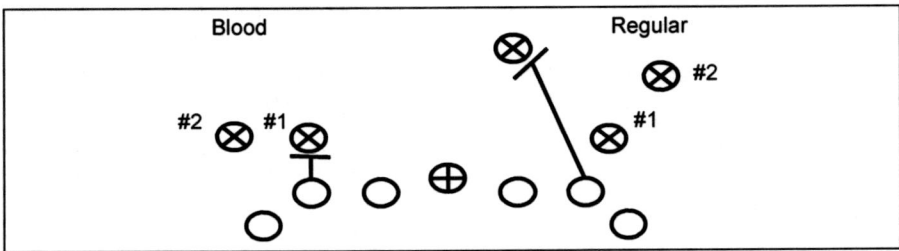

Figure 4-25. Tackle's speed option blocking assignments

Counter Speed

Counter speed is the complementary play to the speed option (Figure 4-26). Teams should add this play for several reasons. The first and most obvious reason is to get a lightning fast tailback on the perimeter as quickly as possible. Many times, in an option attack, the dive back strictly runs between the tackles. However, if an option team has a tailback that has the ability to change the game, it's important to have a way to feed him the ball to the outside.

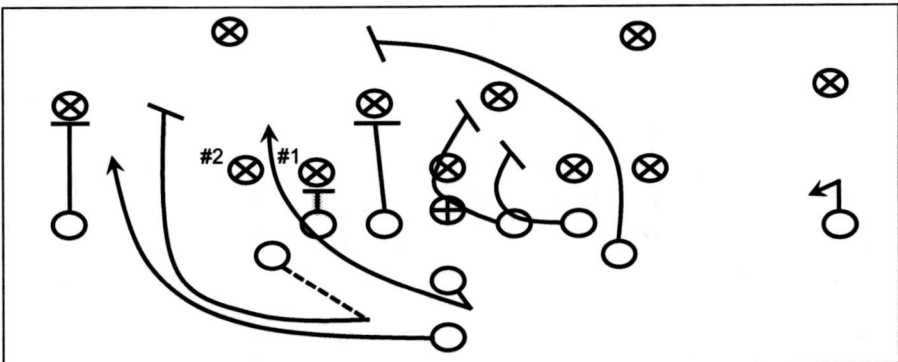

Figure 4-26. Counter speed option

Second, it combats a defense's unsound secondary rotation. Many secondaries against the spread option like to roll their safeties to the motion, which can sometimes leave the offense outnumbered. Thus, when this occurs, counter speed will be open. Being able to counter unsound secondary rotation is a must for the spread option offense. When a team is in the pistol, this play is enhanced for the same reason the regular speed option is enhanced. The three-yard depth away from the line of scrimmage puts the quarterback on an automatic path downhill. Also, because the tailback is in a two-point stance, he's able to move laterally better than if he's in a stance with his hand in the ground.

Third, this goes hand in hand with the second point but is more specific. It's an essential play that uses counter motion. The spread option should strive to counter motion as much as possible and to use regular motion as little as possible. This provides a way to control the defense from simply running to the motion side on everything.

Two specific techniques must be understood when running this play. The first is the technique of the tailback. The option path of the tailback is similar to the slot's option path. The tailback will take three lateral steps to the sidelines. These steps must gain ground. Once the tailback has performed three lateral steps, he'll turn it up with the quarterback (Figure 4-27).

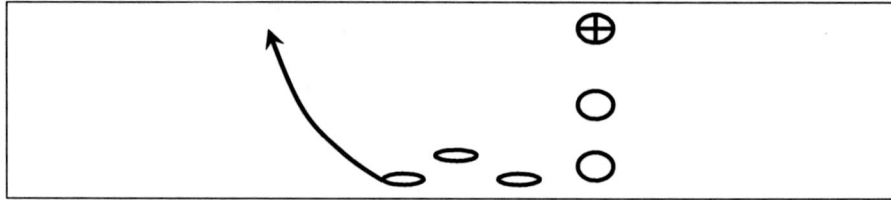

Figure 4-27. Tailback's option path

The tailback doesn't retreat back nor does he perform his steps slowly. Most of the time on this play, it will be a quick pitch. The tailback must be ready to take it to the house. The next important technique is twirl motion for the playside slot. This technique is very important and needs to be practiced every day. No matter the snap count, cadence, or speed of cadence from the quarterback, the slot will take three steps toward the tailback's heels. These steps must be legitimate and they can't be lazy. The ideal scenario is that the slot motions through the cadence. That scenario makes the defense believe the play is going the opposite way. Defensive football players are smart. If a slot has lazy motion, any half-brained defender will immediately pick up on that. The slot will take three steps. On his third step, he'll turn inside and open up laterally and perform his arc block. The slot must inside turn so he can immediately eye the defender he's responsible for. Without crisp/believable twirl motion, this offense is easy to key (Figure 4-28).

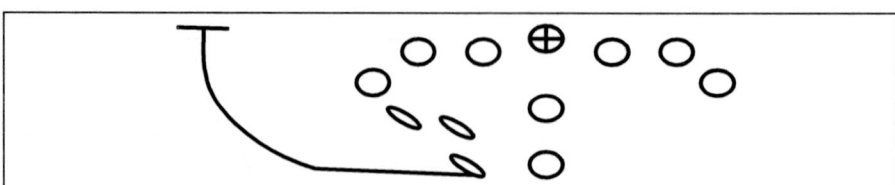

Figure 4-28. Slot's twirl motion

Iso

Every offense—whether it's an option, wing-T, spread, run-and-shoot, air raid, or West Coast—needs a downhill physical play that gives the offense a good chance to convert on short-yardage situations. The original iso gives this offense many different facets (Figure 4-29 and Table 4-3). The first is that it's a play that pre-determines a between-the-tackles run with the tailback. This gets the tailback in a mode of grinding and overpowering defenders. Some offenses simply forget the value of having a simple smashmouth football play. Teams should always have room for one or two downhill plays in their offense.

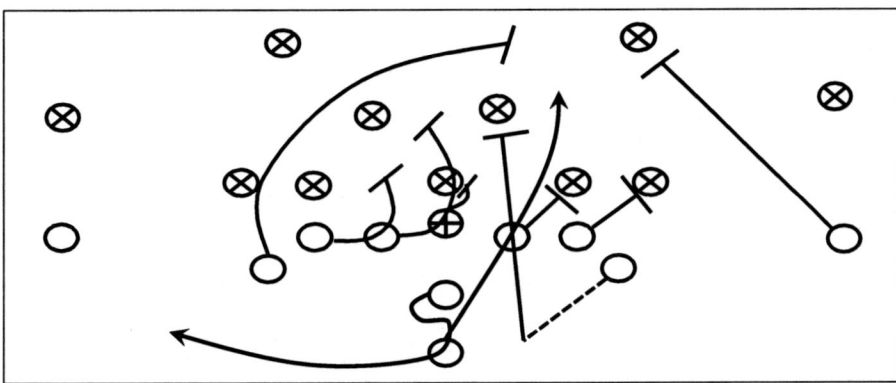

Figure 4-29. Iso

QB	Whirlybirds (reverses out), hands the ball off and boots away
TB	Triple steps, follows lead blocker and runs to daylight
PSSB	Twirl motion, blocks playside linebacker
BSSB	Touchdown block
PSWR	Two high: blocks safety; one high: stalks corner
BSWR	Cuts off
PST	Base to out
PSG	Base to out
C	Covered: 0-scoop; uncovered: playside backside technique
BSG	Vs. nose: scoops through the nose; vs. no nose: scoops, cuts if possible
BST	Scoops, cuts if possible

Table 4-3. Assignments for the iso

Second, this play runs with twirl motion. Twirl motion gives the defense a false key. The significant factor of twirl motion has already been explained. Because the spread option offense runs with quick motion, countering that motion is important. The next reason goes with the second reason: This play is a non-option counter motion. This puts the defense in a bind. All game, the defense is thinking option, option, option—and then suddenly, it's a smashmouth play right down their throats.

The quarterback on this play "whirlybirds" the handoff to the tailback. This gives the play slight misdirection. On the regular iso play, misdirection isn't the goal. However, it does enhance the play even if the linebackers hesitate for a split second. At one point on this play, three of the four backfield indicators tell the defense that the play is being run the opposite way. This enhances the downhill effectiveness of this play (Figure 4-30).

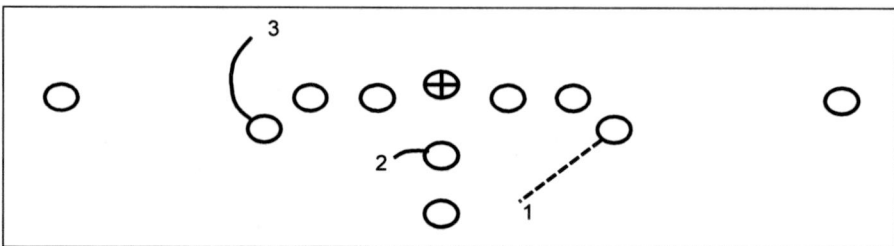

Figure 4-30. Triple indicators

This puts defensive instincts in conflict with each other. Most of the time, seeing 75 percent of the picture tells a player that what he's seeing is correct. However, the art of defense is detecting the subtle difference. With all the areas of the field this offense attacks, this play can be a game changer by accident.

Slot Iso

This play is the number one counter play for this offense (Figure 4-31). Teams have several reasons for adding this play to the option offensive attack. The first is that this play takes the aggressiveness away from a defense that's keying motion. Second, this play has great misdirection because it's faking the base play of this offense. Also,

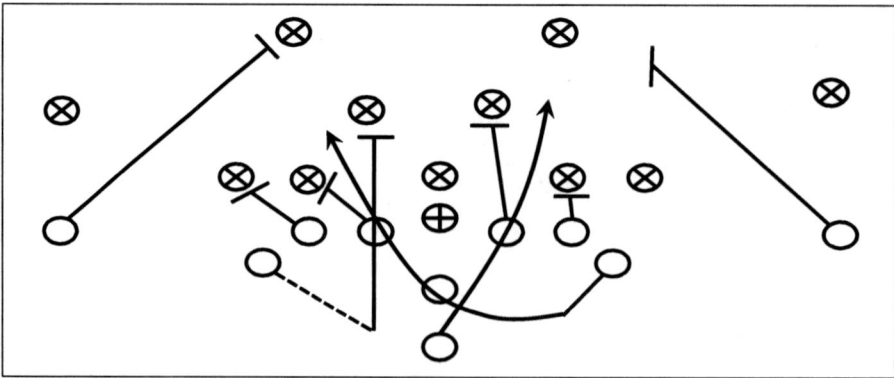

Figure 4-31. Slot iso

sustaining the points of attack is vital for the success of this offense. The offense must threaten each inch of the field vertically and horizontally so a defender can't leave his area without a huge play going his way. This play's original goal was a restraint on the defense. However, teams can employ this play for other reasons. Another reason for slot iso is to get the slots involved between the tackles. This can be a positive or a negative depending on personnel. However, if a slot has in-between athletic abilities, this play can be a positive. Setting the expectation that a slot will have to run between the tackles will make him into a better runner.

Flash Fake vs. a Real Fake

Something that many football coaches—including some of the best ones—have been sold on is the idea of giving a "flash" fake on a misdirection play. The thought process behind this idea is twofold. The first is that it minimizes the risk of fumbles. The second is that the flash fake is adequate enough misdirection to get what the play caller wants. It's believed that those are fallacies.

The first is the idea that fumbles might occur with a full ride fake. This is not well-thought-out. An option offense works on ballhandling every day all practice long. To illustrate the point further, consider how much work has been placed on ballhandling. For example, a team runs the option for four years without a change in scheme and runs its base plays every practice for an hour. The inputs for this example will be three weeks before game week, only one hour is included for offense, and practices are only during the week. The amount of time spent on ballhandling without counting in-season practices, two-a-days, spring football, and team camp would be 60 hours of handling the football in the same offense over the span of four years. The logic of saying there might be fumbles does have some credence to it. However, when a team specializes in running the option, it's hard to say that ballhandling will be a problem. Ballhandling is generally a problem for several possible reasons. First, the coaches aren't coaching it right. Second, the offense is trying to run too many plays. It's true that if an offense is trying to run a million plays that a flash fake is probably the way to go. However, specialization of the option makes this argument hogwash.

The second point also has some credence to it. It's true that a flash fake can adequately fake the defense out enough for the play to work. However, a problem with this thought process is the word *adequate*. The offense doesn't want to be adequate. It wants to be great. The goal of offensive coaches is not to lead the league/district/region in offense. The goal is to lead the entire state or country in offense. When coaches show the difference between a flash fake and a full ride fake, it's pretty obvious which one would fool somebody the most. A quarterback stepping downhill and meshing like he normally would and then handing the ball off makes deception deadly. Mediocrity isn't acceptable. Being the best is the expectation—and it starts with subtle coaching details.

Scoop Block

When discussing slot iso, coaches must go over what the backside of the offensive line is supposed to do. Instead of performing a regular scoop, the offensive line will simply base block. The reason is simple: The goal of any offense is to eliminate as many keys as possible that a defense can use against the offense. If the defense steps to the tailback and then reads a "scoop" block from the guards, it will be easy for them to key when it's a misdirection play or not. The goal is to give the defense a cloudy read for its linebackers and defensive line. This makes the defense play slower than it would have otherwise. Figures 4-32 and 4-33 show the difference between the two.

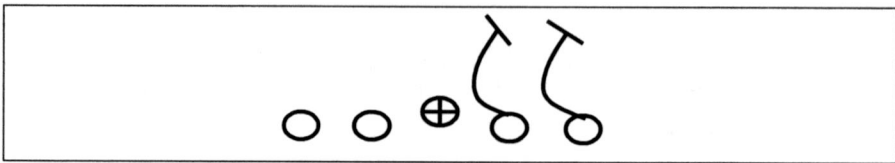

Figure 4-32. Scoop

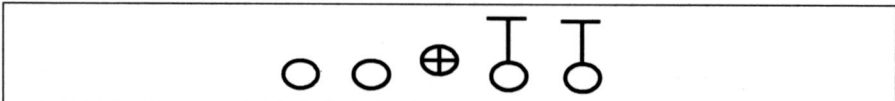

Figure 4-33. Base

The point illustrated is obvious: Taking away the linebackers' ability to key a scoop block and run over the top to stop the counter is difficult. Taking little things away from the defense is the difference between a five-yard gain and a 60-yard touchdown.

The slot's steps are illustrated in Figure 4-34. The slot will take a "bucket" step and come around the quarterback. This play is another play that's enhanced with the three-yard depth away from the quarterback. Because the slot is deeper receiving the handoff in the pistol than under center, he's able to work downhill faster, with his shoulders becoming parallel to the line of scrimmage as fast as possible.

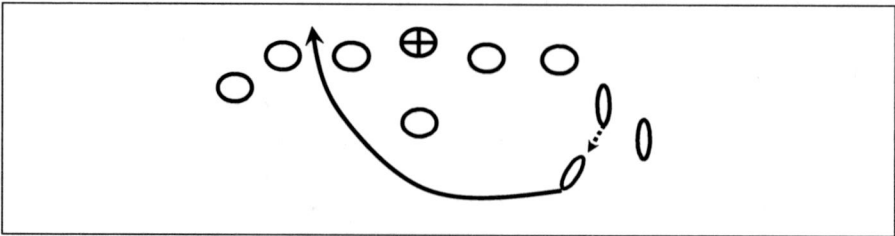

Figure 4-34. Slot's path on slot iso

On both regular and slot iso, the isoing slot needs to be sure about what he's supposed to be doing. As in counter speed, he'll perform three motion steps regardless of the cadence. Once his third step hits the ground, he'll dig his backside foot into the ground and quickly go through the B gap, expecting to block the playside linebacker. A couple of thought processes come with this. The first thought process is that the slot won't directionally attack the defender. Ninety percent of the time, because slots are the smallest players on the field, they'll directionally block somebody. This isn't the case on iso. The slot will blow up the linebacker and take him wherever he wants to go.

The second thought process is important. The blocking slot must act as if he's carrying the football. He'll "run to daylight" to block the linebacker. If not, he could erroneously run right by the defender he's responsible for. The same blocking fundamentals for the offensive line apply for slot. He'll shoot his hands from the beltline, have tight elbows, will roll his hips, and will have a wide base on contact.

Slot Iso vs. Eight-Man Fronts

Versus eight-man fronts, iso is actually outnumbered at the point of attack. When running regular iso, the offense shouldn't necessarily care about always winning the numbers battle because everybody except the "hinge" player will be accounted for. However, the offense must be prepared to block the extra defender in the picture. When playing against a 4-4 defense (Figure 4-35), the center will be responsible for the playside linebacker. The reason the offense believes this is feasible is because of the counter action and the personnel decision of choosing who'll be the center. Thus, the center must stay on the track he performs on his "playside backside" technique and expect to block the linebacker. The slot will check the linebackers "inside out" and block the most dangerous man who appears.

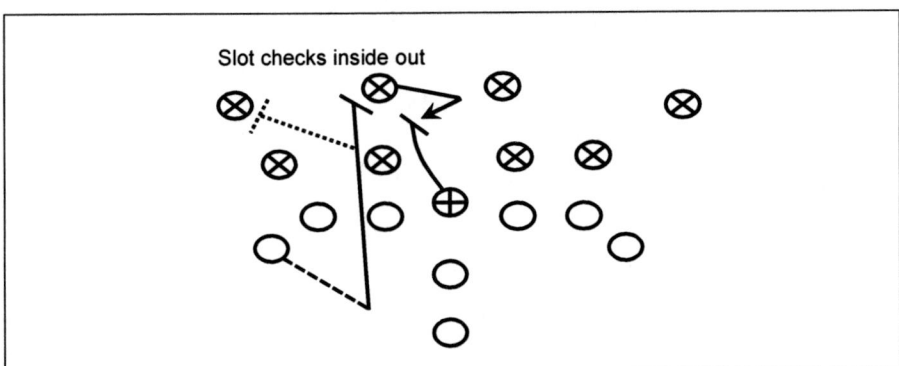

Figure 4-35. Vs. 4-4 defense

Against a 5-3 defense (Figure 4-36), the center is covered, so this blocking scheme isn't feasible. In this case, the guard will be the one who comes over and blocks the middle linebacker. Against this front, the slot doesn't need to check the linebackers inside out like he does against a 4-4. He'll simply take the playside linebacker.

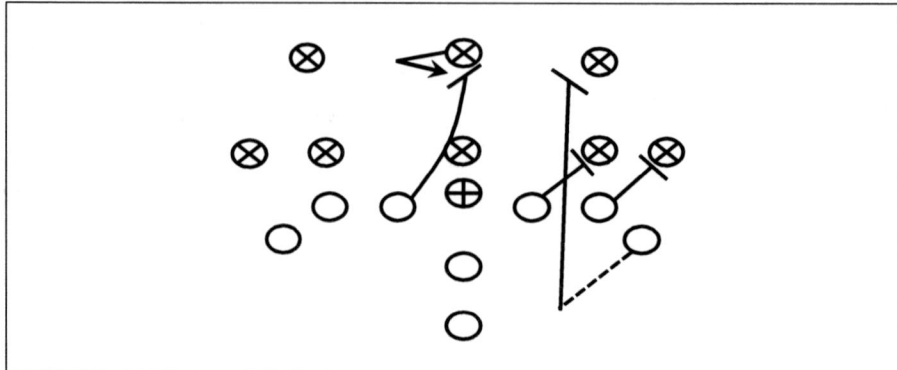

Figure 4-36. Vs. 5-3 defense

Counter Option

An integral play in the spread option offense is the counter option (Figure 4-37 and Table 4-4). The counter option out of the spread is the staple counter play in the Paul Johnson coaching tree. Out of the pistol, a quarterback's depth away from the line of scrimmage helps his steps better than under center. In this version of the spread, the counter option play has subtle differences for specific reasons.

The first reason to install this version of the counter option is to have a counter play against eight-man fronts. As previously talked about, it's hard to run slot iso against an eight-man front. In those cases, a backside lineman sometimes has to take a playside linebacker. Having this play solves that problem. Numbers become even and the offense has a numerical counter play against eight-man fronts.

Another reason to install this play is the fact that it's an option play with counter action automatically gives this play a surplus. Anytime a defender can be eliminated by reading him rather than blocking him gives the offense a huge advantage. It also allows the slot to get in open space off counter action, which can lead to many huge plays on the ground.

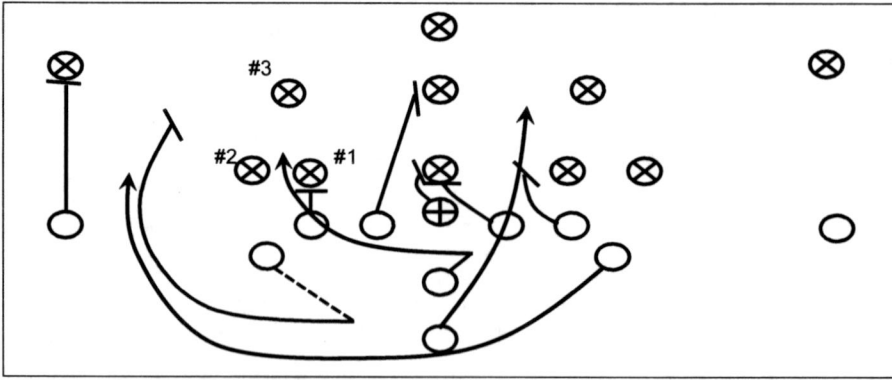

Figure 4-37. Counter option

QB	Fakes triple opposite, fully meshes with the tailback, inside pivot and option either #2 or #3
TB	Fakes triple, stays on triple path, then looks for work
PSSB	Twirl motion, opens up and blocks #2; vs. blood: blocks #3
BSSB	On the snap of the ball, gets into a pitch relationship
PSWR	Stalks the near deep defender
BSWR	Cuts off
PST	Veer; vs. blood: base #1
PSG	Base
C	Base
BSG	Base
BST	Base

Table 4-4. Assignments for the counter option

The first obvious difference between the traditional spread counter option and this version is that it doesn't use a pulling guard. A distinct reason for this is because when an offense pulls a guard, it's telling the defense where the ball is headed. That's something that must be taken away from the defense to use as a key against the offense. Many coaches simply say they don't care and that in most situations it doesn't matter. However, the goal is to eliminate as many keys as possible that the defense can use against the offense. The difference is shown in Figures 4-38 and 4-39. The Oklahoma defense presents a big problem. The backside linebacker can easily step to the tailback and then run over the top and be an unaccounted-for player.

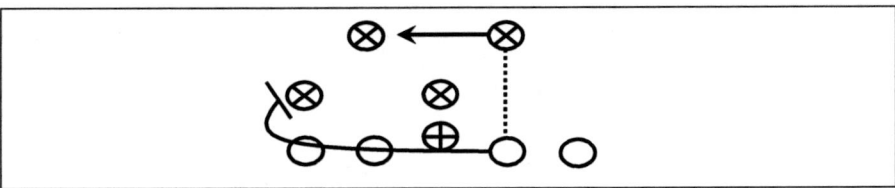

Figure 4-38. Counter option with pulling guard

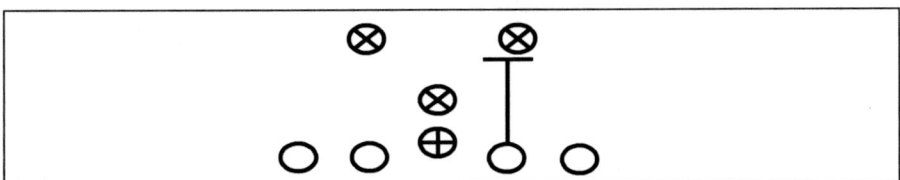

Figure 4-39. Counter option without a pulling guard

The point is obvious. The defense has less keys to use against the offense. It's true that without utilizing a pulling guard, the fronts that counter option can be used against is limited. However, this offense deals with those defenses differently.

This play has three key elements. The first is how the tackle deals with a 4-4 defense. As shown in Figure 4-40, the pitch off #1 is dangerously quick.

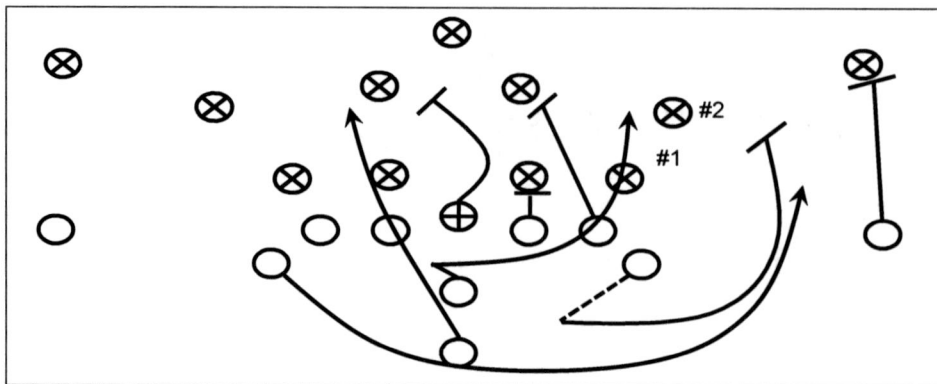

Figure 4-40. Counter option vs. 4-4 defense

The obvious problem with this play against this defense is that the pitch will be so quick that the quarterback might get his head taken off and the slot might not be in pitch relationship that fast. A solution to this problem is that the tackle will base block the defensive end for one second and then veer inside to the playside linebacker. This should give the quarterback enough time to fake, get his head around, and then pitch the football (Figure 4-41).

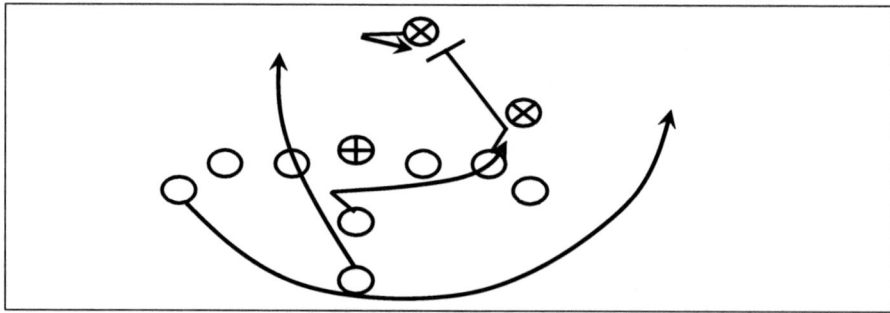

Figure 4-41. Tackle adjustment vs. 4-4 defense

The difference between a flash fake and a full fake has already been talked about. However, it's important to emphasize here that the quarterback must put more of an emphasis on his fake. The reason? The more time the quarterback spends on his fake, the more time the slot getting in his option route on the snap of the ball has to get in proper pitch relationship. A happy medium definitely exists for this relationship. The quarterback can't merely fake forever and then get his head around because that will cause the play to die. But the quarterback can't get his head around so fast that the slot isn't in a good relationship to option the defensive end. This relationship takes repetition in practice to perfect.

The last detail to talk about with this play is the quarterback's footwork. For the counter option footwork, the quarterback will ride the tailback as he would on triple. Once this has happened, the quarterback will pivot inside and option the defensive end. If the quarterback reversed out after the fake, he'd be too deep and his angle attacking the defensive end would be skewed. However, it's a perfect attack relationship to the defense if the quarterback inside pivots and options the end in that manner (Figure 4-42).

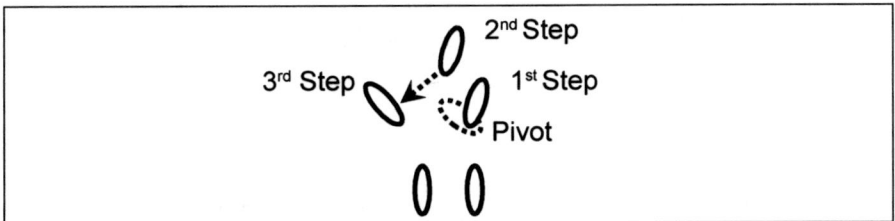

Figure 4-42. Quarterback footwork on counter option

The footwork is unnatural and confusing at first, but this is only a repetition problem and not a teaching problem. After many repetitions, the quarterback won't have a problem with this footwork.

Jet

This play has a special place in this offense (Figure 4-43 and Table 4-5). The jet sweep provides the offense an automatic outside presence. This is important for several reasons. The first is that it's another blitz control. This helps prevent the defense from simply blitzing up the middle every play. Second and most importantly, speed option is used in this same scenario. However, it's true that because it's still an option play that the defense can react and make the quarterback cut it up the middle. If a defense does that and the offense wants to get outside, jet is a phenomenal play. This gets the ball directly out on the perimeter.

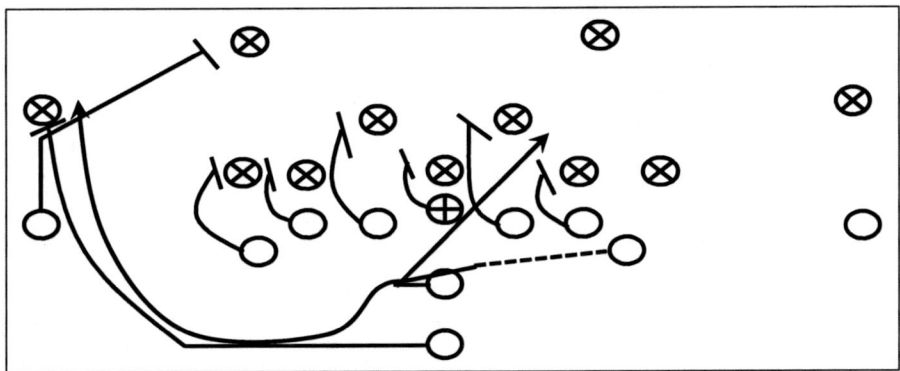

Figure 4-43. Jet

QB	Gives the ball on the jet, runs backside hard
TB	Works laterally, then kicks the corner inside out
PSSB	Reach
BSSB	Jet path
PSWR	Two high: cracks safety; one high: cracks outside linebacker
BSWR	Flash
PST	Pulls and overtakes
PSG	Pulls and overtakes
C	Pulls and overtakes
BSG	Pulls and overtakes
BST	Pulls and overtakes

Table 4-5. Assignments for the jet

The tailback's block on this play is important. The tailback's block here resembles his arc block, except it needs to be exaggerated because the man he's responsible for is farther away. As a rule of thumb, the tailback will take five lateral steps and then turn it upfield and attack the corner inside out. In general, the farther away the defender, the more width the tailback must work for. It's important to attack the corner inside out. If he doesn't, the block will be harder for the tailback. Giving him an aiming point helps because this block is blind. With an aiming point, the block is no longer blind (Figure 4-44).

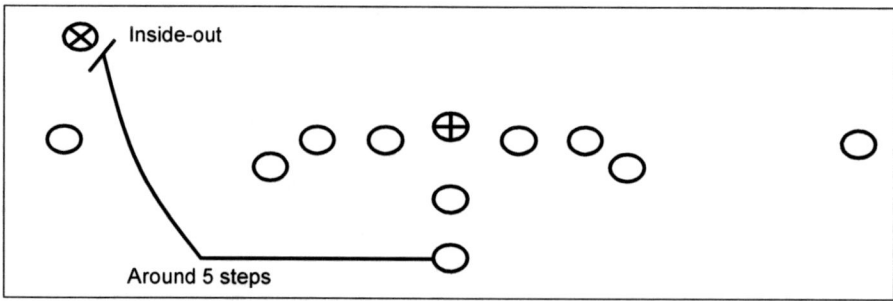

Figure 4-44. Tailback's blocking path

The jet path of the slot must be explained. The slot will motion underneath the quarterback. Once he receives the football, he'll "slide step" to gain depth away from the line of scrimmage and then catch the outside hip of the tailback. A good example is asking the players whether they've ever played baseball. In baseball, the player who has just gotten a hit rounds the bases. In short, the slots can be told to "round" first base and get behind the tailback. The next step is that the slot will run directly at the corner. The slot is responsible for setting up the tailback's block. Even though the tailback has an aiming point, this is still a difficult block to perform. The tailback needs a static defender to perform his block on. The slot will run at the corner. Once the pads click, the slot will cut it up and score (Figure 4-45).

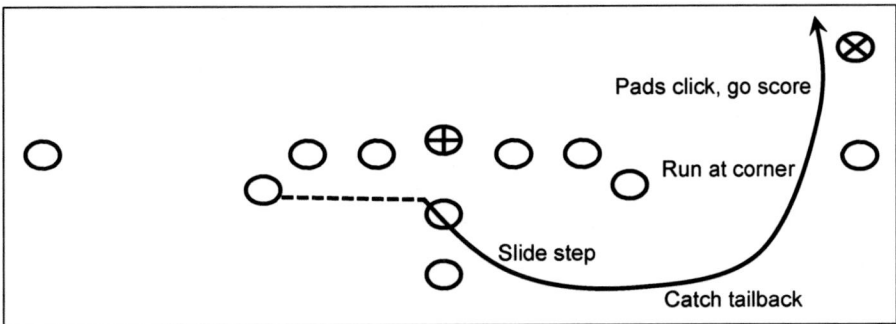

Figure 4-45. Slot's jet path

The next aspect of this play is for the blocking. Each lineman will pull and overtake the lineman closest to him on the playside. His aiming point is to place his outside arm underneath the outside shoulder pad of the defender he's blocking. The goal is to one-leg the defender. If a lineman can get a defender's leg in the air, the block is done. The same is done with the slot reaching the defensive end. The slot has the most crucial block on the perimeter. He must set the edge. Because this is a complementary play for the option offense, that indirectly makes this block much easier for him.

The reason why this block is easier for the slot is because of the nature of this offense. When the triple is called, the defensive end is unblocked. Throughout the course of the game, it becomes second nature to the defensive end that he'll be unblocked and read. Thus, it's very difficult for him to react to being reached by the onside slot. This puts the defensive end in a bind. Setting the edge is the most important part of this play. If the defensive end even hints at coming hard at the quarterback, the slot will have an easy block. In triple and jet, an arc step and a reach step are basically the same. This shows how difficult it is for the defense to key the slot's approach to the defensive end. It must react on the fly (Figure 4-46).

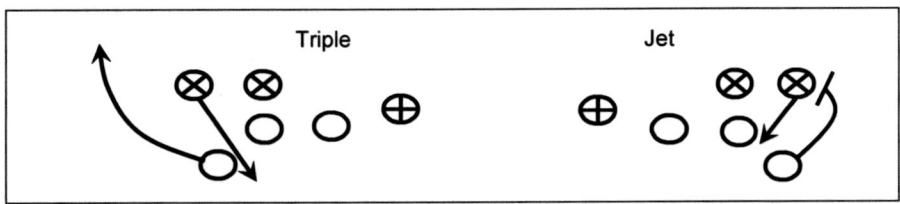

Figure 4-46. Predicament a 9 technique has in jet

The under-center spread pre-determined outside play is rocket toss. Some have a belief that jet and rocket toss are good for their respective structures. However, the argument put forth here is that the jet sweep out of the pistol is better than rocket toss for one reason: numbers. It's true that rocket toss hits so quickly to the perimeter of the defense that most of the time, the offense isn't necessarily worried about numbers. However, it's true that if a seven-man front reacts appropriately to rocket toss, the play can be dead in its tracks (Figure 4-47). Unless the tackle can overtake the outside linebacker and the slot can work for secondary run support, this play is at a numerical disadvantage. Under-center option coaches would counter and say that they run rocket if the linebackers are blitzing inside or the defensive ends are squeezing their tackles inside release. That's a great way to enhance the mechanics of the under-center option game and a great way to combat those defensive tactics. As it will be stated again, running jet sweep with the tailback lead blocking means the offense will almost never have a numbers problem on the perimeter. *If the pistol jet has any downside compared with an under-center toss, it's that jet hits considerably slower.*

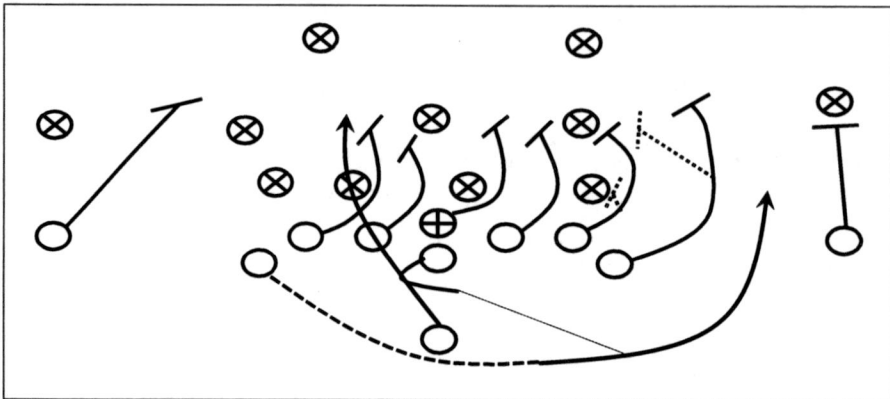

Figure 4-47. Under-center rocket toss

Dart

Not long ago, the inverted veer was invented in college football. This play in particular shows how fast the evolution of football is possible through the information exchange of technology. Teams can run this play in many ways. However, this play is run for specific reasons (Figures 4-48 and 4-49 and Table 4-6).

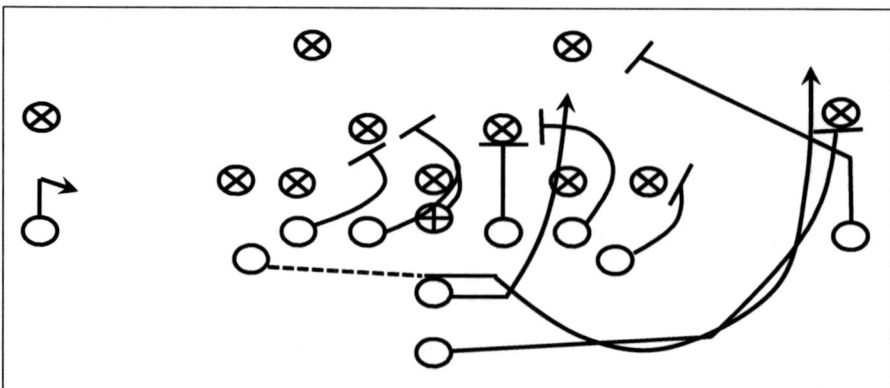

Figure 4-48. Dart vs. 50

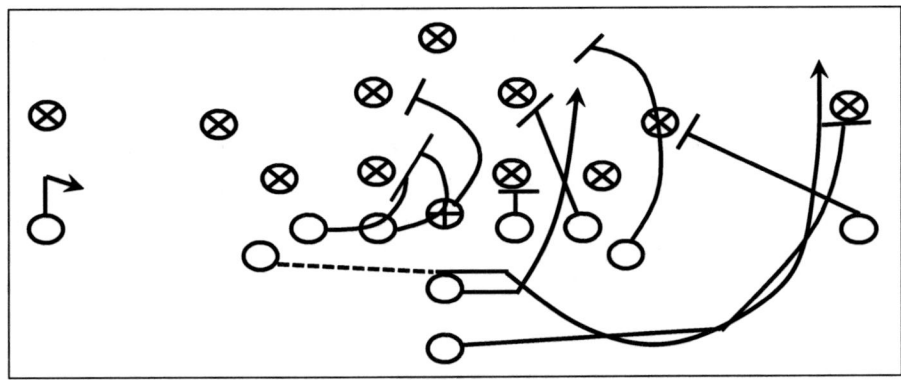

Figure 4-49. Dart vs. 4-4

QB	Slides and decides, gives and replaces, pulls and replaces; runs the wall
TB	Works laterally, then kicks the corner inside out
PSSB	Two high: blocks outside linebacker; one high: blocks #3; vs. blood: reach the end man on the line
BSSB	Jet path
PSWR	Two high: cracks safety; one high: cracks outside linebacker
BSWR	Flash
PST	Triple blocking rules
PSG	Base
C	Triple blocking rules
BSG	Scoops
BST	Scoops

Table 4-6. Assignments for the dart

The first reason to install this play is for the system to operate more functionally. A technique that some defenses use against the option is to squeeze the tackle's inside release. This way, the defense can disrupt his path to the linebacker. Many different outcomes could result from this—and most of them are good. However, a way to deal with that is to run dart. Running the inverted veer, the defensive end takes himself out of the play (Figure 4-50).

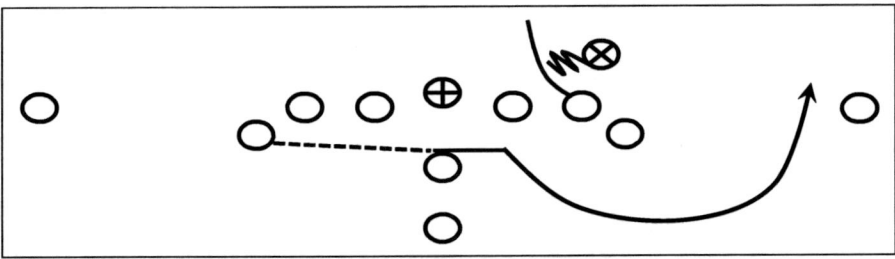

Figure 4-50. Defensive end getting hands on the tackle's veer release

Even though this technique can be combated with the tackle veer releasing, grabbing grass, and getting upfield, this directly puts a disincentive on a defensive end who does this. The ball will automatically go outside.

The next reason for this play to be implemented in this offense is to give the quarterback a play where he's the wall runner. If the team has a quarterback who's a great downhill runner, this is his play. This is a different look given to the defense. When the defense sees triple, triple, triple and then the offense suddenly goes out the door with the inverted veer, it changes how perimeter defenders approach the way they're blocked.

Zone

Zone has a special place in this offense (Figure 4-51 and Table 4-7). Unlike in the under-center game, this offense has the ability to run zone backside of motion. This play is in the playbook for two specific reasons.

To make it simple, the linemen won't "fully" zone block the front. That takes too much time to perfect when time is scarce and they must perfect all techniques that go with running the triple option. The offensive line technique will be simple. Each man will take a 45-degree step and block the gap he's assigned to. *Block the gap, not the defender.* If that point can be pounded into every lineman's head, this play will be successful.

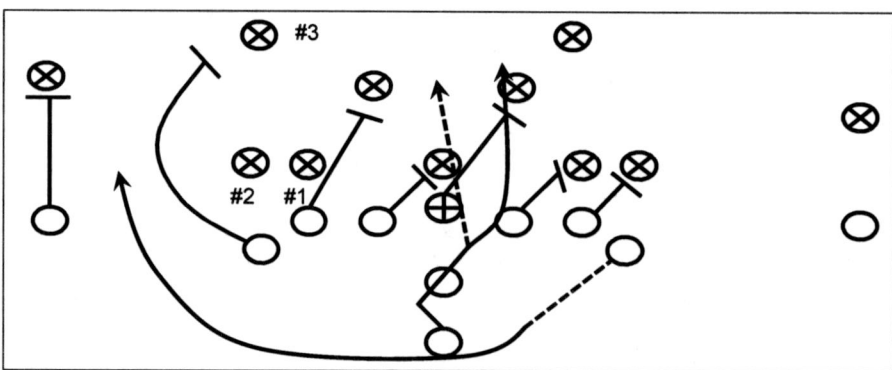

Figure 4-51. Zone

QB	Midline footwork, except doesn't work downhill; reads #1, gives/pulls and replaces, leverages pitch off #2
TB	Zone step, aiming point is the inside leg of the backside guard; reads the first down lineman at the center, makes one cut and goes to score
PSSB	Arc #3
BSSB	Option path
PSWR	Stalks
BSWR	Flash
PST	Blocks the B gap player
PSG	Blocks the A gap player
C	Blocks the A gap player
BSG	Blocks the B gap player
BST	Blocks the C gap player

Table 4-7. Assignments for the zone

The main reason to install this play is to combat defenses who are playing unsound gap defense. Many times, defenses will try to "cheat" a backside linebacker to the playside to outnumber the option game. Or they'll run an interior player to the motion. When those situations happen, zone is a huge play. Offensive coaches must recognize defenses trying to play games against the option. Figure 4-52 shows an example of a defense trying to cheat the option.

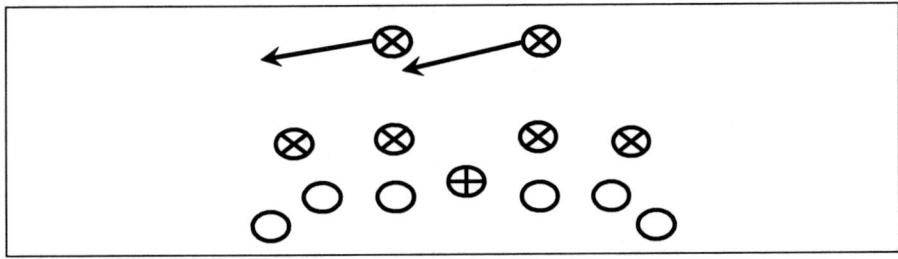

Figure 4-52. Unsound linebacker play

The defense is down a gap on this play. This means that zone is wide open. When defenses become desperate trying to win the numbers game, they become unsound in structure. The offensive staff must be able to know and understand when the defense has become desperate to the point where it's trying to cheat another player to the playside of the option game.

5

Game Management

Every coach lives and dies for game day. No better feeling exists than knowing that the offense outschemed the opposing defense. When a team runs the option, the coach already has superior knowledge. He knows and understands that he's already eliminated players in the numbers game. Why waste energy blocking people when the offense can read them and have better results?

This section will be divided into three parts. It's imperative to know and understand the theoretical realms being placed here. The first is to fundamentally understand defensive structures. Knowing a couple factors gives a coach a much better feel of how to react to different defenses he'll see. Second, when and why to use this formation will be addressed. Running different formations in this offense has specific roles. Third, play calling philosophy will be gone over. Most of them are universal play calling principles that will be addressed and a small cheat sheet will be given at the end.

The specific play calling won't be covered for a reason. A book could be written on every situation that will be seen within the structure of this offense. A basic play calling list will be covered last in this chapter.

Defensive Structures

Running the option, a specific principle should be used directly to know what the offense will be going against. *Coverage determines the front, not the other way around.* This principle is very important to understand. Many defensive coaches are "front" guys. And nothing is wrong with that if the defense is playing a predominately run or pass team. However, the problem is when it's playing a balanced offense. The pistol spread option offense is very much a balanced offense. If the defensive coordinator is more worried about stunts and blitzes than being sound in coverage, he'll be burned by this offense.

Several reasons make this is a great starting point. The first is that some collegiate teams teach the opposite. They teach that the front determines the coverage. This started in that form is incorrect. It's true that the front can determine the coverage, but it's easier and much more clear when the offensive staff and the quarterback only have to look at three to four people in the secondary and determine the coverage by only the few alignments those defenders can line up in than to look at seven to eight guys and figure out what coverage they're in. When it comes to messing around with a defensive front, a defense has a million different ways its front can stunt, blitz, slant and confuse the offense. The thought process being placed here is that it's much easier and much more convenient to look the defense from the back to the front than the other way around. As will be covered in a little bit, defenders in the secondary can do very few things.

The next reason is the overall principle of what sound football is. When talking about playing sound football, this means being schematically sound against everything. If a defense decides it's a front-oriented defense, it's putting a massive burden on the players in the secondary to play efficiently because they're now put on an island with no help. The easiest way to defeat an unsound defense is to pick apart its unsound secondary play. Coaching the defensive front is easy because minus playing an option football team, the only plays the defense has to defend against are zone, power, iso, maybe a trap, and counter trey. Besides that, the offense has very few things it can do to directly attack the defense. The true test of a defense isn't how it performs against an I formation power running team but how it performs against every kind of offense the defense will see. This offense will pick apart teams that are unsound in coverage and decide that running a front is more important than structurally sound defensive football.

That principle is a good starting point because it puts the offensive staff's mind in the right place. Many advantages are given to the offense when running this offense. One of them is knowing and understanding the coverage being given. As already discussed, a triple option team won't see difficult coverages because of the original theory of running the triple option that Emory Bellard developed. Right now, the structures that will be covered will be the differences between a seven- and eight-man front.

Seven-Man Fronts

Coverages

The starting point for seven-man fronts will be the coverages that will be played in the defense. Because of the seven-man structure, a defense has only four coverages it can play against an option offense: cover 2, 3, 4, and 6. As already explained, option theory makes it difficult for a team to play outside rotation against the option. However, that must be put aside for right now. The differences between cover 2 and cover 4 must be understood.

The difference between those coverages is who's playing run support. In a cover 4 shell, the safeties are run support all the way. In cover 2, the corners are run support (Figures 5-1 and 5-2).

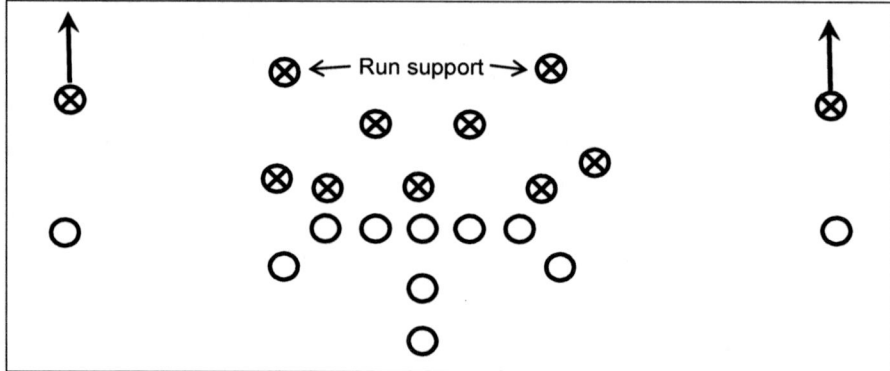

Figure 5-1. Cover 4 run support

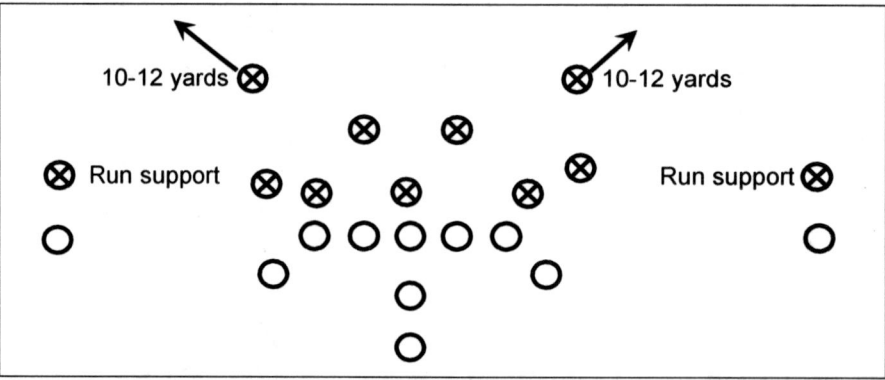

Figure 5-2. Cover 2 run support

Most of the time, it's very easy to decipher the difference between the two. The first thing to look at is where the safeties align. If the safeties are seven to eight yards away from the line of scrimmage, it's most likely cover 4. If the safeties are aligned 12 yards deep and are on the hashes, it's cover 2. Reading where the corners are aligned is also helpful. Whichever one is more convenient for a coach or quarterback to identify is fine. If the corners are playing uptight to the line of scrimmage or are playing inside leverage on the wide receiver, most of the time, it's cover 2. If the corners are playing off, it's most likely cover 4.

Another advantage of running the option is that the offense will never see the best type of cover 4: palms coverage. When cover 4 palms is being run, the corners are reading the release of the #2 receiver—much like a Tampa 2 defense. Because the offense is running the option and the corner must be worried about defending the deep third of the field, this defensive technique is obsolete.

The next coverage the offense must be worried about is cover 6—more commonly called quarter, quarter, half. Many times, seven-man fronts will want to run cover 2 to the boundary and cover 4 to the field. It's important to be able to identify this defense. Because it's a combination of cover 2 and cover 4, the run support correspondingly adheres to those coverage rules. To the cover 2 side, the corner is primary run support. To the cover 4 side, the safety is primary run support (Figure 5-3).

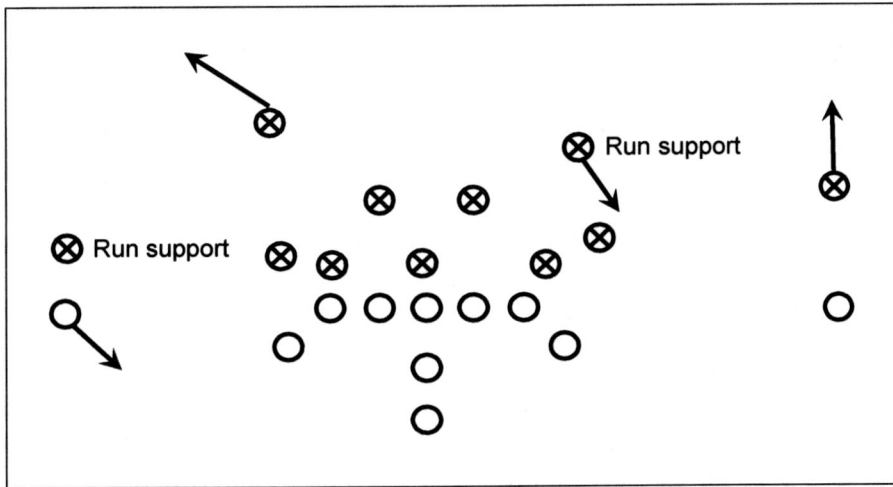

Figure 5-3. Cover 6 run support

The last coverage a seven-man front will give to the offense is a cover 3. This is very easy to figure out and it must be stated that cover 3 in a seven-man front is much different from in an eight-man front. In a seven-man front, cover 3 can be run several different ways. The first is that the safeties roll to motion. They'll "sky" the strong safety to the side where motion is also leading. The second is the strong safety will be "in the hole" to the wideside of the field in order to play his force responsibilities. Running the option offers yet another advantage. No difference exists between a strong safety "buzzing" or "skying" because of the count system. It doesn't matter how the defense plays its force players in a cover 3 because of the nature of this offense. Illustrating a rolling safety is pointless, but the illustration in Figure 5-4 shows the nature of a cover 3 without rolling to motion. The strong safety will be at a shallower depth level than the free safety. The free safety will be near the middle of the field and will be around 10 to 12 yards deep. His first steps will be backward.

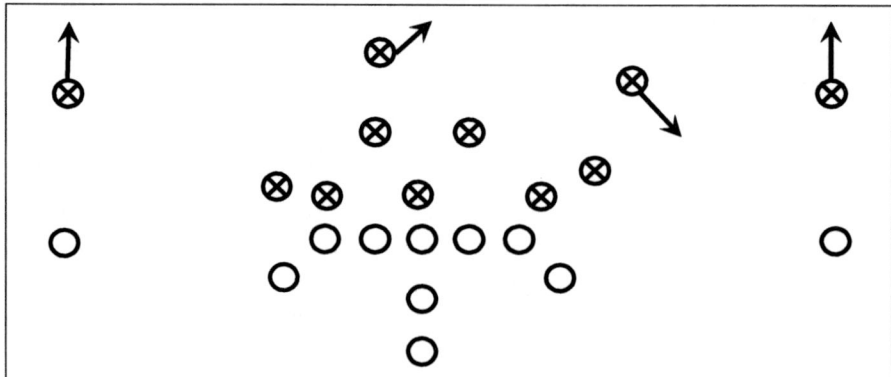

Figure 5-4. Seven-man front rolling to cover 3

Blitzes/Stunts/Gap Control

Seven-man fronts honestly vary from coach to coach on how much they blitz or stunt or how they control gaps. Theoretically, against the option, blitzing and stunting aren't smart. Gap control varies. Most cover 2 and 4 defenses are one-gap defenses. A one-gap defense means a defender is assigned to one gap and controls it on the snap. Cover 3 teams vary by either running a one-gap or a two-gap scheme. It all depends on the coach's philosophy of how to stop the run and how to control gaps.

Eight-Man Fronts

The first goal and mission of an eight-man front defense is to stop the run first and defend the pass second, even though most eight-man front coaches would probably refute that and say they want to defend both adequately. From an offensive perspective, it's a run defense first.

Coverages

Only two real coverages can be run in an eight-man front: cover 1 and cover 3. Because the structure of the defense puts eight defenders in the box without a disguise, it limits the coverages that can be run through it. It's important to note that both these defenses have built-in force players near the line of scrimmage. This is different in contrast to seven-man fronts where the secondary sets the force for the defense. Usually, against a 5-3 defense, the defensive ends are the force players, and in a 4-4, the outside linebackers are the force players.

The first coverage to discuss is cover 1. This is man coverage with one defender playing center field. It's as simple as it sounds. The corners man up and the linebackers will play the slots man on man. Sometimes, these defenses will have the Mike spy the tailback and be an extra player in the middle of the field. However, for simplicity's sake, it's man coverage (Figure 5-5).

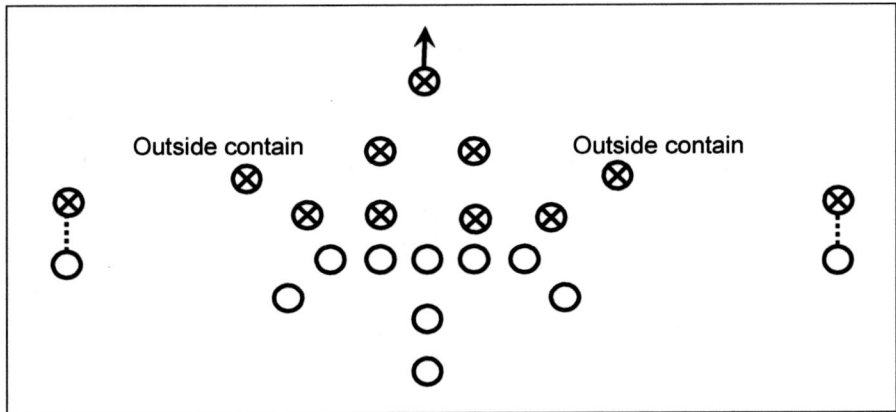

Figure 5-5. Cover 1

The next coverage that an eight-man front will employ will be cover 3. Cover 3 is a "play it safe" defensive coverage. It has three deep, with either three or four underneath defenders. The three secondary players' first steps will be backward, performing read steps. The outside linebackers will play the curl and run to the flat. The inside linebacker play varies. Sometimes, in a 4-4 defense, the linebackers will play the seam first and then work to anything underneath them. Sometimes, they'll simply perform a spot drop and scan for incoming offenders coming their way. This coverage is shown in Figure 5-6.

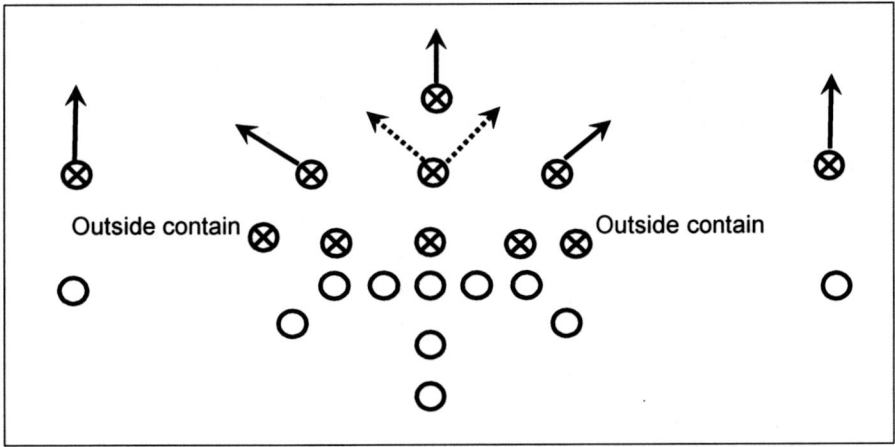

Figure 5-6. Cover 3

Blitzes/Stunts/Gap Control

The nature of an eight-man front means more blitzes and stunts will likely occur. As discussed before, front guys love blitzes and stunts because that's what they live for. Lining up in an eight-man front makes most of those exotic fronts come alive. As talked about with running the option, blitzing and stunting aren't very smart from a theoretical and practical approach with defensing the triple option.

When it comes to gap control, most of these defenses are one-gap defenses. Some 4-4 defenses use a two-gap technique to let their interior linebackers run free. Because of the structure of eight men down to defend the run, sometimes it's best for the defense to simply let its linebackers run around and make plays. Knowing and understanding what kind of gap control the defense is using are vital in running the option.

It's true to say that the way this has been illustrated is simple and doesn't necessarily hit all points of how defensive structures exist. However, the point is that no matter what other front the offense will go up against, it will fall under the categories talked about. It's true that the Gary Patterson 4-2-5 defense is a mix of a lot of different defenses and is very sound in structure. It's true that the hybrid 3-3-5 defense developed by Gordon Elliott is much different from the base structures talked about. But again, the defenses will fit into the categories talked about. Teams might have a mix and many exotic defenses will claim they're a nine-man front. Identifying run support in a defense and coverage is important before the offense is ready to attack the defense. Knowing a defense inside and out is critical for the option mission statement to work.

Changing the Formation

When teams started with the wishbone, the theory of the triple option with its components is one of the soundest offenses ever devised. With the wishbone and now the spread, the formations are the shape they are for a reason. The goal of both formations is to theoretically and strategically force the defense to cover most of the grass on the field horizontally and vertically. As previously talked about, the more an offense can stretch the field. the more the advantage goes to the offense. As many defensive coordinators will talk about, space is the enemy of defense. If the defense can shrink the field and force the offense to gain five yards every play in order to score, the defense has more of an advantage.

With that being said, it's important to say that changing the shape of the spread should be used carefully and for a purpose. The triple option offense is so theoretical and philosophical that an offensive coordinator can divert the original mission of an option offense if he's too worried about changing formations to get different looks from defenses. Too many times, option football coaches get away from what they do. They practice running the option over and over again all spring football, summer, and two-a-days, but in the middle of a game, they abandon the option and the best formation to run it with for things they're coming up with on the sidelines. It's true that circumstances exist in which changing the formation can enhance the attack. However, the theory being put out here is that changing formations is the start to a long dark road. It's okay to do. However, it should be done with great caution.

It's true that some option football teams run a bunch of different formations and have great success with them. The first team that comes to mind is Troy Calhoun's Air Force Falcons. Air Force runs a lot of different plays and runs a lot of different formations. Anyone who has watched college football knows Air Force is good at what it does and it leaves defenses clueless. Using different formations in the option game has some pros. The first is that by formationing the defense, the offense can gain a strategic advantage in numbers and angles. It's true that by coming out in a formation that the defense wasn't prepared for, the defense will generally run its base defense and the offense can exploit exactly what it knows the defense will line up in. It's true that if a defense is more of a "technique" defense and the offense finds the two or three formations in which it has numbers and angles, the defense can be helpless to the offensive attack. The next reason is twofold. It catches the defense off-guard and creates a panic preparing for those teams. If a team runs a lot of different formations, the opposing defensive coordinator will have to take extra time to prepare for that team. If his defense misaligns with the formation, the offense will have a big gain. Also, if a team uses a new formation, it can catch the defense off-guard. For example, if the offense comes out in an unbalanced jumbo set that the defense hasn't prepared for, the offense most likely will have a good offensive play because of numbers and angles.

That kind of thought process can lead to some negatives. The first is play calling. What's the play calling mechanism used when a team runs a lot of different formations and plays? The honest answer is that it becomes a casino with less luck and more education involved. When it comes to calling plays, how is the offensive coordinator going to make subtle adjustments running 20 different formations? He only has a few seconds to completely see how a defense aligns to his formation, shift, or motion. Coming back and taking advantage of an alignment is possible and can lead to a huge gain or a touchdown drive. However, the thought process that's being put out here is that there is an easier way to do things. The next negative is game planning, it's true that extensive game planning will usually lead to great things, but again, what's being put forward here that a better way to run an offense than to watch more than 50 hours of film a week exists. It's true to say that film study is important and should be the cornerstone of a coach's weekend and week leading up to game time, but he can find better ways to prepare than constantly watching a TV screen. The last negative is what if the preparation for specific defenses are wrong? Now the offensive staff has a playsheet full of information that's useless because the defense is now defending them differently either because it's defending an option team or it's simply chosen to defend something differently. Most of the time, the offense can prepare well for what it's going to see, but sometimes, when an offense has prepared for the wrong defense, running multiple formations only amplifies this problem.

Most critics of the option offense say that the option isn't a good offense because the defense knows the few plays the offense will run. However, that criticism misses the point: Self-adjusting plays are the basis of the option and run-and-shoot offenses. Plays that adjust after the snap eliminate the need for a fat playbook. This is called "strategic flexibility." This is what Sun Tzu called a "formless attack"—an attack that attacked the enemy like water attacked rock, adjusting as it flowed. The more plays in the playbook that have built-in answers, the fewer plays the offense needs.

The point that should be taken away from the philosophical and theoretical realm of this chapter is that *the pistol spread option offense is a built-in game plan*. The built-in game plan consists of maintaining the width of the field to 53.3 yards wide and 30 to 40 yards vertical. Every part of the defense is threatened, so if a defender is flatfooted or leaves his respected area, the offense will formlessly attack that area and put up six points.

To start off the discussion of formationing to attack a defense is to figure out specific defensive principles. As discussed, several factors should be considered when deciding how to attack a seven-man front or an eight-man front. It first includes coverage. The second is whether it's an odd or even front. Mostly, the coverage is what the offense should be looking for. Two other formations can be utilized because they seem to naturally fit with the spread: trips, which is a formation with a three-receiver side and a one-receiver side (Figure 5-7). The second would be an unbalanced look, bringing the wide receiver over to try to overload the defense (Figure 5-8).

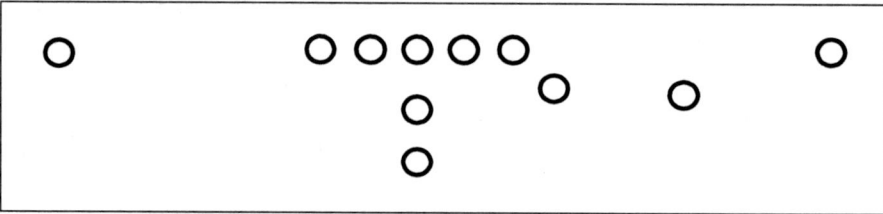

Figure 5-7. Trips

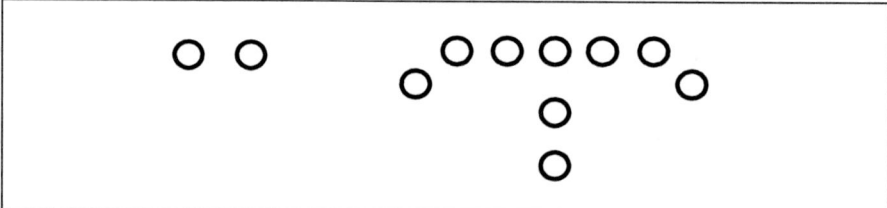

Figure 5-8. Unbalanced over

Trips

When and how to utilize the trips formation will be covered first. The first reason to line up in trips is to manipulate an eight-man front. When the offense sends an extra receiver to a side, it puts the defense in a predicament. Something has to give. Most likely, the defense will send an outside linebacker to split the difference between the #2 and #3 receivers. This opens up running the football in the interior (Figure 5-9).

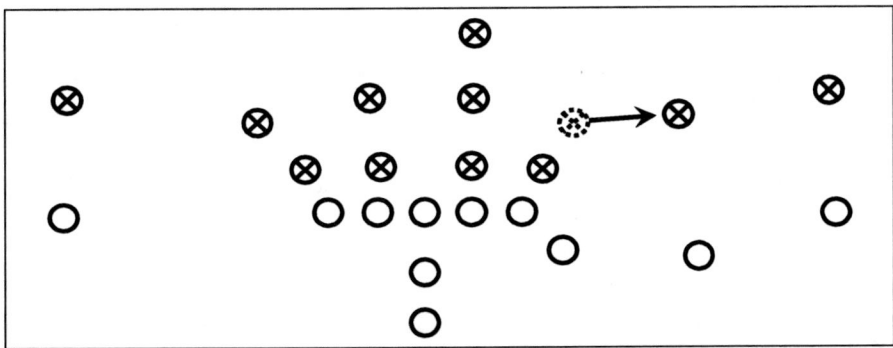

Figure 5-9. Eight-man front adjustment

If the defense slides and overcompensates to the trips side, this opens up the backdoor running game for the offense. Running the triple to the weakside can be a great play if the defense sends defenders over to cover the trips (Figure 5-10).

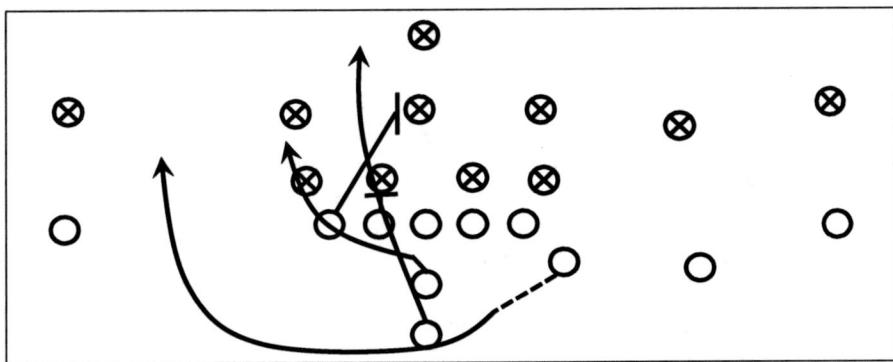

Figure 5-10. Linebackers slide to trips

The most foolish thing a defense can do against this set is to not change its front at all and send the free safety to cover the #2 receiver. If it does this, it's gambling big time. Running play-action stretch will burn the defense (Figure 5-11).

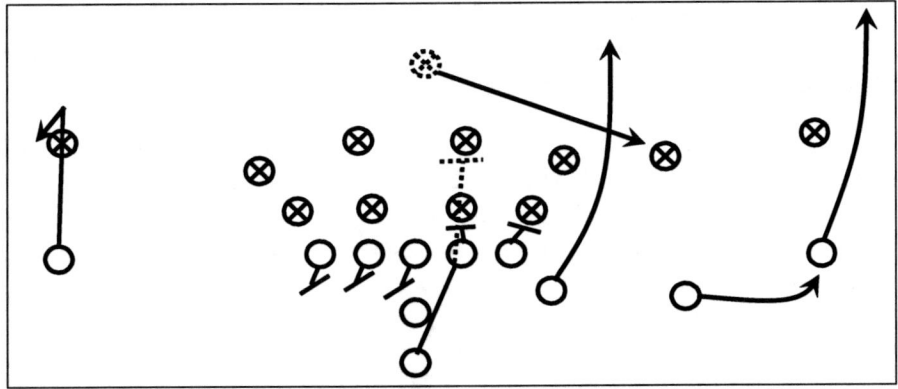

Figure 5-11. Unsound secondary adjustment

Seven-Man Fronts

When going up against a seven-man front, the offense has the advantage of knowing the coverage principles of that defense. Coverages can be aligned in just a few different ways to a trips formation without changing the base defense the opponent normally runs. The first coverage to go over is how to outformation cover 4. Cover 4 is really just off man because palms coverage is out of the question for a triple option team. Cover 4 could really just be called off man. When going into a trips formation, cover 4 is very effective to the three-receiver side. Running is a headache and throwing is a headache against this coverage in trips. However, what's lacking in a cover 4 defense is backside run support (Figure 5-12).

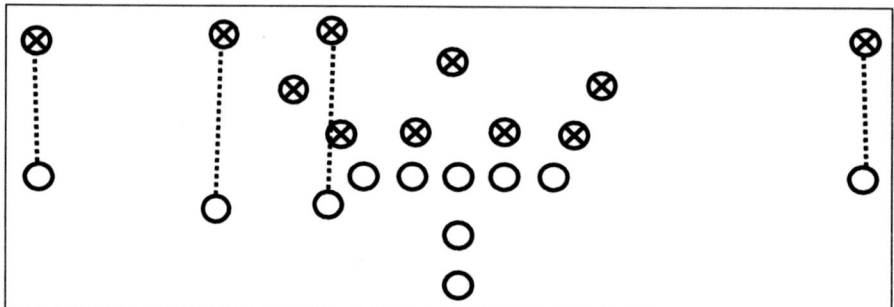

Figure 5-12. Cover 4 trips adjustment

The offense must know what the defense is doing when it aligns in a trips formation against this defense. Running backside—whether it be triple, speed, or midline—the backside running game is open all day against this.

Formationing against a seven-man front and an eight-man front is different. When going against an eight-man front, the offense is lining up in trips in order to run between the tackles. When a seven-man front is confronted with a trips look, the better idea is to run backside of trips. The reasoning is because of the way a cover 3 team would adjust against a trips look. Instead of widening a linebacker out to cover the trips, it will rock down a safety to either line up on the #2 receiver or to split the difference between the #2 and #3 receivers. Some value still remains to running to the trips side because of shades the defense will give the offense. However, the better theoretical idea is to run the backside of the formation (Figure 5-13).

Sometimes, teams who run cover 3 as a base defense will automatically lock up the backside receiver with the backside corner. When scouting a team, take note if that's what the defense is doing. If the offense can put its best wideout on the backside of the trips side and get a one-on-one match-up, that's ideal. Don't be afraid to take a shot at that match-up.

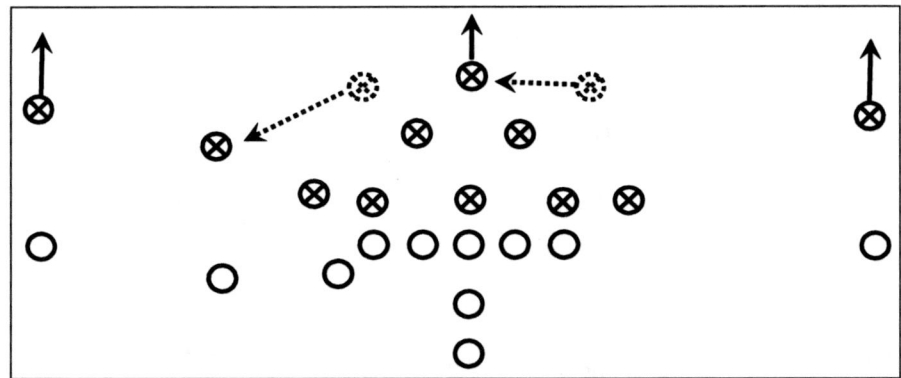

Figure 5-13. Seven-man front—cover 3 vs. trips

Merit and good possibilities exist when running trips against cover 2. The first is that it adds a receiver to the hardest coverage in football to throw against. It's true that a notion of cover 2 is to put three defenders on a two-receiver side and four defenders on a three-receiver side. However, careful design can make it two receivers on one defender. It's difficult, but it's possible. The best part about lining up in trips against cover 2 is that it opens up the interior running game. Because cover 2 is worried about having four defenders on three receivers and this offense is able and willing to throw the ball, the defense becomes vulnerable to the interior running game. The example in Figure 5-14 shows a 3-3 stack cover 2 defense.

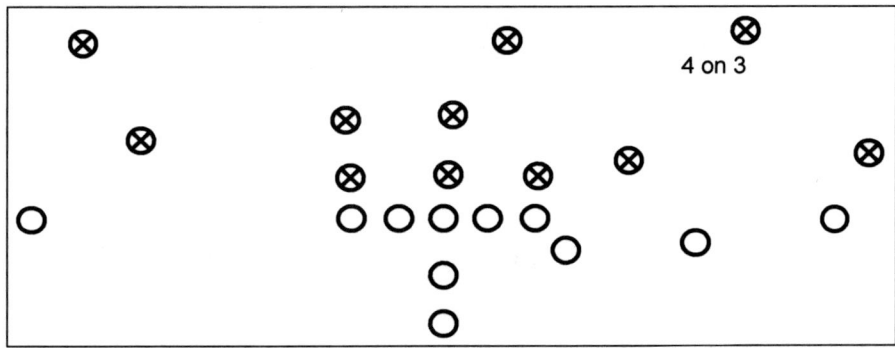

Figure 5-14. 4-on-3 coverage

It's possible to open up the interior running game against this kind of defense. When a team faces certain cover 2 defenses, running to the backside is beautiful because the defense will default into another coverage automatically against a trips set.

Versus man, trips is used in order to set the defender away from the trips and to run backside. This is essentially already shown with cover 4. When man coverage is used, it's better to run where the defenders aren't rather than relying on holding blocks for a couple seconds.

Unbalanced Over

The unbalanced over formation has several facets to it. The main goal of the formation is to gain an extra blocker and gap. If the offense can gain a numbers advantage because the defense didn't adjust to the unbalanced over, the offense should keep running it until the defense decides to make a change (Figure 5-15).

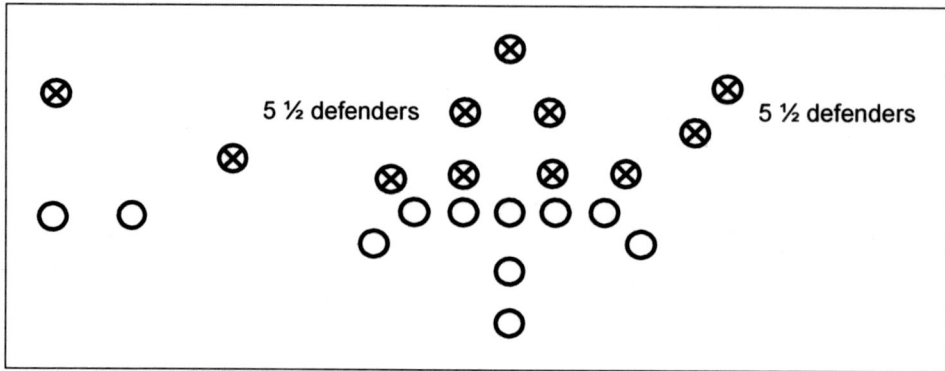

Figure 5-15. Defense doesn't adjust

The numbers advantage that the offense gains is obvious. Depending on the specific shades and front, a specific play can exploit the defense for not adjusting properly to the unbalanced over. The next way to exploit a defense through this alignment is if it overadjusts or if it's strictly a man defense. In these situations, the backside running game can be golden. If a defense has a "corner over" rule, the backside should be run every play (Figure 5-16).

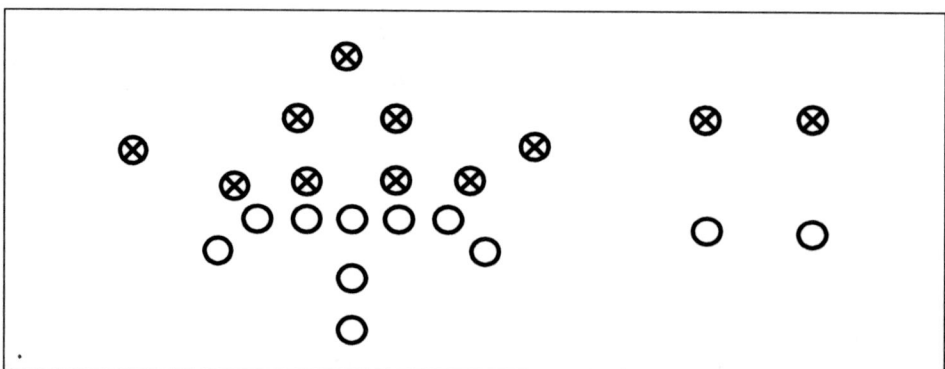

Figure 5-16. Corner over adjustment

The point of attacking corner over is simple. The defense believes it's playing "sound" football by matching numbers with numbers, which in most instances is true. However, against an option football team, it's playing with fire. The offense already doesn't block two defenders on a given play, so this gives the offense more rounds in its arsenal.

Play Calling Philosophy

It's true to say no magic play calling formula exists for this offense. Coaches should have principles they keep at all times. However, they don't exist just for an option offense. Most of them apply to all offenses. It's true that some basic situations call for adjustments. (A short list will be provided at the end of this chapter.) It's true that running this offense has a goal: to establish the option game at all costs. If a play isn't working, another play will work. That's how the system of option football works. It's an offense that's already molded. If something isn't working, something else will work. Some key differences exist when calling plays with an option offense compared with other offenses.

The first key difference is the idea of "feeding the beast." This philosophy is mainly in the West Coast offense. Much of the West Coast offense is about match-ups. When the offense believes it has a match-up, it will go to it over and over and over again. However, false premises can happen with this kind of thinking. If an offense is strictly designed to give the ball to very specific players, this simplifies a defensive game plan immensely. The defense knows and understands who'll be getting the football in the run game and the passing game. Instead of defending an offense with built-in answers, the defense is simply defending players. Also, a fault with this kind of thinking is the idea if a key player goes down. The offense has now designed an entire offense based on feeding one player the football and he's injured. Many examples exist of offenses that are based on match-ups faltering because the player who has been the centerpiece of the offense has gone down.

The next fallacy with scripted play calling is if the offense is wrong in its analysis of the defense. Many times, a defense will change how it plays a different offensive look week to week. If an offensive coordinator has put in a bunch of three-deep beaters out of trips because he's expecting three-deep coverage and the defense comes out in a cover 2 look, the offense has prepared its play calling sheet wrong. It's true that the argument could be made that simple play calling adjustments can be made based off what the coach has seen through the first quarter of the game, but that's one quarter too late. The offense never wants to wait an entire quarter to finally figure out what the game plan looks like. The option offense doesn't have this problem because of its built-in game plan.

Numerous principles should be followed when running an option offense. Of course, this is all subjective. However, it's believed that these guidelines will help any offensive coordinator run an option offense correctly.

Establish the triple as the team's base play.

This is the first and obvious rule to follow. The triple option is the best play ever devised and is worked on over and over again in practice. It only makes common sense that the play that's worked on the most must be the establishment point for the offensive attack. Something is profoundly wrong if the offense isn't running the triple option a lot during the course of a game. If the play callers aren't running it in a game but are repping it in practice, they're running the wrong offense. If the offensive coordinator isn't completely sold on what this offense can do for him, he needs to change the offense. This is an all-or-nothing offense, which must be understood when a coaching staff has decided to turn to this offense.

Maintain all points of attack.

As previously stated, the pistol spread option offense is a built-in attack plan. The offense has been designed so every area of the field is attacked to the point where a defender can't leave his area or a big play will occur. If maintaining all points of attack aren't kept, the field has shrunk greatly and that gives the advantage to the defense. For a defense, space is the enemy. It wants to shrink the field as much as possible in order to make it harder for the offense to move the football. At all costs, the offense must expand the field to operate in the most efficient manner possible. Keeping the defense guessing where the ball is going is important.

Use numbers, angles, and grass.

This is a critical part of calling plays for an option offense. These are the three ingredients that help an option offense succeed. The first is numbers. Offensive football is a numbers game. If the offense can outnumber the defense at the point of attack, the offense has a better chance of succeeding. Because the pistol spread is a balanced formation, the defense in most cases is forced to play 5.5 defenders on each side of the ball. If the defense has six on one side and five on the other, the offense should run at the five-defender side. Remember, the triple option can handle four perimeter defenders (on or outside the offensive tackle). If the defense can get a fifth perimeter defender, the offense needs to account for that defender in a different manner. Numbers is the number one priority when it comes to play calling.

Angles is the next important factor to bring into the play calling realm. Many times, just by alignment, the defense becomes vulnerable to angle blocks. It's also true that the triple is better run against a 1 technique instead of a 3 technique. It's true that running midline against a 3 technique is much easier to do than a 1 technique. Speed is great against a blood call when the tackle can easily base the pinching 4 technique. The base plays in this offense handle various angles that the defense will come out in.

Grass is the third factor. If the numbers are even and the angles are even, the offense should look to run to the wideside of the field. As stated before, the more grass, the more advantage for the offense if the numbers battle between the offense and defense is even. However, this should be the last factor to be considered when running this offense. Running the option into the boundary shouldn't scare play callers because the fact of the matter is that big plays are still able to happen running to the boundary.

Aggressively attack the defense.

Too many play callers are passive and not aggressive enough. Defensive coordinators are very smart. They know whether an offense is going to attack. If the offense isn't going to be aggressive and keep the defense on its heels, the defense will have a field day all over them. Also, from another angle, football players want their coaches to be aggressive. It motivates football players that the coach is trying to score now instead of 10 plays later. Being a passive play caller can be demoralizing because the players can feel like they're not being given the best chance to win.

Another point must be addressed: A difference exists between attacking the defense and being aggressive and being plain stupid. The problem with this is that it's all subjective to the coach's personal preference. It's true that many times on third-and-long, the triple option is the best play in the playbook because the defense isn't expecting it. However, this doesn't mean on fourth-and-inches that the offense throws up a Hail Mary and expects to score. Throwing on third-and-short or fourth-and-short does have some merit, but it must be smart and for a reason. It shouldn't be for the sake of throwing on fourth-and-inches but because a passing play is open that will result in an easy completion.

Figure out what the defense is doing and attack it appropriately.

This in some respects is already done within the structure of the option offense. However, it's true that some plays are better in some situations than others. As already talked about in this book, good situations do exist in which to run plays in this offense. Knowing and understanding this offense from front to back is the only way to know when and how to appropriately attack the defense. Eye control for a coach is important to develop. This comes from hundreds of hours of film study and years of coaching this offense. The coach must immediately know and understand why a play worked or it failed. Knowing that, it then becomes easy for the offense to counter the defense.

Have the ability to "feel" the defense.

In all honesty, this is something that must be learned through years of experience with this offense. The offensive coaches need to know this offense like the back of their hands in order for them to know how to call plays. It's true that calling defense is much more of a "feel" than calling offense. But feel comes from years of experience and thousands of hours of watching film. The best feeling in the world is knowing exactly what the defense is trying to accomplish through naturally feeling them out. This is like two boxers at the beginning of the fight. Feeling the opponent out is important for calling offensive plays.

If the defense is doing random things or trying to be unpredictable, the offense must counter and become more unpredictable than the opposing defense.

Many times, offensive play callers get confused by multiple stunts, blitzes, slants, and coverage change-ups. However, this offense puts those coaches in their place. When the defense is in unpredictable mode, the offense must counter and become even more unpredictable. This isn't just for an option offense but for any offense. However, the argument being put out here is that running an option offense is much easier to be unpredictable with because of its built-in game plan. When a defense is being unpredictable, still adhere to the numbers, angles, and grass theory, but hit every point of attack to punish the defense for not playing sound. This offense is most successful when adhering to this principle against defenses that are throwing random fronts, stunts, and coverages.

It's also important to note that when a defense is unpredictable, *the offense must remain unpredictable.* Many times, when a defense is playing unsound football like this, the coaching staff will try to attack a previous defense for which it just saw. This can be dangerous because the defense isn't running a philosophical defense. It's just out to confuse 16- to 18-year-old players with random stuff. Sometimes, it's necessary to suspend "good ideas" and adhere to the numbers, angles, and grass theory and hit all points of attack.

Don't necessarily repeat plays. Doing so makes a play caller predictable. But come back to plays, especially option plays.

A common rule in football is that if an offense repeats a play, the defense will be ready for it the next time. Especially in the option offense, if a play is repeated three or four times, the defense will be ready for it. It's true that the triple option must be called a lot, along with the midline option and the speed option. It's also true that counter plays must be called to keep the defense from cheating. Especially with counter plays, don't repeat those. Those are to serve a purpose. The worst thing a play caller can do is to repeat a misdirection play. When a misdirection play is called and creates a huge gain for the offense, it has served its purpose and keeps the defense from playing unsound against the triple. Repeating it isn't smart because more than likely, the defense will be ready for misdirection. Misdirection must be used. However, don't repeat it and expect another huge gain.

A ball thrown deep is easy to defend when the defense knows it's coming.

One of the easiest plays to defend in football is a deep pass that the defense knows is coming. It knows it's coming because certain scenarios exist when that's the only feasible call for the offense. But in regular circumstances, the deep ball must be thrown as a surprise against the defense. Attacking the deep third of the defense is a staple of this offense, but it must be a surprise. When it comes as a surprise, huge gains come about. When it comes up in an obvious situation, that's when interceptions happen.

When running screen or draw, limit running those plays to twice a game.

The ultimate trick plays in football are the screen and draw. They're the ultimate trick plays because they take advantage of natural reactions when a linebacker sees pass and a defensive end is coming free to clean the clock of the quarterback. However, they're trick plays. Calling them more than twice in a game is a mistake. Many football coaches learn the hard way that running draw too many times in a game is a mistake. It's true that this is subjective analysis, but it's also common sense. If the defense has been burned by a screen or draw play, most likely it won't be burned by it again.

Another golden rule regarding screen and draw is that many times, these plays don't work against well-coached teams and poorly coached teams. Well-coached teams defend this well because they're coached day in and day out to recognize screen and draw. Poorly coached teams aren't necessarily burned by it because the defenders are like a deer in the headlights—they stay at home because they don't know any better. Usually, these plays are best against an average to an above-average team. The last input about screen and draw is to self-scout when the offense runs them. Many times, teams will only run these plays on third down. Smart defenses will figure this out and alert teammates that on third down, screen and draw are coming. Use these plays smartly and realize they'll only work once or twice a game at best.

When a play is successful, run the next play quickly.

The analogy that can be used here is that of a fighter who lands a good punch against his opponent. When the opponent has been hit with a haymaker, he's been put in a position where he could be put away. He's on his heels and is most vulnerable at this point. This is where the virtues of a no-huddle offense come in. The no-huddle offense is successful when big plays happen because the defense just got sucker-punched in the face and is forced to immediately rebound from a right hook. When the defense is on its heels, keep it there and finish the job. Don't let the defense get a chance to regroup. Human beings tend to cower into a corner when they're hit unexpectedly and they also usually recover when they're given time to put a play or situation in perspective and learn from it. Don't let the defense learn from its mistakes. Once it makes a mistake, put the pedal to the metal and score.

Self-scout tendencies.

Although it has been preached throughout this book that the offense has built-in game planning and play calling, the idea of self-scouting tendencies still has merit. A distinction should be made though. Don't simply self-scout and call plays differently because of the self-scout. Sometimes, because of the way the defense is playing, the reason for calling that play may be skewed in the analysis. If the defense keeps bringing pressure inside and speed option keeps being repeated, that's not a bad thing. However, if in the analysis a specific tendency to run a very specific play in a very specific situation is noticed, then having an alternative plan for the next game in that same situation is reasonable.

Be smart and don't be stubborn.

Many play callers proudly profess they don't care if the defense knows what's coming because they still have to stop it. It's true that in the option offense, the defense is going to know that some kind of option play is coming. However, a point does come where stubbornness hurts the offense's chance of winning. If the defense lines up in a 7-2 defense and the play caller wants to call iso, it's probably not the best call. If on first-and-10 the defense aligns with five deep in the secondary, calling a deep pass is probably not the best play call.

From another angle, players are smart. Coaches oftentimes don't take into consideration that players talk and have opinions too. They're actually the ones performing the tasks the coaches are telling them to do. With that said, it can be demoralizing for a player if a coach is stubborn in his play calling and believes he's not being given the best chance to win. This happens to almost everyone at some point in his life with some kind of activity. He believes that no matter how hard he works, the leadership direction is wrong and he'll fail regardless of how hard he works. Be smart. If the defense is blitzing eight guys up the middle, do what will correspondingly hurt the defense instead of yelling at players to drive those eight defenders out of there. The offense is an option team that's nonnegotiable. What's negotiable is specific plays for specific situations.

Be able to explain when and why a play has been called, why it has failed, and what the adjustment is.

Something that motivates players is their knowing the offensive staff is on the same page with the players. The coaches must sell the strategy of the option offense to their team. If a play fails, don't be afraid to explain to a player why it failed and what the coming adjustment will be. Having open communication with the players on the field to what they believe will work and what won't will only help possibilities of success.

It's better to have two play callers than one who makes all the decisions.

It's believed that having two informative play callers collaborating with each other works out beautifully because sometimes one coach's mind is looking at one thing and the other is looking at another. It's only common sense that collaboration in play calling between two coaches is more logical than having one autocratic play caller. But a catch-22 comes with this. Both coaches must know, understand, believe, and be on the same page with what the offense is trying to accomplish. Sometimes, the play caller on the field is seeing one thing and wants to call something and the play caller in the press box sees that the play might not work. Or the play caller in the press box believes that a play will work and the play caller on the field has a better vision and decides that another play will give the team a better chance. It's true to say that it's tougher to call plays from the field. The play caller can't see everything. Calling plays from the field is more of a feel and has a rhythm to it. Calling plays from the press box is more educated in terms of knowing exactly what the defense is doing. Sometimes, virtues exist to calling according to the rhythm of the game. Other times, calling the game specifically because of what the defense is doing also has virtue.

It's understandable that giving up some authority is hard for some people to fathom, but it's honestly for the best. Feeding off two smart coaches is better than having one sole play caller leading the team. The play caller on the field feels the rhythm of the game, while the play caller in the press box knows the specifics of what the defense is doing.

When the team has the lead, it should finish the job.

Too many times, offensive play callers at all levels and with multiple offensive styles become complacent when they have the lead in the third and fourth quarters and get the ball back. If the offense is only up by one or two scores, the play caller must not take his foot off the gas. It's a natural human characteristic that people relax when they're in the lead. If it's in the fourth quarter and the offense just got the ball back, don't experiment with plays. Run the offense that got the team in the lead. Still be aggressive. Most if not all play callers at some point have lost a game because they become complacent with the lead late in the game.

When in doubt, run triple.

This is pretty self-explanatory. The triple option is the best play ever created in football. Many times, when an offense is sputtering, it's because it's gotten away from its base offense. Or sometimes, it's just difficult to call plays in some games. If a coach has any doubt about a situation, running the triple is the best play call. The worst thing a play caller can do is to be in doubt and to call a companion play. Believe and trust in what the offense's mission statement is. Keeping the width of the field 53.3 yards wide and 30 to 40 yards deep. The option play is the best instrument to attack the field's full 53.3-yard width.

Introductory Specific Play Calling Guide

As talked about earlier, an enormous option book could be written about detailed play calling specifics. This guide is just the basics that many spread (flexbone) coaches use on game day:
- Establish triple.
- If a backside linebacker makes the play, run the slot iso or the counter option.
- Run triple to a 1 technique.
- Run midline to a 3 technique.
- Speed vs. a blood stunt is the best situation to get the ball outside.
- Blitz inside = jet or speed

- Corner force = stretch
- Safety force = choice
- Cover 3 = scat, stretch, quick game
- Unsound defensive line or linebacker play = zone
- Rolling secondary = counter speed/zone
- Team keying motion = midline kill, twirl midline, twirl triple, slot iso, or counter option

6

Option-Specific Drills

There could be an encyclopedia weighing 25 pounds containing all the football drills that have been created since football became a sport. This chapter is here to provide clearance to good option-specific drills that will help out anytime the offense runs the option. This section will be divided by the skill positions first and the second part will be on the offensive line.

Quarterback Drills

Down the Line

The down the line drill is a drill used in order to perfect the fundamentals of a quarterback pitching the ball on the option. The drill is simply set up on one of the field markers on the field. Two partners are involved. They'll jog down and back, pitching the ball to each other. When they get to the end of the field, they'll turn around and work on pitching the ball with their other hand (Figure 6-1).

This drill has several points of emphasis. The first is that the quarterbacks don't stop until they get to the end. The second is that the quarterbacks are performing the correct technique for pitching the football. The quarterback must have his thumb underneath

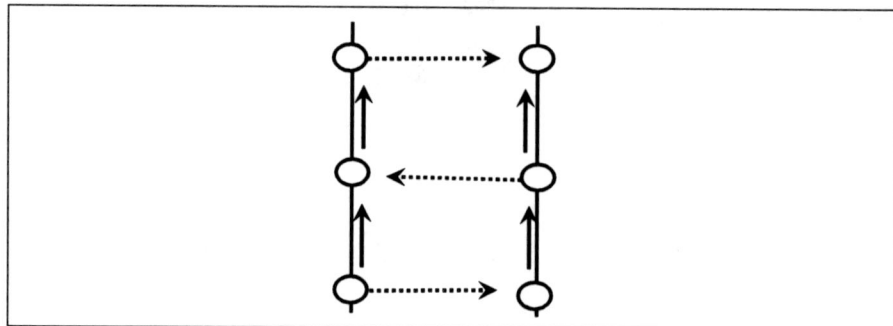

Figure 6-1. Down the line

the football, pitch the ball heart to heart, and have a loose wrist to help keep the pitch dead. The last emphasis is that the quarterbacks are stepping toward their target while they're still on their path down the line. This helps perform the movement pitch. The fadeaway method isn't taught in this offense for reasons already talked about. This drill can make it easier for a quarterback to perfect the muscle memory of the movement pitch. The quarterbacks need to go slow enough to where they're perfecting these small coaching points. The point of the drill is to not be first but to perfect the details of being an option quarterback.

Chop and Pitch

This drill helps emphasize the workings of the movement pitch. It's unnatural for an athlete to step and pitch while staying on his path. This drill helps the quarterback learn how to attack downhill once he pulls the football and gives him muscle memory on how to perform a movement pitch. The drill is shown in Figure 6-2.

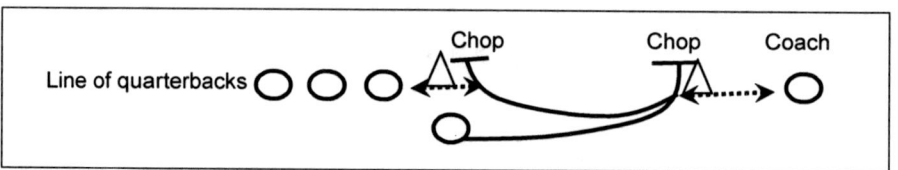

Figure 6-2. Chop and pitch

The quarterback who's up will be attacking downfield toward the cone. Once he gets to the other side, he'll pitch the football to his coach and chop his feet waiting for the ball to be pitched back to him. The quarterback will then roundly attack the other cone and pitch the ball to the next quarterback in line and will chop his feet until the quarterback pitches him the ball back. The quarterback goes until the coach says the next in line is up.

This is a good drill for several reasons. The first is that it helps get the quarterback thinking about attacking downhill and being an aggressive runner. The next is that he's getting a lot of reps at pitching the football. Also, it's a smooth transition to getting the quarterback's muscle memory right on the movement pitch. It's a stepping-stone in order to get to that point. He pitches the football and then chops his feet for about another yard. If the quarterback can be "weaned" into muscle memory, then this drill serves its purpose. The last reason for this drill is that it's something that helps with hand-eye coordination for quarterbacks. Many quarterback coaches proclaimed that the quarterback must have the best hands on the team. That statement isn't necessarily true, but as a position group is concerned, quarterbacks must practice as if they must have the best hands on the team.

The only real error that can be made during this drill is the quarterback not attacking the cone at the appropriate angle. If he simply runs to the cone back and forth, this drill is worthless because it's engraining bad muscle memory into the quarterback.

Bad Snap Drill

This drill is important because the snap to the quarterback must be consistent or the advantage of going to the pistol are lost. In this drill, the quarterback will be in his ready position prepared to take the snap. He'll secure the bad snap and perform whatever play the coach had called on him to perform. If the ball touches any part of the quarterback's hands, it's expected that he'll control the ball and performs the play with 100 percent proficiency.

Footwork Steps

This doesn't necessarily need an explanation. Before practice, the quarterback needs to be working on his triple, midline, three-step drop, three-step play-action drop, speed footwork, and zone footwork. Footwork must be a top priority for an option quarterback to succeed. It must become second nature for a quarterback.

Tailback Drills

Wall Path

As an introductory tool for teaching the tailbacks how to "run the wall," setting up cones and having the coach be the quarterback can be effective. The main point of this drill is to get a tailback to understand that he'll run the wall first. This is the angle of how the offensive line blocks will align. Once he clears the wall, his shoulders becomes square with the goal line and he'll score a touchdown. This needs to be drilled over, over, over, and over again (Figure 6-3).

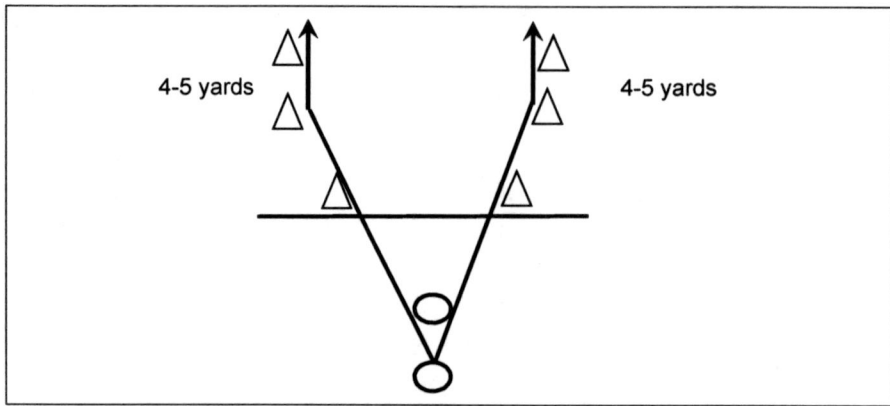

Figure 6-3. Running the wall with cones

Midline Path

The midline path drill is easier to set up because no cones are needed. The emphasis with this drill is to keep the tailback on the midline against a noseguard. As already stated, when running midline against a nose, the tailback will change his aiming point slightly from the rear end of the center to the right/left thigh of the center. The coach will be the center in this drill and the tailback will simply make one subtle cut from where the coach's rear end goes and immediately get back on the midline (Figure 6-4).

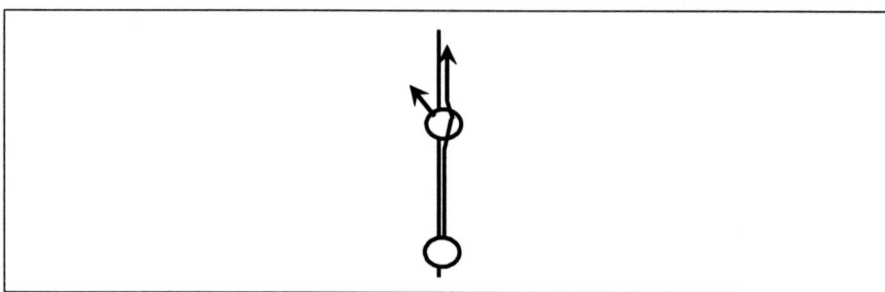

Figure 6-4. Midline path with coach

Perimeter Blocking

Whether this drill is set up for blocking jet or speed (which it needs to touch both), this is integral to getting the tailback's path correct for blocking on the perimeter. Blocking on the perimeter starting from the backfield is much different from being a wide receiver stalk blocking. The emphasis—whether it be speed or jet—is that the tailback must start off laterally. The reasoning has already been explained. But the tailback on either speed or jet must take four to seven steps laterally before engaging his man. This is the main emphasis for this drill, along with the emphasis of blocking fundamentals (Figure 6-5).

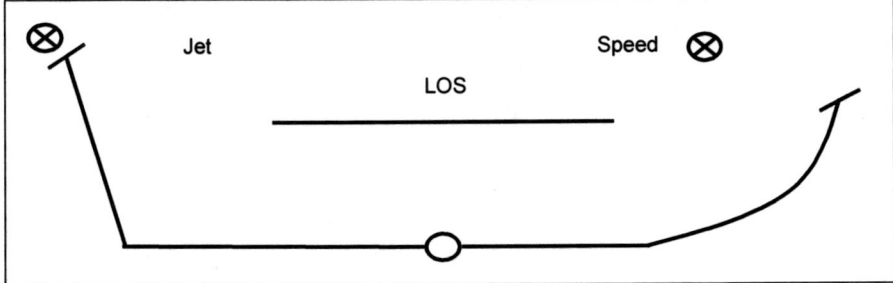

Figure 6-5. Tailback perimeter blocking

Slotback Drills

Bad Pitch

This drill should be performed with tailbacks too. However, this drill is more specifically for slotbacks. During this drill, players will stand in a line. The coach will face the line, wildly throwing high, low, sideways, and up in the air balls at the players. This is radical, but it emphasizes an important point. The slot must be prepared to catch everything the quarterback can muster up.

Arc Drill

This is the single most important drill the slots must do during practice. If applicable, this drill should be done every day. The act of arc blocking is so tough that it must become second nature to the slots performing this task. This drill is shown in Figure 6-6.

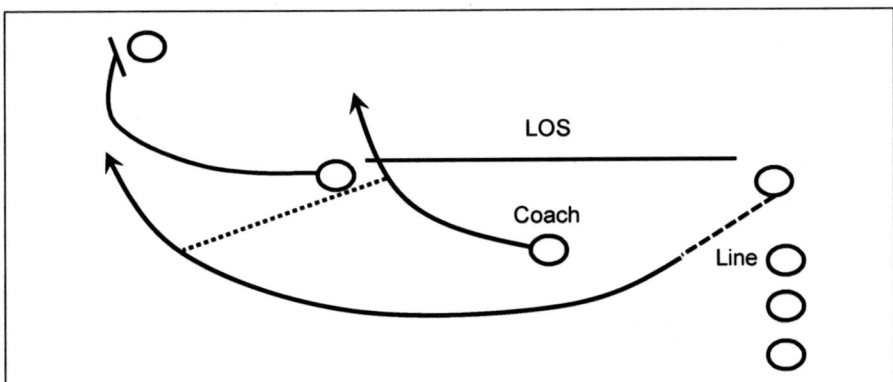

Figure 6-6. Arc drill

The actual drill will be explained first. Once done, the slot arc blocking goes and plays safety, the safety goes to the back of the line, and the slot catching the pitch becomes the arc blocker. The coach will be the quarterback and will pitch the ball to the slots.

This is the best way to simulate an actual arc block. Having dummies set up doesn't adequately prepare the players for actual game situations because it's a stationary target. It needs to be a moving target actually trying to get to the pitch. This gets the slot to understand the principles of arc blocking. He needs to perform a good arc step and he needs to work on his curve-shaped path, mirroring the defender while working to his outside shoulder. This also works really well when the defender tries to "knife" (undercut) the block. If the slot performs his block correctly, this technique performed by the defense won't destroy the pitch phase. Also, this drill helps the slot catching the pitch and gets reps at a real look at how to react to perimeter blocks. Anyone can run in open grass when he's running read drill on air, but once a defender with a blocker is in the picture, the ballcarrier has a better and real look at how it will look once the game starts.

Ball Security Running Back Drills

The number one priority for an offense is ball security. As already talked about, if a team has the turnover bug, it's a direct result of coaches not putting the highest priority on being a good ball security team. Before diving into the ball security drill, one drill (which isn't a drill) should be done with every team in America. During 80 percent of practice, all skill positions should be carrying a football with proper ball carrying fundamentals. When thought is put into it, how often do players carry a football during practice? The honest truth is not very much. Yes, they catch it and carry it during team and 7-on-7 drills, but they immediately give the ball back. Some collegiate wide receiver coaches have done studies on how much a receiver in college actually catches a football during the course of a practice and the results are shocking. Some college teams catch the football fewer than 15 times a practice. The exact same can be said for ball security. When it comes down to it, how often does a player have a ball in his hands? A football play averages around six to seven seconds, then the ball is back to the referee. It's a coach's responsibility to make sure the skill positions carrying a football with proper ball carrying fundamentals all throughout practice: high and tight, wrist above the elbow, middle finger over the top of the football, the ball compressed to the player's chest, and the ball invisible to players behind him. These are the standards that must be met if a coach expects his team to have a good turnover ratio.

Monkey Rolls

Monkey rolls don't necessarily need to be explained except for why they're significant to ball security. Most fumbles occur when a ballcarrier is going to the ground. This happens because the ballcarrier is bracing himself for the downfall. The emphasis on monkey rolls needs to be that the ballcarrier doesn't brace himself when he goes to the ground. When he's on his way down, he needs to go from four points of pressure to five points of pressure on the football. Ballcarriers must become numb to contact with defenders and with the ground. That might sound cold, but it's the truth. It must become natural for a ballcarrier to expect contact with the ground while he keeps good ball security.

Lunge and Pop

This ball security drill starts like this: Players form groups of three and one is a ballcarrier with a football in both of his arms in a good ball security position. Two players are next to him. The ballcarrier will lunge for 10 yards while his two partners are trying to pry the balls out of his arms. The emphasis for this drill is that most offensive players tend to carry the ball in their dominate arm. This drill forces players to be proficient at carrying the football with both arms consistently.

Bag Rolls

This drill starts with vertical padded bags lined up for about five yards. The ballcarrier will fall onto the beginning of the bags with good ball security. He won't brace himself to the ground but keep five points of contact on the ball. He'll slowly roll off the end of the bags, pop up, and sprint to finish the drill. This drill is here to emphasize being in a crowded area. It's also here to simulate being in a pile where dirty tricks happen.

Ball Security Tunnel

In this drill, players form two lines of backs through which one ballcarrier will run. The players who are on each side of the tunnel try to pry the ball out of the ballcarrier's hands. This drill is pretty self-explanatory. The best coaching point is that this drill can sometimes get out of hand, so it must be emphasized to not tackle or grab the ballcarrier. This drill becomes worthless once it becomes a garbage show of tackling and grabbing (Figure 6-7).

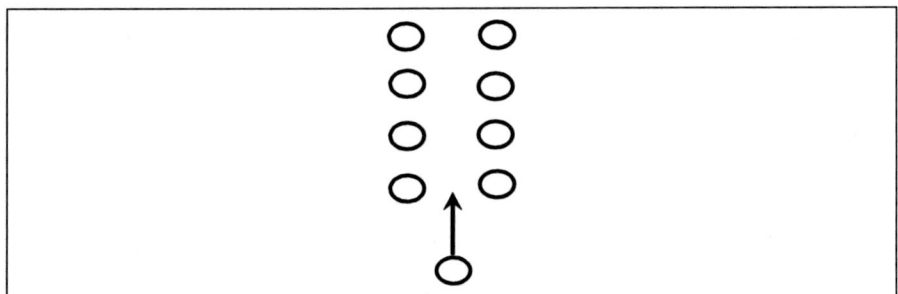

Figure 6-7. Ball security tunnel

Wide Receiver Drills

Vertical Release

As explained several times in this book, the job of the wide receiver is to create a vertical stem in order for the options machinery to properly function. This drill isn't unique to the option. However, it's very important so the offense can flourish. The drill is simple: Every day—whether it be a huge line spread across the field or a single file line—the receivers will create a fast vertical stem to their route. All the techniques need to be employed. The receivers should lean the upper body over the front foot, place the majority of the weight on the front foot, and then quickly release by rolling off the front foot. This drill should be performed every day. It's of great importance that the receivers become a vertical stem.

Progression to Stalk

This drill can be simply explained as working on the fundamentals of a stalk block. The key here is for everyone to be stationary so the receivers can work on the specific fundamentals of creating contact with the defender. This drill is simply performed with two partners. One has a bag and the other is the receiver. And the act of initiating contact is used.

Stalk Drill

This drill is similar to the arc drill in the way it's set up. It will employ three players and a coach. The coach will set up as the quarterback, one will be the motioning slot, and the other two will be the receiver and defender. The coach will pitch the ball to the motioning slot while the receiver is stalk blocking the defender (Figure 6-8).

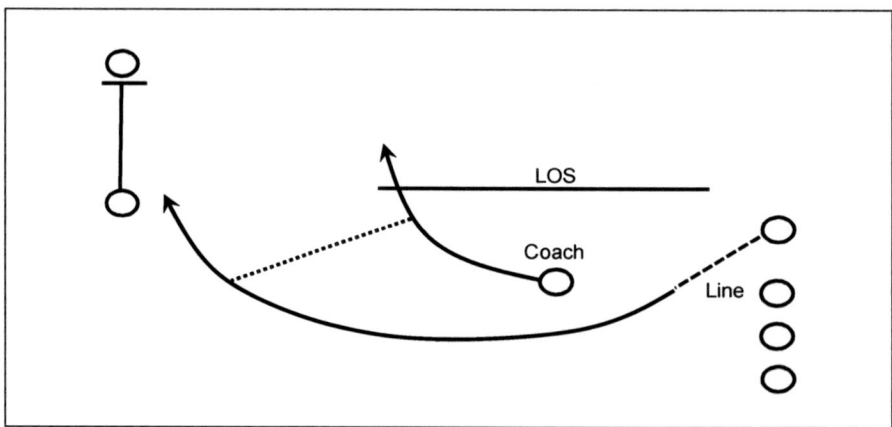

Figure 6-8. Stalk drill

The purpose of this drill is the same as for the arc drill. It's easy for a blocker to have a great block on an easy stationary target with no runner behind him. Once a defender tries to get to the ballcarrier, the entire process of stalk blocking and arc blocking is changed. Both blocks are blind and hard to accomplish. Performing these drills with an actual ballcarrier is the only sure way to get quality reps with this skill. Without good perimeter blocking, this offense is dead in its tracks.

Offensive Line Drills

6/4/3 Point of Contact

In the option offense, base blocking fundamentals are vital. What's vital about base blocking is getting the lineman's hips to roll on contact. This drill enormously helps get linemen to roll their hips naturally. During the first part of the drill, they line up with their helmets about a yard in front of a popsicle or sled. The linemen will have six points of contact on the ground. Their toes, knees, and hands will all be on the ground. On the whistle, they'll explode and strike the popsicle, hitting the bag. They'll explode to the point where they'll fall on their bellies. It must be emphasized that they won't brace their fall. The point of this drill is to get their hips to roll as far as possible. The next part of the drill is to do the same thing except in a four-point stance. This is where the coach must emphasize not to brace the fall to the ground. The next step is the three-point stance. As already explained, the goal of a base block is to create lift. The way to create lift from the ground is for hip roll. Offensive linemen must be used to rolling their hips on contact and lifting their defenders.

Veer Release

This drill is used by the guards and the tackles, although it's mainly for the tackles. The guards on the midline must veer so they're also part of this. Coaches can conduct this drill in a couple different ways. The first that will be explained involves using a goal post. Tackles and guards will line up facing the goal post. They'll get in their stance while having their inside foot at the same point as the goal post. They'll take a step with their inside foot and perform their veer technique, grabbing grass with their backside hand and becoming skinny. The goal of using the goal post is to enhance the idea of becoming skinny. The more a tackle or guard can become skinny the less likely an outside defender can compress his release so he can't get to the linebacker he's assigned to. Once he's become skinny, the tackle will block a moving target to get him in the thought process of having a perfect release and then blocking the linebacker he's assigned to.

The next veer release drill is done through a blaster. The drill is set up exactly like the goal post, except the inside leg will line up with the outside of the blaster. On the whistle, the linemen will veer release while staying low through the blaster. They'll come out of the blaster and block moving linebackers. The blaster portion of this drill is used to simulate a tough release for the tackle being compressed. It's by no means perfect, but it serves the purpose that the guards and tackles must be tough in their releases to the linebackers. If they're not, the offense will be at a disadvantage because linebackers will be running free all game long.

Two other drills are used to enhance a veer release. They're simply offsets of the goal post drill. The lineman will be in his stance and there will be a towel or a tennis ball on the ground. The lineman will release and will be forced to grab grass, get skinny, and pick up either the tennis ball or the towel. This is useful if a goal post isn't available.

Playside Backside Drill

This drill involves the centers. If the center is uncovered, he'll perform his playside backside technique. This is important because he must be able to work his playside step and then work backside in order to pick up the backside linebacker. Against one linebacker, this is easy. The problem is when two middle linebackers are there and the center is covered. Thus, this drill should be set up as the technique he would be performing in the game. Have two linebackers set up as if they were aligned in a 4-4 defense. The center will perform triple right and triple left. If the linebacker runs over the top, he'll go to the backside backer. If the backer runs to the A gap, the center must pick him up (Figure 6-9).

Figure 6-9. Playside backside drill

0-Scoop Drill

This is one of the most difficult techniques in the option's repertoire. With that being said, it must be practiced over and over and over again. This drill is simple. It's simply the act of what the center and backside guard perform on triple (Figure 6-10).

Figure 6-10. 0-scoop drill

The fundamentals need to be addressed over and over again. If the nose goes backside, he's no longer the center's responsibility. The guard will pick him up and vice versa. This is aggressive and the lineman should be stressed a thousand times that this block is essentially a double-team on the nose—it's just different in nature. When it's explained as a reverse double-team, a light goes off in their heads and they better understand what the offense is trying to accomplish.

Drills With Multiple Position Groups

Running an option offense has to include immense collaborations with different position groups. Individual time is very important, but group work must be done in order to perfect the intricacies of this offense.

Fit Drill

This drill is performed with the quarterback and the tailbacks. This drill is simply to get the mesh in order on triple and midline. Both of these groups will do this individually and then come together to perfect this. Several coaching points must be emphasized here. The first is when meshing on midline. This is most effective on a line. The reason is because this gives the quarterback a landmark for how far he has to get off the midline and where his hands need to be for the mesh. The tailback needs to remain on the line. The coaching point is: if the quarterback doesn't get off the midline, the tailback needs to run him over. It's the quarterback's responsibility to get off the midline while working downhill.

The next coaching point has to do with the triple. It's imperative with the triple that landmarks are used. They need to be used because if they're not, during the mesh/read drill, the quarterback's steps will be too wide or too shallow. They need to be perfect every time. Landmarks are a must or the timing and mechanics of this offense are skewed with regard to the most important part of the offense: the mesh between the quarterback and tailback.

The quarterback must give and pull. He must create a credible feel between the two so the mesh can be constant and well done. The quarterback must also work on the most important aspect of his footwork: the rapid acceleration off the mesh. As already talked about, whether the quarterback has the ball or not, he must come off the tail of the tailback at 100 mph. This drill helps serve this emphasis in technique.

Mesh/Read Drill

This drill can be called a lot of things. The name isn't important, but the action done with the backfield is. This drill has all the backs combined into one group: quarterbacks, tailbacks, and slotbacks. If at all possible, the goal line will work perfectly as a landmark. It works perfectly because the quarterback's heels will be on the two-point conversion line and the tailback's heels will be on the five-yard line. A line of tape can mark the offensive line in order to create good spacing. In order to create the perfect spacing, the tape should be placed on the goal line. The coaches will be the read and pitch key for the quarterbacks.

The backs will work on all the footwork and execution of the option plays and the complementary plays. A natural bias exists for coaches to work on the right side more than the left, so it's imperative that equal amount of work be done on both sides. Many option football coaches work a "two ball" drill into this drill. It's believed here that it's unnecessary to include this in the drill. The reason is simple: The quarterback must be used to accelerating whether he has the ball or not. In a game, if he gives the ball, a magical second ball won't be tossed to him for him to perfect the pitch phase of the option. The rationale behind the two-ball drill is that it will maximize the number of reps the quarterback will have executing the pitch phase of the option, which is an excellent point to be made. However, in reality, the quarterback needs to be proficient at working on the acceleration off the tail whether he has the ball or not. Also, when a coach is busy with tossing a ball to the quarterback, he's less concerned with getting his quarterback ready for tough reads. This drill is prominent in many option football DVDs, but this is unnecessary. Acceleration—whether the quarterback has the ball or not—must be stressed to the fullest degree. The two-ball drill doesn't help with this coaching point.

Option Period (Half Line)

This drill is a must-have in an option practice. This drill is a live contact drill with the offensive line, quarterbacks, tailbacks, slots, and a live defense. This drill is shown in Figure 6-11.

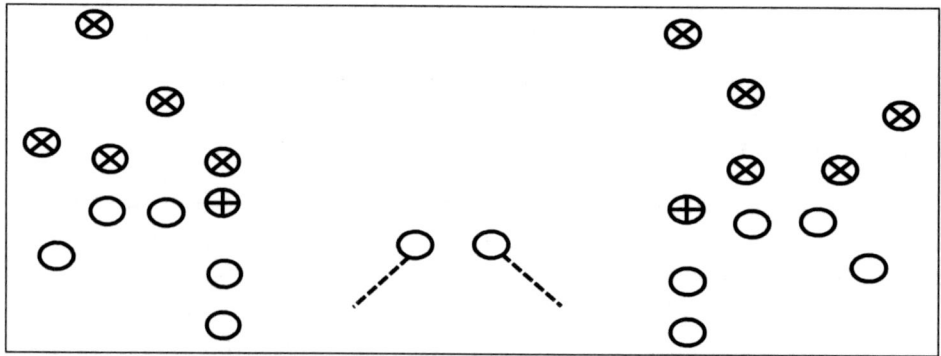

Figure 6-11. Option period

The beauty of this drill is that it maximizes reps with a live look on defense. A rotation should occur to make sure all skill positions get in on offense. Quarterbacks need to work both sides and with different centers. Tailbacks need to be rotated so they're working both sides and with both quarterbacks. As already stated, the goal is to maximize live reps of running triple, midline, speed, counter speed, etc.

Inside Run Period

This drill helps the tailback and offensive line be in sync with each other. They can perform their individual tasks. However, without extensive work together, it can become hard for a tailback to have a feel for how to actually run his paths in this offense. This also gives the offensive line a better feel for where the tailback will run in relation to their blocks. This drill is shown in Figure 6-12.

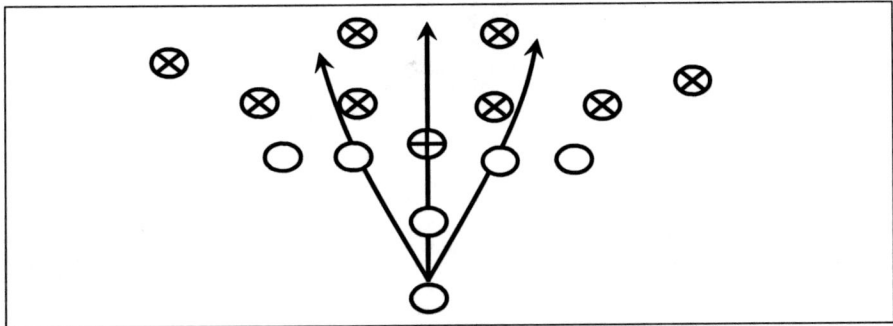
Figure 6-12. Inside run period

Some coaches add a quarterback to this drill in order to get the quarterbacks more reads. However, this drill should be looked at in a different manner. It's so the tailback and the offensive line mesh together on their efforts. This isn't for the quarterback to get good at reads. That's why the coach is the quarterback in this situation.

Routes on Air

This isn't necessarily option-specific, but it's important for this attack. The reason to be in the formation prescribed is because of the ability to throw the ball, not only run. Thus, it's important that the skill positions are consistently throwing routes every day. One suggestion for how to do this is that the quarterbacks should be alone with each position group at a time—wide receivers, slotbacks, and tailbacks—in order to perfect the specific routes they'll perform.

7

Option Offense Practice Schedule

Managing the mechanical aspects of this offense is important. This is done throughout the practice week—whether it's spring football, two-a-days, or in-season practice. Some anecdotes and clichés will be talked about (although this publication is trying to avoid clichés or anecdotes). Then, some important aspects must be specifically considered when running an option offense.

Principles of Practice

Principle #1: The Team Gets What's Emphasized

This seems elementary and obvious, but however elementary in understanding, many coaches seem to miss this point. Many coaches during or after a game will make the statement "I don't know why he did that." He did it because the skill that he was asked to perform during the game wasn't emphasized enough during practice. That answer might seem cold, but it's the truth. Human beings have a tendency to come up with a reason why a failure isn't their fault. Phrases like "We would have won the game, but____" or "They only won because of a bad call." It's natural for human beings to do this—find a way to place blame on everyone except the person blaming everyone. The problem with this approach as a coach is that it's a copout. If a coach doesn't emphasize ball security, the team will most likely have a fumble problem. If a coach doesn't drill tackling in practice, the team will mostly likely not be a good tackling team. If a quarterback is struggling perfecting selected pass plays, the odds are they're not run enough during practice on a consistent basis.

Practice time is scarce. Only so much can be taught during the course of one practice. Thus, an emphasis on practice must be that *what happens on Friday night happens during the week.* When it comes down to it, football is a simple game. NFL coaches love to make football seem very complicated, but it's not. Every team has a small amount of time in which skills and techniques can be taught. The basic skills of football must never be sacrificed for the sake of scheme. A huge difference exists between teams that emphasize fundamentals every day and teams that put a priority on schemes every day. Teams that put a priority on scheme start to deteriorate at the middle to the end of the season. Emphasizing the basic fundamentals every day is important for the longevity of a season.

Principle #2: A Coach Needs to Teach, Not Yell

This is another fallacy that many coaches fall into. Another basic human characteristic is that when a player thinks a leader is acting foolish, he's a jerk and doesn't know what he's doing. However, that same player becomes a coach and finds it perfectly okay to yell and scream at his players. Because his viewpoint has changed, he feels he's right because he now has power and authority over other human beings. This is a form of mental gymnastics. A coach must take into account what his experiences were as a player and use them to mold his coaching style. The point here is not to make a coach soft or to have a coach coddle his players, which is also foolish, but what's trying to be illustrated is the idea that a coach is a teacher. If a coach can't adequately teach his players the skills needed, he's not a good coach.

Coaches yell for several reasons. The first is they simply love to be in charge and dwell in their own authority. Everybody has experienced a boss like that. The next is that yelling is a coach masking his failures as a teacher and is taking out his frustrations on his students, to whom he's failed to teach the basic skills needed to succeed. Coaches absolutely need to get on their players and hold them to the highest standards, but yelling isn't the most effective way to do that. The last reason why a coach yells is he doesn't have an answer for what an opposing team is doing to his team during a game. Many coaches who yell during a game simply don't have an offensive or defensive answer for what the other team is doing. To mask this, a coach yells at his players to cover up his failure as a strategist. Giving an inspiring pre-game/halftime speech won't help the cause of a penetrating 4-3 defense getting torched by a wing-T team running trap every play.

Principle #3: Coaches Set the Tempo in Practice

All coaches and players have been a part of a practice that seemed dead from the start. Most coaches directly blame their players and, more specifically, senior captains for the practices that don't have energy. The truth is that if coaches have a low level of energy, the team has a low level of energy. The coach who took this idea to its maximum achievement was Pete Carroll when he was the head coach at the University of Southern California. Carroll took the idea that coaches must be energetic, enthusiastic, and pumped. This energy would then be transferred directly to the players. He took the idea that the coaches, not the players, were responsible for the energy level of practice. The results of Pete Carroll's tenure at USC speaks for itself. Anyone who watched the University of Miami when it was "the U" under Jimmy Johnson knows how much of a difference energy level has on how a team plays. Coaches need to understand that they're the ones who have the greatest impact on the success of a practice. It's true that a team either gets better or worse at the end of every practice. An extraordinary positive energy level—even if it's fake—will lead to a practice that gets the most out of every player and the team can then accomplish that day's goals.

Principle #4: High Energy Levels From the Coaches Must Be Positive

Yet another human characteristic is that people respond better to a positive environment than a negative environment. A coach can have a high energy level during practice, but if it's negative, it can do much more damage than a practice of players simply going through the motions. Players are much more motivated when their coaches get pumped and hyped up after they made a great play. This must occur in practice. If a player gets a high five or a chest bump while players and coaches are going crazy after a good play, it motivates players. The worst possible thing that can happen to a football team is that players are dreading practice because they're going to get yelled at and have negativity thrown in their face. It's much more appealing to players to go into an everyday environment that's high energy and is very positive.

Principle #5: Teaching Is a Progression

Coaches have two extraordinary ways to teach players the skills needed to succeed. They come from two great coaches. The first is the greatest coach who has ever lived: John Wooden. He had eight laws of learning, which are explanation, demonstration, imitation, repetition, repetition, repetition, repetition, and repetition. This gives players a full understanding of what he's doing and why he's doing it and then gaining muscle memory performing each skill. The next comes from Chip Kelly, the former head coach at the University of Oregon and the current head coach for the Philadelphia Eagles. He has four points to his teaching philosophy. The first is "I see and I forget." Simply seeing something doesn't necessarily mean the player will understand and comprehend the skill necessary to perform it. The next is "I hear and I forget." Simply telling a player something doesn't mean he knows the content of what he's being told. To a football coach, the skill might be second nature, but to a new football player, it's brand new to him. This leads to the next two points, which are the most significant: "I see and I remember" and "I do and I remember." When a coach actually shows a player what to do, it's much easier to comprehend. Then, the ultimate is having the player perform the skill. Repetition is the only way to get good at a skill. That's why it's crucial for a coach to limit the skills a player needs in order for the team to be successful.

Principle #6: Practice Time Is Scarce—Don't Waste It

It's obvious to say that what players have done during the week is exactly what they do on Friday/Saturday nights. Many coaches simply do drills to kill time, when the truth is, they need to do drills that emphasizes the importance of the offensive/defensive fundamentals/schemes that will make the team better. Practice time is scarce. Players have too many things they have to perfect before game time. Standing around waiting for something is unacceptable. Efficiently allocating practice time to the drills needed to succeed is a must for a team to be successful.

From another angle, practice needs to be fast and up tempo. This is the only proven way to maximize repetitions. Many teams have a lot of standing around when they can get in 10 to 15 more plays during a team time or they're still explaining a drill or technique during practice. The truth is, no skills or techniques should be taught during practice. That must occur during pre-practice so time isn't wasted in practice teaching a skill or technique. Maximizing practice time is the ultimate goal of every coach—not only in football but in all sports.

Principle #7: Don't Overload Team Time

Team time is often overrated. It's believed here that too much time can be allocated to this and not enough to teaching the specific techniques and skills needed to win. Individual time is needed and mixing position groups is needed along with team time. But 30 minutes of team time is a lot. The last 10 minutes end up being a waste of time because the players are tired and practice is almost over. The maximum amount of team time believed to maximize team cohesion is no more than 20 minutes.

Principle #8: Don't Yell Obvious Things

Many coaches believe pointing out the obvious makes them good coaches. Or if they say very broad things, their players will play better. The bottom line is that a coach is a coach because he's supposed to have a specialize understanding of football. The following is a list of sayings a coach should avoid:
- "Catch the ball."
- "Block somebody."
- "You're lunging."
- "Move your feet."
- "Tackle!!!"

The point trying to be illustrated here is that those phrases aren't coaching. If they were, every football fan in America would be Bill Walsh. When a player drops the football, he knows he dropped the ball. He doesn't need six coaches telling him he dropped the ball. Being a coach is telling a player why he dropped the ball. Saying he didn't catch the ball isn't coaching.

Option-Specific Practice Setup

Each position has skills that should be placed above the others for the simple fact that some skills will be performed more than others. Thus, it's important to have a list of the most important skills that every position group must have. The following is a list of the most important skills every offensive position group must perform when running this offense.

Quarterbacks

- Footwork
- Read on #1
- Pull and replace
- Acceleration off the mesh
- Leverage pitching
- Three-step drop
- Throwing stretch and choice

Tailbacks

- Footwork
- Running the wall
- Running and staying on the midline
- Understanding the blocking scheme
- Pass protection

Slotbacks

- Footwork
- Arc blocking, arc blocking, arc blocking (The importance of this skill can't be overemphasized.)
- Switch blocking
- Two- to three-step motion
- Pitch relationship
- Running through the pitch
- Catching passes

Wide Receivers

- Footwork
- Threatening the deep third
- Stalk blocking
- Switch/crack blocking
- Routes
- Catching

Offensive Line

- Footwork
- Base blocking
- Correct fundamentals on all blocks
- Scoop block (including 0-scoop)
- Playside backside
- Veer/loop release
- Kick-out for tackles
- Midline blocking technique
- Knowing and understanding *rules, not fronts*

The purpose of this list is to give specifics about what should be a priority for this offense. Many of the skills listed have great carryover from play to play. That's why they're a priority for running this offense. The following sections are some more suggestions for drills and how often they should be employed.

Mesh

This drill with the running backs and quarterbacks must be done every day. Combining the skills necessary to make the triple option work is of the utmost importance in this offense. At first, it's good enough for the coaches to give the quarterback easy reads and so forth so they can perfect their footwork, timing, and decision making. However, once this stage is over, the coaches need to make this drill harder for the quarterback. The coach needs to try to play the quarterback and the tailback and then the quarterback and the pitchback. Making it hard in practice will make running the option during a game much easier.

Routes on Air

This should be performed every day because throwing the ball is important for this offense to work. Doing it individually between the position groups will emphasize perfecting the specific routes they'll run. Most option football teams throw scarcely, and when they do, they miss the pass. That must be avoided. When a throwing opportunity is given to the offense, it must take advantage. Nothing is more frustrating than a coach calling the perfect passing play and the offense doesn't execute it. It directly comes from not making it an emphasis in practice every day.

Inside Run Period

This should be performed at least once a week. As stated, the emphasis of this is to get the tailback and the offensive line to become a cohesive unit. They need to gel in order for the dive portion of this offense to succeed. The tailback needs to understand the blocking schemes well enough so he can play fast through the line.

Option Period (Half Line)

This should be done at least once a week. It's similar to the inside run period. However, because it's only three linemen, the emphasis isn't necessarily on the tailback but on the offensive unit as a whole. Maximizing reps is the most important aspect of this period. It's full contact and the defense will be bringing it to the offense.

Arc Drill

This should be performed every day for at least five minutes. This is one of the most difficult skills to perform in football, so it should be treated as such. Although many principles and techniques are involved, infusing a sense of feel for this block is important in order for it to be consistently accomplished by the slotback.

One Ball Security Drill per Day

This goes for all the skill positions. Whether it's the monkey rolls (preferred) or the step and lunge, ball security needs to be emphasized all the time. Carrying a football all throughout practice has already been discussed, but an emphasis should always remain on good ball security. The difference between a perfect season and a .500 season is turnovers. This eliminates turnovers from the source.

Conclusion

The Principle of a Winner

The principle of a winner can be summarized in two words: no excuses. Losers and cowards have excuses for why they didn't win, why their specific player did the wrong thing, or why the refs stole the game from them. The honest truth is that none of that matters. The only thing that matters is if you win. Cowards and losers are always looking to place blame upon somebody else for their failures. Most people in the world always have an excuse for why they failed. To be trapped into a cycle of excuses is like being trapped inside a black hole—you will never get out of it. When people make excuses, it seems justified. Excuses are never justified. Winners are always finding ways to get better and to correct mistakes. Winners win the close games instead of losing them. Ultimately, winners have no excuses.

About the Authors

Chris Paulson has been the head football coach at Kentlake High School in Kent, Washington, since 2010. During that time, the Falcons have enjoyed unprecedented success and have consistently ranked as one of the top offenses in the state. A former linebacker and graduate of Washington State University, Chris previously coached at two other Washington high schools: Mount Rainier High School and Auburn Riverside High School.

Jeff (Jefferson) Glessner is the offensive coordinator and running backs coach at Kentlake High School in Kent, Washington. In 2012, the Kentlake offense led the state in offensive yards and was third in points scored per game. Jeff is also currently serving in the Washington Army National Guard, which he joined in 2009. Born in Arlington, Virginia, Jeff was raised in Fredericksburg, Virginia, where he attended Chancellor High School. He played football at Chancellor for four years. He recently received a bachelor's degree in law, economics, and public policy from the University of Washington. He is currently pursuing a master's degree in education. After he receives his master's, Jeff plans to pursue a career coaching college football.